$\langle$

Liberation and purity

Liberation and Purity

The rise of new religious movements has raised important questions about how race, ethnicity and the lives of black minority communities in the West are to be understood. In *Liberation and purity*, Chetan Bhatt critically examines the ideas and organization of new Hindu and Islamic movements and relates this to contemporary debates in philosophy, social theory and cultural studies. He considers the creation of new traditions and new ethnicities by these movements and explores how ideas of purity, pollution, the body, sexuality and gender are key themes in their ideas of emancipation. Bhatt explores the relationship between right-wing and progressive social movements in modern civil societies, and examines the influence on these movements of new globally-organized communications technologies.

Chetan Bhatt is ESRC Research Fellow at the University of Southampton

Race and Representation

A series edited by John Solomos, Michael Keith and David Goldberg

Race and Representation is a series of books designed to open up new ways of thinking about race, racism and ethnicity in contemporary societies. International and multidisciplinary in focus, it aims to establish a dialogue between contending theoretical and political perspectives and to provide a forum for the most innovative contemporary work in the field.

Also in the series:

New ethnicities and urban culture by Les Back

Liberation and purity

Race, new religious movements and the ethics of postmodernity

Chetan Bhatt

PRESS

London – Bristol, Pennsylvania

First published in 1997 by UCL Press

UCL Press Limited
1 Gunpowder Square
London EC4A 3DE
UK

and

1900 Frost Road, Suite 101
Bristol
Pennsylvania 19007–1598
USA

The name of University College London (UCL) is a registered
trade mark used by UCL Press with the consent of the owner.

British Library Cataloguing in Publication Data
A CIP catalogue record for this book is available from the British
Library.

Library of Congress Cataloging-in-Publication Data are available

ISBNs: 1-85728-423-2 HB
        1-85728-424-4 PB

Printed and bound in Great Britain.

For Stephen Cross with love . . .
. . . and for Robert Mitchell, Parul, Bina, Narendra and Lilavati

Contents

Acknowledgements

Many people have helped in various ways with this book though they are not responsible for any errors nor would they necessarily agree with all the conclusions. I would like to thank John Solomos, Paul Gilroy, Clive Harris and especially Jeffrey Weeks for their encouragement and for their critical comments on previous drafts of the book. Sabiha Aanchawan's stimulating commentaries on several of the chapters, as well as her support have helped me greatly. Lata Mani and Ruth Frankenberg were an ocean away but always deep in my heart. The numerous discussions with Robert Lee and Gita Sahgal were important in guiding and framing some of the more difficult arguments. I am very grateful to Hansa Chudasama and Kum Kum Bhavnani for their support and for many of their critical insights that helped in several parts of the book. A huge thank you to all of you.

I want to acknowledge the generous support of the Economic and Social Research Council (reference: H53627500395) and the University of Southampton during some of the stages of research that were made use of in the book. I would also like to thank Caroline Wintersgill, Justin Vaughan, Sandy Anthony and the staff at UCL Press for their assistance and patience, and Woodrow Phoenix for the book cover.

Various people selflessly assisted me with materials, discussions, comments, translations and support. Lilavati Bhatt, Prataprai Bhatt and Pushpa Dave provided extensive support, though they are not to blame for any incongruous conclusions I may have reached. Patti Wallace, Nanda Sirker and Leena Sevak provided help and support when it was particularly needed – thank you. The late Siddhartha

ACKNOWLEDGEMENTS

Gautam remains in our hearts as a constant source of inspiration for innumerable local and global political projects. He is deeply missed.

The members of the real and pretended family have in each of their ways made this book possible. Robert Mitchell generously and unstintingly assisted me throughout the course of writing. Stephen Cowden, Vivek Sajip, Zahid Dar, Parul Huston, Bina Bhatt and John Huston provided encouragement and support, critical comments and endless, but welcome distractions. A major bundle of love to all of you. Finally, I want to express my deepest gratitude to Stephen Cross for his intellectual support and his emotional sustenance during difficult modern times.

Introduction

Faith and reason have had an intimate historical association. Reason, indeed unrelenting rationalities, have frequently been the basis of the restoration of primeval faith in the Supernatural, the God, the Infinite, the Ineffable or the Sublime. There is, for example, short epistemological distance between some interpretations of modern science and the rationalities of religious faith. The latter somehow easily manage to encapsulate the former, even if dogmatically. However, the tensions of reason and faith, or of rationalities and religions, have usually been seen as more important. These have been frequently articulated as the tensions between Enlightenment rationality and Romantic mystery that still continue to plague the modern world. The Third Reich and the Holocaust against European Jewry are seen as prime examples of this murderous coupling of scientific-technical rationality and Romantic mystification. There is indeed something troubling about Enlightenment reason (and its scientism and its humanism) that can deny its own existence in these horrifying moments. It is perhaps another version of the Cartesian axiom that reason comes into being by virtue of its capacity to doubt its existence.

Faith in God and Gods and Goddesses is itself endlessly rationalized. Most contemporary religious formations have systematic authoritative discursive strategies that are founded on continual appeal to some form of reason, as well as some resonant versions of the real or empirical. They are coherent discursive regimes, apparently consistent, mechanically rational, deeply concerned with the social, political, economic and cultural domains. For example, Islamic social and political philosophies, as well as various New Age religious metaphysics and the new cultish Hinduisms all share a remarkable concern with being rational. They also seem to give considerable privilege to natural science. What is the difference between their reason and the reason of Enlightenment? When does their "science" depart from the products of Enlightenment science? When are the claims of Vedic "science" wrong? At what stage does the intimate, parasitic relationship between New Age metaphysical environmentalism and the discoveries of environmental natural science become so contradictory as to become meaningless?

Religious ideologies do reach a point when their reason becomes exhausted. This point, both dogmatic and infinitely malleable, is a moveable feast called "faith". Faith entails a profound decentring of the subject that puts poststructuralist theory to shame. The political consequences of human agency enacted with the authority of faith or the will of God have been tragic. They fill newspaper columns and TV bulletins daily. This distinction between faith and reason in modern Islamic, Hindu and Christian political discourse is hugely important in informing its foundations for agency, action and politics, and ultimately in deriving its authority. It is an Augustinian conception, recombined with Aristotelian teleo-totalities. It can be said to exist in a very strong tension with non-algorithmic, open-ended, anti-teleological natural and human science, its only real intellectual enemy. For St Augustine, there were limits to reason, and the human capacities for the discovery of truth were inherently fallible. If the limit-point was faith, then its exteriority, the reason or cause, was the will of God outside time that was also manifest in everything human and earthly. The latter is well put by someone who did indeed create a City of God, Ruhollah Khomeini:

> Philosophy itself is a means, not an end; a means for you to convey truths and forms of knowledge to your reason through proofs. This is its sole scope. It has been said "Those who seek proofs have wooden legs". This means that the leg of rational proof is wooden, while the leg that conveys man and actually enables him to walk is his knowledge of himself as a manifestation of God; it is the faith that enters his heart and his conscience (Khomeini 1981: 376).

In Hinduism, the limit of reason by faith, and its resolution through the will and manifestation of God is dramatically played out in the fourth poem of the *Bhagavad gita*. The dilemma for the soul, torn by reason on the one hand and belief in a predestined infinite totality that controverts the reasons for this-worldly action on the other, are resolved by a greater faith, the manifestation of another God outside time and causality, and his will.

> But he who has no faith and no wisdom, and whose soul is in doubt, is lost. For neither this world, nor the world to come, nor joy is ever for the man who doubts.... Kill therefore with the sword of wisdom the doubt born of ignorance that lies in thy heart. Be one in self-harmony, in Yoga, and arise, great warrior, arise. (*The Bhagavad gita* [trans. Mascaro] 1962: 64–5)

This extratemporal extraspatial resolution to the troubles that one's faith faces when confronted by one's reason is recursive and emphatically dogmatic. Its repetitive or iterative form is one basis for its authority: its authorization derives from the act of repetition itself. It also hints at the kinds of divisions between high religion ("ecclesiastical" forms of faith and knowledge) and popular religion (faith and devotion). Most importantly, it is an identification with God, the human as a manifestation of God or his will, that demands both human agency (political agency) and a decentring of the human subject through its identification with something "extra-discursive".

There is an epistemological structure to this limit point of reason and its relation to faith. The Infinite and Unknowable is placed at an arbitrary distance from oneself, beyond the boundary of reason or beyond the limits of human knowledge or knowability, though religious discourses rarely define where this boundary should lie. However, there is also a deep sense of ineffability within oneself, most importantly in the capacity of the human mind to have enigmatic, incomprehensible, mysterious and mystical experiences. The mystical experience is comprehended as decentring, destructive of the ego-sense of identity – there is no "I". Time and space do not exist or are not corrigible – there is no "is". Mystical experience can be sublime, blissful and terrifying, apparently infinite and boundless, where everything is apprehended as understood, all knowledge is known, there is no interior or exterior, no discreteness, only what might subsequently be called a unity. The important step in much religious discourse is to create a relation between the inner mystical experience and the Infinite that resides beyond the arbitrarily limited capacity of the human intellect. This relation can be one of identity, as in much mystical Hinduism or in the sufi tradition, or can be mediated by other devices, most important of which is a discipline of faith.

These themes of reason and faith are central to each of the chapters in this book. The book is about authoritarian religious movements and their political ideologies. But it is also about how these ideas have been shaped by very modern political and socio-logical problems – very much Enlightenment problems, despite the shrill "anti-Western" exhortations of many of their adherents. Hence the book draws upon current theoretical debates and issues in sociology, political theory, cultural studies and philosophy. In particular, ideas about globalization, new communications tech-nology and the body are generously employed. Implicitly, it is also a book about the problems that racial or black liberation politics have faced when dealing with religious movements. It is necessary to emphasize that the authoritarian religious movements described in the book are not to be considered equivalent to the wide religious traditions they claim hegemony over. It is also extremely important to note that neither the authoritarian religious movements described in the book, nor religious tradition *per se* completes the political, social or cultural organization of South Asian communities in the UK. Each chapter of the book generally stands on its own as a self-contained essay. However, several themes, elaborated in detail in the first two more theoretical chapters, run throughout the book.

It may appear surprising that there are very few political-sociological, philosophical or even cultural studies paradigms for assessing authoritarian religious movements and fundamentalism. To be sure, there are numerous descriptive and analytical texts within the disciplines of politics and international relations, espe-cially about Islamic movements. But it is striking that what should perhaps be the most relevant paradigms in modern social theory – such as postmodernism theory, cultural studies, race and ethnic relations, neo-Marxism and the burgeoning field of postcolonial discourse analysis – have barely looked at religious affiliation or religious fundamentalism though, as shall be argued, the political problems thrown up by fundamentalism have been germane to, and in some cases directly formative of, these disciplines.

In the first two chapters, I look at some broad theoretical issues that I think are relevant for an understanding of authoritarian religious movements. If nothing else, religious movements and regimes force us to rethink foundational issues in knowledge, ethics and the utopias we can strive for. If these conveniently Kantian questions are at the core of the "postmodern crisis" in Western culture, they are just as important (though barely thought through) in authoritarian religious movements. Hence it is worth examining the problems with postmodernism theory, deconstruction and neo-Marxism, mainly to try and understand why they have posed such weak political challenges to religious authoritarianism. A more recent offspring, "postcolonial discourse analysis" or "postcolonial theory" (or its variously hyphenated and parenthesized syllabic permutations) should ostensibly be more challenging to the foundations of religious authoritarianism. After all, its main concern is with the same time and space of metropolis and colony from which non-Judeo-Christian fundamentalism has arisen. Its political imaginary, like that of much postmodernism theory, claims some deep affiliation with the concerns or struggles of the subaltern, the Third World, women, those marked by "difference". It may then be asked why it has failed to challenge the religious authoritarianism that is speaking in the name of those same "Third World" subalterns. This is examined in the first chapter through a critical assessment of postcolonial theory.

In virtually all authoritarian religious discourse, the control of the gendered body, its sexuality, the uniforms it should be clothed in, its fertility, its masculinity or femininity, its legitimate spaces for voyage and passage, and the use of the religious body for performance, display and exhibition are hugely important characteristics. In several chapters I explore why authoritarian religious movements recreate new modern anthropologies of the body and its rituals of exhibitionism, pollution and purity. There are indeed some striking similarities between these absolutist anthropologies and those of more progressive movements (such as black and gay liberation) and these are drawn out through some discussions of sexuality and its interface with the South Asian communities in Britain.

It should perhaps be obvious that religious authoritarian movements will be considered to be modern in their strictest sense, and this is an important theme of the book. Virtually all the tropes of Enlightenment political discourse appear *foundationally* in (Hindu and Islamic) authoritarian religious movements: identity, liberation, emancipation, liberty, rights, freedom, revolution, political power and the state, hybrid variants of nationalism and "socialism/communism", anti-imperialism, even, on occasion, equality, fraternity, "women's emancipation" and "individualism".

Religious discourse usually claims a special privilege for itself over and above that of any other modern discourse. This can derive from its repetitive authority, often linked to the idea, will or manifestation of the Supernatural. However, the political projects represented by religious authoritarianism are simply that and need to be criticized and analyzed on that basis, just as any other secular political claim would. To be sure, there are distinctive sociological features of religious ideology and its structuring of both utopian and empiricist world-views, rituals, suffering, emotion, agency and belief. But these are not in themselves reason for giving religious ideology an *a priori* epistemic, ethical or moral privilege in comparison with any secular or atheistic discourse.

Some of these areas are explored in the four middle chapters of the book through an assessment of just how novel the political claims of authoritarian Hindu and Islamic movements are. Despite their vigorous claims to tradition and continuity, virtually all the Hindu and Islamic movements active today were formed in two recent and distinct periods: the middle to latter part of the last century (during the global colonial period) and from the 1920s to the 1960s (during the phase of decolonization). They are remarkable examples of "the invention of tradition", and of ethnogenesis, but now structured into the modern urban city and the arrangement of communal identity-territorial spaces within it. Chapter 3 explores the social and political thought of Khomeini, as a prelude to the discussion of the Rushdie affair in Chapter 4. Chapters 5 and 6 extend the discussion of new traditions through an examination of Hindu nationalism and the thought of Vinayak Damodar Savarkar, perhaps the most important influence on right-wing Aryan-Hindu revival this century.

The cross-national aspect and velocity of, say, the Rushdie affair in 1989 or the Ganesh "milk miracle" in 1995 (during which idols of the Hindu God Ganesh across the world started to absorb milk) highlighted how various social spaces – such as community, city, nation and the "global" – were connected in some non-systematic way and, in their connection, they told us something about "globalization" and "time–space compression". Hence, social time–space compression and its impact on the meaning of politics in the contemporary period is an important theme of this book. Time–space compression and globalization have entailed novel forms of political agency, novel political languages and new sociological formations. Some of the political formations that are discussed in the book cross the boundaries of the sociological body (equivalent to, say, a nation-state and its civil society). For example, an analysis of contemporary Islamic and Hindu movements cannot easily be undertaken using a methodology based on a single social formation ("a sociology") or on a localized methodology of "community" or "social movement". However, many of these "Third World" religious movements cannot be viewed within a global conceptual framework either, since they are not "global" in the way that, say, Western multinational corporations, the organizations of inter-national finance capital or electronic communications industries and services are. Similarly, very few people in the "Third World" have access to electronic Internet-based "Cyberspace". However, the movements operate at the level of civil society but are not contained within one civil society. An important argument of the book is that these social movements acquired their greatest impact precisely because they were not local and that their non-local nature said something about "globalization" or "modernity" and its differential meaning for the "Third World". Their agency in different civil societies may be very uneven and differentiated, but, in their different manifestations, they constitute some kind of common and related phenomenon. However, is there an overall conceptual, aesthetic or methodological scheme – a "cognitive mapping" – into which these spatially non-contiguous but highly connected activities fall naturally or logically into place? This means facing issues of relativism and "incommensurability" and proposing some general evaluative criteria, a task that necessarily works against the postmodern injunction to study "small", "local" or "private" narratives. These theoretical areas are discussed in Chapters 1 and 2 and the issue of local agency and translocal or global reception is explored in detail in Chapter 4 through an extended examination of the new political ideas and formations that intervened dramatically during the Rushdie affair itself.

The manifest modes of affiliation across different civil societies during the Rushdie affair were often based on electronic communications. However, while there is a sociology of mass communications and there are several methodological approaches – such as literary criticism, semiology, cultural studies and ethnography – to the study of the cultural products of mass communications, there are important methodological issues that lie somewhere in between these two areas. What conceptual framework can be used to describe the sociological and political relationships between collectives that use, or are subject to, the field of mass communication? And what are the methodological concepts one can use to analyze the interactive sociological relationships created inside as well as through the medium of electronic communications? For example, there is an intrinsic relationship between the televising of Khomeini's speeches and Shiʿa Muslim mobilization that goes beyond and is irreducible to simply the *existence* of a mass audience brought about by visual or print technology. In an important way, television changes the social and political function of the Imam and creates a new social relationship between him and Shiʿa followers. Similarly, the televising of Hindu epics sweepingly transforms the meaning of the Hindu devotional religious idiom itself. This is something that an unreconstructed ethnographic approach could not easily capture – the cultural rituals and signs may appear to have only changed their medium but are otherwise the same. In these examples, existing sociological relationships are not simply displaced into a new medium of communication but drastically transformed so that they bear only a resemblance to (they are not just a simulacrum of) the social relationships that existed before. Chapters 4 and 7 look at some examples of how the medium of electronic communications has been used by Islamic and Hindu religious movements to crystallize new traditions. Of particular interest is how the global medium of electronic communications allows for the rehearsal of non-local "cyberspatial" identities and "communities".

The discussion of invented traditions and their relationship to modernity is continued in Chapters 5 and 6, where some of the mythologies of contemporary Hindu movements are excavated. I examine how "truth" and "tradition" were fabricated through a discussion of the campaign by Hindu fundamentalists to destroy the Babri masjid (mosque) in the early 1990s. These chapters expand the themes of body, identity and purity that were introduced earlier and link them to some of the theoretical discussions on post-coloniality and foundationalism in Chapter 1. Contemporary Hindu fundamentalism conspicuously demonstrates the will to archaeological and anthropological "authenticity" and the "return" to ethnicities that have never existed. It also ties together the body-related themes of religious purity with racial purity that are invoked separately in the respective activities of Islamic fundamentalists and right-wing black nationalists.

There are indeed some superficial links between modern religious authoritarianism and the natural and human race pseudoscience represented by some variants of black nationalism, such as some tendencies in Afrocentricity. The latter's stress on archaeology and anthropology, notions of purity and mysticism, and associated ideas about the gendered body form tentative links with the remarkably similar concerns of religious demagogues. There is clearly a political danger being highlighted in these various areas which only a few writers have repeatedly signalled (for example, Gilroy 1993). The most abhorrent aspects of Enlightenment and Romantic race pseudoscience have re-appeared today in the guise of the (white) "Bell curve" and the (black) "Cress theory of color-confrontation with racism" (Kohn 1995). More importantly for the concerns of this book, the shared epistemic spaces between variants of Afro-Asian nationalism, religious authoritarianism and classical Nazi and fascist ideologies are striking. These spaces seem to be informed by a dogmatic appropriation of liberation discourse (Enlightenment) and ideas of purity (Romanticism). Important to most of these ideologies is their placement of originary genesis within an emancipatory framework of land, blood and emotion. They can also selectively incorporate the themes and occasionally the methods of the natural and human sciences. The manner in which modern Hinduism has done this is explored in Chapters 6 and 7.

The concluding chapter is less a conclusion and more a presentation of diverse areas of discussion and intervention, including a broad assessment of new communications technology and the impact of natural science, both of which are increasingly important for cultivating new ethnicities among authoritarian religious movements. Several of the other themes of the book, including communalism and the gendered body, are revisited, especially where they relate to the themes of relativism, cultural difference, multiculturalism and issues of ethics. Questions of universalism and particularism, difference and sameness can be congruent with ideas of national community but may have been partially eclipsed by new, enduring non-local communities. The traffic across different civil societies and the formation of non-contiguous communities and movements can disrupt the practice of national-democratic authority. Generally, within the UK, black and multiracial feminism has been virtually alone in creating an activist political challenge to fundamentalism. But while black feminism in the UK has remained the dominant challenge in activist and community circles, black Marxism has, with very few exceptions, traditionally kept silent about, and perhaps failed to come to grips with, religious issues. However, many of the absolutist movements have also thrown up other transgressive resistances to themselves in marginal, interstitial sites within and across different civil societies. I briefly explore the possibilities of these challenges and what they might mean for the more earnest politics of socialism, feminism and black liberation.

CHAPTER 1

Knowledge and its alternatives

What explains the difficulty of the "human sciences", their precariousness, their uncertainty as sciences, their dangerous familiarity with philosophy, their ill-defined reliance upon other domains of knowledge, their perpetually secondary and derived character, and also their claim to universality, is not, as is often stated, the extreme density of their object; it is not the metaphysical status or the inerasable transcendence of this man they speak of, but rather the complexity of the epistemological configuration in which they find themselves placed ...
(Michel Foucault, *The order of things*, p. 348)

'Tis evident, that the identity, which we attribute to the human mind, however perfect we may imagine it to be, is not able to run the several different perceptions into one, and make them lose their characters of distinction and difference, which are essential to them.
(David Hume, *A treatise of human nature*, p. 259)

Some popular Indian gurus have taken to answering the increasingly desperate question "What is the Answer?" with a giggle and a soothing "What is the Question?" From the lips of an Indian guru this reply is merely a polite way of finding out where it hurts and when the ache is established, the guru will produce an equally polite, if banal remedy.
(Gita Mehta, *Karma cola*, p. 71)

Introduction

If the philosophical schemes of Enlightenment – let's group them as rationalism, empiricism, idealism – were the definitive challenges to eighteenth and nineteenth century clerical authority and religion-based "knowledge", why have they apparently failed now? How do postmodern or postcolonial theories offer better challenges to religious authoritarianism? Conversely, do religious authoritarian movements have an investment in modernity or are they simply a return to pre-Enlightenment "nativism" and "primitivism"? This chapter is preoccupied with looking at these three difficult questions mainly in general epistemological terms. Some sections of the chapter are digressive and look more closely at theoretical issues, particularly in the areas of knowledge, rationality and culture that have preoccupied postmodern and postcolonial theory. The chapter begins with a discussion of postmodern theory and its critique of Enlightenment rationality.

The postmodern assault on Enlightenment

There are, at the very least, warranted reasons for criticizing the Enlightenment tradition from the side of those historically denied – or subjugated because of – its universal and ethical products. It is necessary to account for the historical relation between the universal "rights of man" and the subjugation of women and black slave and colonial populations, between Mill's liberalism and his history of India, between Macaulay's Whiggish liberalism at home and his execrable racism abroad, between "liberty, equality" and slavery. The very best liberal and liberal-democratic traditions arising from (or before) the Enlightenment explicitly and in an endogenous manner denied women the universal franchise and excluded non-property owning working masses from their discourse of liberty. Thomas Jefferson's slave owning *did* circumscribe the "self-evident truths" of his discourse. Similarly, the modern human and natural sciences must account for the creation of subjugated racial and gendered subjects. The disassociation of the periods of Renaissance, Enlightenment, Romanticism and industrialization from their complex relation to slavery and colonialism, the frequent collapsing of Enlightenment thought with actually existing modernity and the wilful amnesia around the non-Western experience of modernity evade a number of difficult historical questions and have allowed (again) for a selective reconstruction of the philosophy of the West.[1] Moreover, a defence of Enlightenment is not helped by the evasive attitude of contemporary champions of that tradition towards "actually existing Enlightenment" and its harsh consequences for many of its subjects. For example, Habermas' silence about life-worlds outside Western capitalist and eastern (post-) state socialist countries, and the refrain that his work is concerned with *modern* societies and therefore has no bearing on the "Third World" is a subterfuge that can leave one in an aporetic state (see Dews 1992: 50–1, 183; Bernstein 1985: 118–19). Conversely, there is nothing new in the "incredulity at the metanarratives of modernity" that postmodern writers have discovered: the latter is less a feature of contemporary postmodernism than of the experiences of women, slaves and colonized populations and working people who were truly incredulous at the universal claims of modernity that were denied to them.

However, the critique of Enlightenment, especially the form of critique that claims to be on the side of the oppressed, the subaltern and the "other" also needs closer critical examination. While it now seems normal to speak of "the Enlightenment", the "Enlightenment tradition" or "project" and while the latter is often simply identified with modernity, there are two factors that disrupt these kinds of assembly and identity. The theorization of what constitutes modernity is very much tied up with the current sociological, political and cultural debates around the Western contemporary period. The Enlightenment is an extremely complex set of influences that cannot simply be reduced to the ideas of reason, autonomy, freedom, progress, humanity and science. The pre-revolution philosophies in France, the Scottish Enlightenment, the American Revolution and English anti-despotic liberty, Newtonian science, as well as the Romantic reaction to scientific rationality contained a highly contradictory set of situated ideas that do not necessarily or always translate into the condensed form ("foundationalism") in the way that much postmodernism theory claims. The post-Enlightenment, nineteenth-century rise of industrially organized capitalist societies – "modernity" – should be at least as important in these discussions. Indeed, the importance of the nineteenth century can get lost in these constructions of Enlightenment.

However, the general products of a collapsed "Enlightenment

tradition" have come under considerable attack from a number of different, though apparently related, tendencies. While these critiques are complex and cannot just be read as if they follow one trajectory and result in one conclusion they do still have common features. In particular, the contiguity of history, progress, the association of change with development, as well as the Enlightenment values of reason and rationality, science and humanity, have been relentlessly criticized from different philosophical and political positions. Similarly, the "grand narratives" and the master texts of modernist political philosophy – liberalism, socialism, democracy, communism, nationalism, fascism (but not capitalism) – have undergone sustained interrogation or have imploded under the weight of their own transcendental truths. The poststructuralist (especially Foucauldian) assault on History has relativized those values of Enlightenment and modernity as belonging to one *episteme* among others (Foucault 1970: 30–2, 51–8). In Foucault's work, the genealogical method, which transcended his earlier "archaeology", is favoured over any delusional pretences to historiography and reveals instead the micropolitics (or "microphysics") of power that is immanent in, as well as a constitutive condition of, all discourse (Gordon 1980: 56–62, 146–65; Foucault 1981). This combination of *episteme* with the methodology of genealogy and power/knowledge is symptomatic of the relativist–universalist tensions that haunt much postmodern and deconstructionist theory.

Postmodern theory has also elaborated upon what the forms and contents of Western political theory could be (Jameson 1991; Bauman 1992; Heller & Feher 1991). Generally, the earlier structuralist obsession with synchronicity (and its prudent avoidance of the signified and the referent) has resulted in a substantial repudiation of the texts of modernist political representation and agency. More recent work, demonstrating a synthesis of deconstructionist, neo-Wittgensteinian, Foucauldian and post-Lacanian methodology, has been able to mount a major critique of the nature of the political project itself, including the nature of political identity and representation, political struggle, the idea of political dichotomy, the nature of political antagonism and especially political necessity, morality and ethics (Laclau & Mouffe 1985: 105–22; Laclau 1990: 89–92, 97–132; Butler 1993, Zizek 1989). In their more popularized form, apparent in much cultural studies work, these tendencies simulate an identity between the limitless play of the signifier and the realm of the political, economic or bodily real. The ease with which differences between signifiers can be remanufactured is aesthetically identified with the task of articulating oppositional political blocs. The harder work of the politically possible, the difficult issues of ethical accountability and moral necessity, the non-transient, often violent presence of institutional power, the endurance of the capital–labour relation and the manifest and real problems of judgement and evaluation seem to disappear under the debris of multiple antagonisms, indeterminate signification or even psychosis. The debt that this tendency owes to (especially Althusserian) structuralism has been especially apparent through its ferocious attacks on humanism and historicism. Another political relativist tendency, owing as much to American pragmatism as to French poststructuralism, urges a "public" attitude of liberalism but a "private", aesthetic or poetic attitude with regard to everything else. The privatized intellectual cannot make public legislative claims over other similar "final vocabularies" (Rorty 1989: 73). It is not clear how these private critical attitudes might deal with ("public") institutions, the state, forms of technical rationality and of technological domination and terror that persist inside and outside (and because of) "liberal-democratic" societies, but do not comply with the arbitrariness of language or signification. Nor is it evident how a "private" disposition defines its contextual boundaries, and knows it has done so, without at least some recourse to more general evaluative criteria (an excessive universal that haunts a particularist centre).

However, much postmodern (and postcolonial) theory repeatedly offers an important but often clandestine political imaginary. This is usually affiliated with the value of social and cultural diversity, (if not just difference) and profound ideas of liberty, radical democracy and, arguably, an ultimate humanism. It is clear, for example, that even though postmodern theorists would disavow the possibility of foundations for freedom or liberty, they would at the very least have a consistent *distaste* for the kind of chauvinism expressed through racism, sexism, homophobia – or religious authoritarianism. Postmodern and, certainly, postcolonial theories are also frequently explicit in their claim that they are disrupting *specifically Western* foundationalism. These strands combine to form a kind of political imaginary, postmodern theory's own utopia, its unintelligible horizon. Pragmatically, it represents an ideal bourgeois liberal democracy (Rorty 1989) or a type of "permanent revolution" radical social democracy (Laclau & Mouffe 1985, Butler 1993, Zizek 1989), with (necessary) democratic structures that prefigure their own persistent critique, which dismantles and reformulates group identities (Butler 1993, Spivak 1993b, Bhabha 1994) or seeks to make connections between them again in persistent narrative forms that privilege class (Jameson 1991, Harvey 1989). Many of these projects are not entirely dissimilar to eighteenth- and nineteenth-century English and American liberalism, though, importantly, their focus has shifted from the classical freeborn individual to the identities of modern groups or collectives.

Enlightenment, identity and difference

Many postmodern and postcolonial critiques imply that the decentreing of the subject, the reduction of agency and history to text, the critique of historicism, humanism and rationalism, perhaps even the revelation of the genealogies of power in all discourse, are *in some way* capable of disrupting new forms of Western economic, political and technological terror and domination or, worse, that this disruption is actually taking place because of these critiques. There is a set of narrative styles deployed in much postmodern and postcolonial writing through which the author can write very suggestively and very evasively about real oppression and domination: "In postcoloniality, every metropolitan definition is dislodged. The general mode for the postcolonial is citation, reinscription, rerouting the historical" (Spivak 1993b: 217).

This sounds good as an allusion to some kind of "Third World" or migrant resistance. It declares that whatever the metropolitan (say, the West) decides and defines is "dislodged" by something called postcoloniality or the postcolonial (which is something to do with the Third World). Aside from ignoring the real political premiums and political stakes that might be involved in actually undertaking these tasks, these theoretical destructions of Western power are constantly troubled by the real activities of the oppressors and the oppressed.

There is an important, and again typically allusive and evasive set of ways in which postmodern and postcolonial theories write both *about* and *for* the oppressed and exploited while denying that the latter is possible. The "other" or "subaltern" is written into the postmodern or deconstructionist melodrama as an entity that has the status of being both a character-actor and a concept-metaphor. The "other" is also not a simple creature, but is heterogeneous. It can be the philosophical "other" of Descartes, John Stuart Mill, Rousseau and Hegel, Freud and Lacan, Levinas, Husserl or Derrida. It can be the *absolute* other of Descartes, the Romantic Rousseau or Levinas. Or it can be the more complex other of Hegel, the deconstructed Rousseau, Lacan or Derrida. It can be, or allude to, "the others" of the West or the Third World. It can also substitute for personality or character – "the Third World Woman" for example.

This is an explicit identification between the philosophical problems around dualism, monism, tautology, interiority and exteriority, and the problems of providing a political analysis of the real oppressed. This identification has influenced much deconstructionist activity partly as a result of Derrida's reading of Rousseau (and Lèvi-Strauss) which exposes the necessary supplement to any binary mythology of origin (Derrida 1976: 220–7). "There is no ethics without the presence *of the other* but also, *and consequently,* without absence, dissimulation, detour, differance, writing" (ibid: 139–40, second emphasis added).

Ethics, and in particular the ethics that naturally arise from self, require the presence of a differentiated other, a presence that disrupts the self's identity as self, and consequently destroys the "ontological mythology" of self and other. If the other is in some way imbricated in the self *and vice versa*, it is only a short step for deconstructionists to argue that the *political* identifications of oppressed and oppressor are already imitated in each other, as most readily evinced in Homi Bhabha's writings on ambivalence, mimicry and hybridity. The interdependency and instability of the categories of self and other also provide an indefinite resource from which to (textually) attack the oppressor (the master, the colonist, the white/Western feminist, imperialism). One creates a critique of the master that is uniquely, and monotonously, based on revealing the elements of slave that it contains. One creates a critique of the slave subject position by revealing its imitative and slippery congruence with the master's discourse that created it. Somewhere in between these two critiques one inserts an ineffable or sublime property that disaggregates the master and slave positions, and the relations between them. This binary method of talking about self–other, oppressor–oppressed relations and subsequently inserting a complexity that disrupts the relation entirely is strikingly reminiscent, and indeed is a variant of, older philosophical debates around the subject–object relation in empiricism, rationalism, realism and idealism.

It is also not clear that this kind of critique and ambiguity reflects the practices of the actual others. Indeed, in their deference to identity, personal experience, dogmatic reasoning, legislative authority, u- or dystopia and the quest for spiritual and transcendental meaning, the many others, in the West at least, sometimes appear to have recast themselves as subjects within an old matrix drawn by Kant, Hegel, Descartes and Hume. One can no longer easily resolve these subjects by inserting a Marxian critique of the commodity form, the anthropology of labour or a coming to self-awareness of alienation. However, it is not clear whether the others want to displace the subject of Enlightenment and humanism, take his white male place, want to squeeze in there with him and share his throne (sometimes against other others) or whether we can even begin to think about this problem in these dichotomous terms. Similarly, it is not at all obvious that the others want to abandon rationality and reason, or history or humanism, or indeed, whether that possibility even exists. One needs to remember that contemporary others have all used reason in their fight for a humanism against the irrationalist reductionism of human and natural, especially biological, science. These battles did not require a transcendental subject of pure reason but did utilize a practical rationality and a powerful appeal to the tribunal of humanism. Those rationalities are very much needed now against emergent forms of physical, biological and genetic determinism. It is troubling that postmodern theory is happier celebrating the electronic products of technical rationality than criticizing the legislative warrants of the increasingly authoritarian natural sciences. This critique cannot be evaded by the rhetorical posture that all one needs to say is that science is equivalent to "positivism" – it is no longer clear that this is the case.

The critique of historicism, humanism and the sovereign subject in postmodern and deconstructionist theory has, however, been frequently undertaken in the name of the *humanism* that has been denied to The Wretched of the Earth (Fanon), The Second Sex (De Beauvoir) or The Love That Dares Not Speak Its Name (Wilde).

Some of these critiques of Enlightenment and modernity frequently reproduce in all their detail the philosophical foundations they attack. This is also a manifestly aestheticized political issue about or against the "superiority of Western reason".[2] Simply stressing the overdetermination of Enlightenment ideas by their endophoric historical association with the West, with Western terror and with contemporary Western domination can evade other problems with these ideas. More importantly, there is the real possibility that the critique or rejection of Enlightenment is not only rooted within the bounds of that normative tradition itself but can also confirm its most obnoxious tendencies. For example, the search for alternative "non-Western" traditions in religion or antiquity can result in the conclusion that cognition, reason and judgement are essentially *Western* qualities, whereas faith, mysticism or renunciation are the only authentic nativist possibilities. This, of course, exactly reproduces one strand of scientific Enlightenment thought itself. Alternatively, reason, validity and the possibility of rationalism are foreign to the native sensibility, freedom, liberty or equality are irrelevant and, worse still, these supposedly *Western attributes* therefore cannot form a basis of resistance to the terror that some "Third World" governments inflict on their subjects.

Another tendency, explored in more detail later in the book, rejects human ideas or capacities that it deems Western, but still considers it legitimate to excavate ancient non-Western texts to prove that Western ideas were, after all, indigenous and hence stolen. It may well be possible to identify very similar constructions, anything from Platonic beauty and the Kantian sublime to empiricism, the cognitive, willing and judging subject, realism, autonomy, the social contract, democracy and probably anything else in the ideas of human science one wants to "find again", *ex post facto*, in other non-Western historical traditions. Ancient Asian texts and artefacts may well reveal similar kinds of metaphysical and practical questions that have confronted humanity and there is no great surprise in this. But many Hindus have found it imperative to show that the *Rig Veda*, the *Upanishads*, the *Bhagavad gita* and the *Ramayana* already contain "everything" that has subsequently been discovered by Western human and natural sciences, including all of Newton, Einstein and quantum physics. The obsession with this kind of activity needs noting and its prophetic form of analysis needs critical examination.

The range and complexity of Enlightenment ideas cannot be reduced from a "standpoint" of postmodern otherness as a simple pejoratively inscribed metaphor that has to be (or can easily be) rejected. The labour that would be involved in "rejecting" the Enlightenment is also considerably underestimated by many of these interventions. "Enlightenment" has not written the scripts that we are perpetually doomed to follow. However, it would be a gross mistake to think either that all the narratives of Enlightenment are exhausted or that the "others" can be so easily situated in alternative affiliations that contest all or, indeed, any of these strands. Indeed, it is striking how frequently Enlightenment ideas are rehearsed in postmodern theory, their rejection only affirming them further. For example, the empiricist tradition of sensate experience as "constitutive" of the subject, which is therefore dispersed through, and is no more than, the external impressions it receives, appears to correspond to the decentred subject of post-structuralism or "postmodern radical difference" (Norris 1993: 79). It was Hume who put it best:

> The mind is a kind of theatre, where several perceptions successively make their appearance; pass, re-pass, glide away, and mingle in an infinite variety of postures and situations. There is properly no *simplicity* in it at one time, nor *identity* in different... (Hume [1888] 1978: 253; emphasis in original)

Similarly, the cynicism of much postmodern theory towards foundations for knowledge bears strong comparison with Hume's scepticism, and in particular his critique of inductive knowledge. Indeed, something remarkably like "the problem of induction" in Hume is often explicitly invoked as a rationale for difference and particularism against commonality and universalism: we have no warrant for believing that what is true for us is also true for them.

Interestingly enough, the vogue for social constructionism in establishing the difference-based identities of new social movements is also frequently coupled with some kind of naïve naturalism. It is symptomatic perhaps of new social movements to have elements of both, to be able to assert from within the same discourse that their identities are both socially constructed and in some way constitutionally natural. Afrocentricity is a good example, but some of the claims of, for example, lesbian and gay liberation or New Age movements exhibit a similar tension. Without wishing to diminish the political importance of these debates, do they not reflect a much older argument about civilization and the natural state?

> It is in fact easy to see that many of the differences between men that are ascribed to nature stem rather from habit and the diverse modes of life of men in society. (Rousseau [1913] 1993: 80)

For Rousseau the social constructionist, these *differences that modern civilization creates* are contrasted with the harmonious state of nature, a utopian community of peace and "equality". This is impressively similar to the primal utopia that at least some in the new social movements wish to return to.

The identities of difference claimed in new social movements also appear to have been formed through the mobilization of rational contemplation in its strongest Enlightenment versions. The rationalist tradition of coming to knowledge or identity through contemplation (Leibnitz) or doubt (Descartes) is easily mirrored in the identity claims of various new social movements. Identities theorized as formed through disavowals of other identities ("I am not that") while coming to a positive realization of themselves ("I am that") seem to be reducible to the methodology of Descartes.

Similarly, the differing ideas of the transcendent that were important to both Kant and Hegel re-appear constantly in the postmodern textual narratives of both progressive and authoritarian social movements. In particular, the anchoring of transient ephemeral existence within a transcendental identity or subject moving through time, ultimately self-realizing, self-determining or autonomous, is Hegel all over again. Similarly, the dialectic, in particular Hegel's master–slave dialectic[3] is a *general form*, what Roy Bhaskar calls "generalized master–slave type relations" (Bhaskar 1993: 175, 332–5), that frequently provides the methodology of time, struggle, prediction and strategy for social movements. The complexities of the Hegelian dialectic additionally prefigure the instability of identity that social movements constantly deal with. The need to rely on what has been theorized as "strategic essentialism", itself disrupted by persistent, repetitive critique, is an allusion to essentially a form of negative dialectics (Spivak 1993b: 3–7). The autonomy of the will in

11

Kant, and the principle of humanity as an end in itself (though perhaps not universal law) would surely have a resonance for those who place a value in their otherness, and seek to create their own autonomous kingdoms.

The special place of the Ineffable

It might be a truism to say that something like the Sublime in Kant is also metaphorically reproduced in virtually all ideologies and theories of plenitude, utopia, lack, faith, aporia, chaos, the Absolute, the Infinite, liberation and so forth. However, a general structure to all these ideologies can be talked about and this becomes relevant in arguing against the view that postmodern or postcolonial theory disrupts Enlightenment foundationalism. In Habermas' exceptional discussion of the condition of philosophy, he shows how identity-thinking in metaphysics is characterized by a conceptual reliance on the removal of origins into an extraspatial extratemporal "object" of unity (Infinity, God, Being) that provides the basis for particularity and difference (Habermas 1992: 28–53). From the idea of one, many is derived and a relation between identity and difference is established for metaphysics. However, philosophy now exists after the event of science, of empiricism and of "procedural rationality". Habermas claims that it therefore does not have an unambiguous choice of turning to classical metaphysics, to forms of irrationality, or to the extraordinary. He distinguishes sharply between classical metaphysics and its forms of rationality, and postmetaphysical philosophy and its necessary disavowal of the extraordinary after the fact of science. However, even if we accept the *post*metaphysical status of modern ideologies, how does this change our political challenge to the striking combination of procedural rationality and empiricism with ideas of totality, infinity and the Sublime that characterize modern authoritarian religious movements? Liberation ideologies also foundationally integrate modern bureaucratic rationality and science into their utopias of plenitude. Does it matter that these are postmetaphysical? Habermas makes a strong claim that metaphysics was shattered by procedural rationality, empiricism, emergent historical consciousness and the overdetermination of theory by practice, among other factors. This implies a typical and powerful optimism about the *de jure*, if not quite *de facto*, triumph of (some kind of presumably communicative) rationality against traditional religious or philosophical metaphysics. How can we make sense, then, of the *possibility* of pronouncements such as the following which claim to integrate rationality, science, modern religion and traditional religious metaphysics:

> ... the Western-Science Paradigm's direction of growth and development has been almost entirely determined by the politicians' need to deter, wage or win wars or the need to land on the moon before anyone else.... Clearly the epistemology of Islam, with a Revealed Paradigm at the centre of human knowledge and behaviour, provides a far superior integrated system of knowledge. The same Revealed Paradigm guides and directs everyone – the scientist and the politician – in a single Grand Paradigm. Indeed, this Grand Paradigm is nothing but Islam itself. It is also the most complete, all-inclusive, open system in which all knowledge and behaviour is simultaneously controlled, directed and set free to seek the highest goals of excellence compatible with all parts of the Grand Paradigm. (Siddiqui 1984: 2–3)

If modern political ideologies are based on reason, then the limit points of reason (the unknowable) and their relation to reason (some method of identity with the unknowable) also require naming, classification and description. In modern religion, the Ultimate or Infinite is usually this transcendental object and faith forms its link with rationality. In liberation ideologies, many of which share a partly Aristotelian, mostly Hegelian schema of totality, teleology, identity and resolution (often combined eclectically with various forms of technical rationality and empiricism), it is their utopia that needs to be named and described. Rationally elaborated epistemology comes into being in circumscribing its boundaries by making immanent a *necessary* ineffable or imagined transcendental object. Put differently, whatever name the horrifying Ineffable is given, it is functionally necessary for concomitant knowledge and reason to exist. It enables a relation with the numinous, and propels the knowledges and the forms of reason that are required. This makes its naming and description in any

13

particular ideology especially important: god, infinity, chaos, the sublime, the world spirit, totality, the ultimate, faith, *Volkgeist*, quantum uncertainty, utopia, liberation. Moreover, this seems to be a consequence rather than a critique of Enlightenment foundationalism, at least in its Kantian and rationalist forms. It is also by no means clear that system-based and evolutionary theories that invoke ideal types, such as undistorted communicative rationality or the ideal speech situation, can escape from this consequence.

Postmodern theory and deconstruction abound with immanent theoretical objects and concept-metaphors that are transcendental (*a priori* or metaphysical) and defined as ineffable. Derrida's object of archewriting has been described by Habermas as renewing "the mystical concept of tradition as an ever delayed event of revelation" (Habermas 1990: 183). This object, highly authoritative in Derrida's work, is unknowable and transcendental and indeed its authority in deconstruction is derived from these qualities that demand endless repetitive interpretation. The same can be said of the status of différance in Derrida, or of the differend in Lyotard. Foucault's conceptions of discourse and power/knowledge, similarly, have the combined properties of immanence, transcendence and ineffability – they immediately invoke a meaning but are defined as impossible to know in themselves or in their origins and yet are foundationally necessary for his epistemology. Lack, plenitude, psychosis and the Lacanian real perform similar functions in psychoanalytic theory. It is also important that the "work" or operation of the theory, literally its hidden hand, and consequently any semblance of human agency that the theory alludes to, takes place as a consequence of these objects.

The postcolonial assault on reason

Postcolonial theory, an increasingly influential academic tendency, overlaps considerably with the above territories. It has been influenced variously by Said's genealogy of "Orientalism", psychoanalysis and its application by Fanon to the colonial condition, the critique of Western feminism, deconstruction, Foucault's genealogical method and the structuralist critique of humanist Indian historiography (Spivak 1988, 1989, 1990, 1993b; Bhabha 1990a, 1994). This tendency often reproduces earlier critiques of colonialism and slavery. Indeed, it seems firmly fixed on the colonial frontier and does not fully engage with contemporary "Third World" political formations (like Hindu nationalism) for which the colonial frontier is of less importance than older "frontiers". In opposition to what it sees as the Western vagaries of postmodernism theory, it has attempted to elaborate a counterdiscourse of "postcoloniality".

Postcolonial theory exhibits many of the epistemic problems of its deconstructionist and poststructuralist parents and these are briefly worth listing here. It adheres to a form of universalism that transgresses human and sometimes natural science disciplinary boundaries. This is not problematic in itself but is undertaken without justifying its own methodological privilege. At its most banal, this reduces to what Peter Dews has called the "nemesis" of all relativist positions (Dews 1987). The claim to be able to deconstruct every methodology ("nothing exists outside the text") creates some kind of equivalence between all methodological positions except the universal, privileged deconstructive one. There are variants of this relativist quandary in postcolonial theory that are highlighted later. More generally, why should textual methodologies be privileged above any others such as empiricist, rationalist, realist or even religious fundamentalist approaches? This universalist claim for the textual method is, nevertheless, highly selective and often privileges the (frequently postmodern) literary novelistic form over other textual styles.

This also means that textual methodologies overreach their epistemic bounds by looking at problems that could never be resolved by, or even have a meaning within their epistemologies. The substances of those problems (such as scientific determinism, sexism, state power, imperialism, colonialism, ecological disaster, the fact of the Holocaust) remain essentially untouched (Norris 1993). It feels odd to have to rehearse the prosaic argument that racism, modernity, sexism, capitalism and imperialism are utterly unchanged by the act of deconstructing them, just as, when one engages in a deconstruction of this beast called "modernity", modernity remains blithely unaffected.

Recent textual methodologies also commit what Roy Bhaskar has called the epistemic and ontic fallacies. The real, in the former case, is identified with knowledge of the real. In the ontic fallacy, knowledge itself is ontologized and naturalized "though its compulsive determination by being" so that the formation of a theoretical object is identified as equivalent with its actual existence or coming into being (Bhaskar 1986: 6, 23–4). Said's Orientalism can be used as such an object. To be sure, textual methodologies can co-exist with an affiliation to some kind of empirical realism but at some stage that cannot just be perpetually deferred, especially if they claim a political purchase, they are *obliged* to identify what the relationship is between their epistemic objects and what exists outside them and indeed is the condition for them. In avoiding this, they share considerable epistemic space with empiricism which itself reduces the real to what is represented of the real. This shared space extends to the conception of history itself. Empiricism also confuses actually existing historical methodology with both "historicism" (as some variant of historical determinism) and Hegelianism (history as any of process, teleology or totality). Indeed, the positivist critique of history seems to have been the original form of the poststructuralist critique of "historicism" (Carr 1990: 91–6).

Modernity, if nothing else, is an historical tendency in which real institutions are reproduced in a manner that is relatively autonomous from the claims within modernity about progress, development and inevitability, and this in itself needs to be explained. One task of historical methodology is to distinguish the historical tendencies in modernity from the discursive claims about history within modernity, rather than assuming an identity between the two, as in much textual method that identifies modernity's iterative compulsion and sense of history with history itself. That history is a text (and humanism is the enemy) can also result in an "anti-ethical", "anti-moral" disposition to historical facts such as slavery, anticolonial resistance, the Holocaust and so forth. This kind of disposition is more strident in postmodern than in postcolonial theory. But there are similar ethical consequences for postcolonial theory. If history is only a text, what are the ethical and moral obligations of or towards those whom the text has deposited in the present? How indeed is historical fact to be distinguished from mythical history or myths about history without at least some critical realist, or even naïve realist, affiliation? How, for example, can the genocidal ideologies of Hindu nationalism, which are politically legitimized through a conception of mythic time, be criticized?

One important challenge that postcolonial theory has tried to face directly is to define the space for knowledge in and of the "Third World" in which Western universal reason and humanism have failed or are incomplete but the return to premodern nativism is also an impossibility after the fact of humanism and science. Gayatri Chakravorty Spivak argues (rather repetitively) that the "Third World" is placed in a relation of catachresis to Western foundationalism. The space in which the marginal or subaltern finds itself in relation to the metropolitan centre is one "that one cannot not want to inhabit and yet must critique" (Spivak 1993a: 161).

> Within the historical frame of exploration, colonization, decolonization, what is being effectively reclaimed today is a series of regulative political concepts, the supposedly authoritative narrative of the production of which was written elsewhere, in the social formations of Western Europe. They are being reclaimed, indeed claimed, as concept-metaphors for which no historically adequate foundation may be advanced from postcolonial space; yet that does not make the claims any less important. A concept-metaphor without an adequate referent is a catachresis. These claims for founding catachreses also make postcoloniality a deconstructive case. (Ibid: 158).

The critical method of "subalterns and ex-slaves" has to be "a catachrestic gesture of reinscription", "the persistent critique of what one must inhabit, the persistent consolidation of claims to founding catachreses". Similarly, for Homi Bhabha, the subaltern must seize the value coding of the spectacle of modernity and transform it from within a non-originary postcolonial locus (Bhabha 1994: 40). The problematic nature of this entity, the "another time, another space" that Fanon imagined (ibid.: 237–8), the postcolonial space of mimicry, ambivalence, hybridity or catachresis should "hopefully" provide a constraint against a return to nativism and ethnic identitarian positions (according to Spivak (1993a: 161)) or, if absolutist nativist positions do emerge they will already be ambivalent (according to Bhabha (1988: 209, 214)).

It is important not to dismiss either the importance of examining "colonial discourse" or the substantive analyses of modernity and "colonialism" that this work has thrown up. In particular, Spivak's argument on "founding catachresis" and Homi Bhabha's corresponding arguments about ambivalence, mimicry, hybridity and a "third space" (Bhabha 1990a) can signal important problems and can be persuasive if we accept the methodology in which they are framed. However, while we can agree with Bhabha's view that theory does not have to translate immediately into politics (Bhabha 1988), I am not convinced that the political or theoretical efforts of this tendency are engaged in the way that is imagined, nor are these efforts undertaking the critical offensives against Western modernity that they set out, or claim, to be. Clearly, the *récits* of this tendency are far from *petit*. Postcolonial criticism constructs quite grandiose and totalizing schemes that can seem very much at odds with its own deconstructive prescriptions. Indeed, it seems to be the case that any methodology (such as rigorous deconstruction) that intimately criticizes the contours and the detail of another complex *episteme* cannot but reproduce a version of that same totality and complexity within itself.

Similarly, its dismissal of universal ethics has not prevented postcolonial theory from making claims that have wide and universal ethical import. For example, the claim to "founding catachresis" is an irreducibly ethical one that makes a stiff judgement on the conditions and forms of knowledge and cultural production in the "Third World". Aside from this, there is another general problem. If postcoloniality has this catachrestic quality, then that is not a sufficient condition for its difference from postmodernity since the latter has the same quality – the critical repetition and transvaluation of the stuff of modernity, since "there is nothing new to be said anymore", but in a way that cannot evade the products of the modernity that preceded it. Indeed, how does one situate the Romantic movement against Enlightenment? Did this not have the same quality of catachresis in relation to, or in response to, the foundationalism that both preceded and gave rise to it? Conversely, what are we to make of the quite real impact on Voltaire, Kant, Hegel and other Enlightenment thinkers of the metaphysical speculations, the philosophies and the civilizational metaphors that came from India and China?

If the issue is that modernity was denied to, or incompletely presented, or presented in a form of terror to the "Third World," then this demands a more careful and substantive historical assessment of the impact of modernity and Enlightenment in the "Third World" and it is not clear that the literary method can provide this. Moreover, the claim that the demand for citizenship, nationalism, democracy and other Enlightenment products from decolonized space is a catachresis because no original nativist position is possible seems circular, because it needs constantly to invoke some idealized but non-existent and impossible nativism as its supplement. In any case, if we begin with a view of the monolithic West and its knowledges, combine it with the West's historical domination of the "Third World" and the West's creation of "complete" knowledges of it (such as Orientalism), then to say the relation between the latter and the former is a catachresis is tautological. Interestingly, Spivak's use of catachresis relates closely to a compounded version of Fredric Jameson's concepts of schizo-phrenia and pastiche in postmodernity. At some remove, it also suggests comparison with the "between two cultures" approach of earlier multiculturalist discourse around second-generation Asians in Britain, a static approach that could only exist by writing Asian and white ethnicized forms out of history.

There is an additional political problem with Spivak's use of catachresis and the project of persistent critique that it entails. This is manifest most directly when we compare progressive and author-itarian critiques of the West, or *of each other*, that arise from within the "Third World". Both may be in debt "to Enlightenment" for the conception of rights, democracy or freedom they use. But the basis of the critique, and the manner in which Enlightenment conceptions are used, is utterly different and has radically opposed aims. Young Muslims UK released a leaflet that criticized Amnesty International's report on human rights violations by the Sudanese government on the following basis:

> ... Amnesty states that "flogging constitutes a cruel, inhuman and degrading punishment". But surely Amnesty is aware that the Hudood punishments are based on the Words of God in the Qur'aan and the example of the blessed Prophet Muhammad (SAAWS) which all Muslims love and strive their utmost to follow and will never abandon? ... Amnesty also rejects "any provisions in any law which contravene internationally-recognised stan-dards protecting human rights" .... What – even if these

supposedly internationally-recognised standards were set by a tiny group of Western nations following the end of the second world war? In effect, Amnesty is declaring its support for a dictatorship of Western values over the entire globe.[4]

To be sure, this persistent critique of Amnesty is not explicitly based on the "rights" of the Sudanese government to torture its people, but other sections of the leaflet mention the *credibility* that Amnesty will lose in the eyes of Muslims, and also implicitly mentions the rights of children conscripted into fighting by the southern Sudanese forces. In these instances, the use of the idea of rights to criticize the rights denied by the West to Muslims actually strengthens the case for *universal* human rights. This is a consistent feature of Hindu and Islamic authoritarian critiques of the West based on exposing "double standards" in the application of rights. Those critiques do use the promises of Enlightenment against its representatives. However, those critics of the West also do not *necessarily* want those Enlightenment products for themselves but want to use them strategically against the West and against dissenters. Similarly, the Young Muslims' critique is not even mostly based on an appeal to rights, but primarily derives its authority from an appeal to what is claimed as God's word. This authority does not necessarily reflect a Western methodology, nor does it make sense to compare it against some ineffable and historically distant "nativism". Against this kind of critique of the West, another directly opposed Muslim democratic tendency, which may itself criticize Western domination, will derive its authority primarily from humanism and rights. This difference is politically definitive and conclusive. It then seems peremptory to label both these postcolonial positions a catachresis, to argue normatively that persistent critique is required, or to suggest that deconstruction is what is being undertaken.

Postcolonial theory also, and paradoxically, has a marked tendency to manufacture its political legitimacy through naked appeals to "other" tribunals of judgement that do not exist, or exist in perpetually deferred form, in the real world of groups, communities and nations. It is easy to criticize Western feminism or Marxism from a position of claimed alterity, typically by mobilizing the judgement of a permanently deferred, unconstitutable tribunal of a racial other and a curious appeal based on its humanism. This, indeed, is similar to the strategic essentialism that black nationalists inside state institutions might employ. For example, Bhabha suggests that Fredric Jameson's "cognitive mappings" may be illuminating when considering the Bonaventura Hotel in Los Angeles but will leave you "somewhat eyeless in Gaza". To reverse this method, would Palestinians be more enlightened if their struggles were revealing "the disjunctive moment of utterance" that signifies the "temporal caesura" from which modernity announces itself as "spectacle", or that their struggles signified the emergence of a contra-modernity (Bhabha 1994: 240, 246)?

This is not to institute an anti-intellectualism, or to insert a backdoor political realism – academia is certainly political. It is to highlight how an evasive but effective metonymic claim to racial and gender alterity is embedded in and constitutive of Bhabha's and Spivak's work and sharply contests their own critique of humanism. Bhabha's and Spivak's own "race" or gender are made to matter in a lively authorial way. Certainly in Spivak's writing her race–gender combinations are rehearsed as a constant supplement to the academic institutions she encounters, even though she is embedded, and possibly canonical, in them. Interestingly, Spivak's personal speculations on race–gender politics within the formal institutions of modernity follow a general form that has been highlighted much earlier, most clearly in the writings of Césaire and Fanon on the administrative and bureaucratic conditions of colonialism. Paul Gilroy has highlighted a similar existential dilemma faced by the professional black other working in state institutions (Gilroy 1987b: 67). "Outside in the machine" is both an existential condition of personal politics and a (very different) sociological condition for some groups and classes inhabiting institutional bureaucracies. To be sure, it is a complex phenomenon that is not completely explained by a recourse either to vulgar Marxism or to some cross-class subaltern or racial affiliation between the academic and the oppressed, though both these are relevant. The neo-Kantian might ask what the conditions of modernity are that have produced relatively powerful classes, groups and institutions that reproduce themselves virtually entirely on the ideological basis of the critique of their exteriority to modernity.

Finding a voice? Or voices already heard![5]

Spivak's uncovering of the problems faced by racial or gendered others employed in performing functions for the institutions of modernity do not just end there. Despite her critique of the conditions in which alterity is claimed, she makes powerful, sometimes metonymic, sometimes metaphoric associations between the condition of herself and the general figure of the "Third World woman". Sometimes these are explicit attempts to recover an affiliation that actually cannot exist, and that she would normally criticize: Shahbano (an Indian woman who challenged Indian law on alimony in the mid-1980s) is "outside in the machine", Spivak is "outside in the teaching machine" (Spivak 1993b: 241). What is the ethical relation this announces between the author and the real constituency that the author employs as a referent?

Postcolonial theory can reproduce the same Foucauldian relations of domination of its subjects that it claims to uncover in other Western epistemologies, though with perhaps one extremely important difference. It implicitly but characteristically claims to know the subaltern consciousness (and its oppression) differently and more genuinely than Western, colonial or racist discourses do. Put differently, postcolonial theory claims to know its subjects differently from Western or colonial ideologies, and this is an ethical and moral difference that contains an indeterminate claim to affiliation with the subaltern and its struggles. This is a political claim about the knowledges that postcolonial theory produces of its subjects.

However, in postcolonial theory, the actual subject referents of fictive constructions like "other" or the "Third World woman" can never be in a position that is constitutive of an ethical court that can judge, criticize or concur with what is said about them. Nevertheless, character-actors are present as important methodological components and have a significance far beyond their heuristic capacities. Typically, and paradoxically, they allude strongly to Cartesian *subjectivities* (the author, the speaker, the reader) or to generalized Hegelian master–slave subject binaries (colonial self – subaltern other, elite – subaltern). The discursive privilege given to "self", "other" and similar constructions is, at some remove, reflective of the methods of the humanist-rationalist Enlightenment tradition that is criticized. The character-actors, the barest trace of "agency" that is found in this approach, also have constitutive features through which they substitute social formations, historical periods, the Third World, the West and so forth. These anthropomorphic constructions have totalizing claims made for them that are at least as momentous as the claims of positivism, rationalism or idealism in the human sciences.[6] An extraordinarily grand *legislative* claim is surely being made in speaking about "the subaltern", the "postcolonial subject" or the "Third World woman" in this way.

It should be apparent why even the asking of the question "can the subaltern speak?" reflects a Cartesian problem (the translation of a collective entity into a sovereign subject) overdetermined by a deconstructivist deferral that could never be answered affirmatively however many screaming subalterns one ceremoniously presented. At its most banal, the question has the answer that if realist historiography fails to find documentary evidence of subaltern voices, then we do not know what those voices said or what those subjects thought (see especially Parry 1987). Postcolonial theory also anthropomorphically refashions concept-metaphors (such as "postcoloniality") so that they substitute for the willing, judging, knowing and wanting subject of humanism. If these concept-metaphors created by postcolonial theory can act as if they were knowledgeable agents, why is that privilege denied to subalterns in their struggles?

There is a more obviously vanguardist aspect to this that appropriates the real referents of "Third World" or Western black struggles and situates them in a theoretical discourse in which they have no agency or voice but are instead explicitly spoken for in a project aimed at a metropolitan audience. This is a legislative and disciplinary "violence" whose consequences are barely registered in postcolonial theory. Consider the following sermon by Spivak regarding the 1995 UN Conference on Women:

> At the end of the day, I pose the same question that I put to a group of Bangladeshi fieldworkers who were about to go to Beijing, and were complaining about their scant English: Do you have any idea how you will be matronized by white and diasporic feminists? Can you get behind their herding smiles? And why, in your opinion – with all your hands-on experience of international exploitation – is it necessary to tabulate our state and local problems at the UN? (Spivak 1996: 4)

All three questions are already concluded. Evidently, they are not questions to Bangladeshi fieldworkers but are statements to the readers of *Radical Philosophy*. The statements elide the several metonymic identifications that are made between Spivak and Bangladeshi fieldworkers, international exploitation, and *our* problems, but also contrive several foreclosures (differences) between Spivak and white and diasporic feminists. The last insidious sentence is hybrid in invoking two gestures: an address to them ("in your opinion") and an identification between her and them ("our"). Perhaps the most important difference Spivak generates is between herself and her readers. None of them are likely to be "Bangladeshi fieldworkers" or "internationally exploited", but the latter are marshalled on the side of Spivak against her metropolitan readers.

This kind of discursive regime is essentially aimed at disciplining the subaltern in the face of the metropolitan audience and the postcolonial theorist and suggests a will to power not entirely dissimilar to the claims made by some liberation movements. The historical existence of subaltern struggles and critiques is the condition for, and has provided the raw materials for, postcolonial theory. This naturally raises a puzzle. How is it that unambiguous struggles against the unmistakably violent instances of colonial domination or slavery can become theorized through tropes such as ambivalence or hybridity? How is it that the condition of subaltern struggles ("utterances") against elites or the metropolitan become theorized as subaltern silence (Parry 1987)?

It is unusual in this respect that Spivak can recast a Shahbano as a silenced or censored figure, even though Shahbano, through her *agency*, overturned the effectiveness of Muslim Personal Law in India by going as far as the Indian Supreme Court. Similarly, Women Against Fundamentalism (WAF), virtually the only multi-racial organization in the UK to protest and demonstrate explicitly against fundamentalism and for Rushdie, is rehearsed in Spivak's work as audible only as "muted ventriloquists". However, Spivak can only re-articulate Shahbano and WAF within her theoretical meditations on subaltern silence because they had already spoken. WAF pointed out that "women's voices had largely been silent" during the Rushdie affair, "where the battle lines had been drawn between liberalism and fundamentalism". But that is exactly the reason why WAF came into being and spoke out forcefully while other voices remained silent. There are extremely important connections between the Shahbano case and the Rushdie affair that are explored later in the book, but women's silence is not one of them. There is a political difference between acknowledging and fighting against the imperialist erasure of exploited and oppressed "voices", and formulating a theory that wilfully seeks to deny those "voices" altogether. "They cannot represent themselves, they must be unrepresentable."

This kind of theoretical vanguardism comes from an unwarranted extrapolation from the syncretic or schizophrenic institutional space that postcolonial academics might necessarily have to inhabit in the West to the catachrestic space that the "Third World" occupies in its relation to the metropolitan. It may also be due to making an unwarranted leap from a reading of selectively ambiguous (post)colonial texts to defining the ambiguous postcolonial state of "Third World" "subalterns" outside of the contemporary political *context*; it may be that no such ambiguity exists, it may be politically irrelevant or may indeed be disciplinary or authoritarian. The metaphoric identity between the aporias in the theory of knowledge that postcolonial theorists may face in Western academia and the condition of the real subaltern is the epistemic fallacy.

Central to much postcolonial theory is the privilege given to marginal, liminal, hybrid, "transitional", migrant cultural spaces, typically those cultural "spaces" created by "Third World" people in the metropolis and written about by authors like Salman Rushdie. Frequently, though, there is a nebulous and indeterminate movement from the experience of postcolonial and generally privileged subjects in the West to the condition of the (contemporary or historical) "Third World" and its relationship to the metropolis. Both Bhabha and especially Spivak would be aware of the problematic and vanguardist nature of this identity between the marginal and the universal. However, Bhabha and Spivak do explicitly attempt to provide grand totalizing theories of culture, domination, temporality, knowledge, reason, the Third World, modernity and the West. Indeed, this projection from the particular space of the postcolonial intellectual/writer/migrant to the universal existential hybrid or catachrestic condition of the "Third World" subject is singularly prominent, often the main or only preoccupation in many postcolonial writings. This constitutes an interesting modernist narcissism that Aijaz Ahmad has highlighted – the privileging of the experience of "Third World" writers in the West as constitutive of, or at the zenith of, the experience of the "Third World" itself. The small migrant intelligentsia, many of whom are South Asian (and reflect precisely the in-betweenness of the gifts of modernity and the brutality of slavery) are at the apex of knowledge production of the Third World. Theirs is a special case that deserves bracketing out (Ahmad 1992: 6–7, 68–9).

Spivak has rhetorically criticized this kind of identity between "Third World" intellectuals, poor migrants in the West and the poor of the Third World, typically by invoking the different relation to "imperialism" of both constituencies and by instituting "the international division of labour" as an absolute marker between them. However, it is the extraordinarily imprecise conception of "imperialism" that she brings to her texts at these moments to function solely as an arbitrary "difference" (Spivak 1993b: 255–8, 77–281). This suggests an instrumental and complacent view of imperialism. For example, an essay on cultural studies begins with a prologue on imperialism and exploitation that not only highlights the invisible "urban or metropolitan, subaltern, the homeworker", but differentiates sharply between the black poor in the West and the poor of the Third World: "The trajectories of the Eurocentric migrant poor and the postcolonial rural poor are not only discontinuous but may be, through the chain-linkage that we are encouraged to ignore, opposed" (ibid: 257).

We may or may not agree with these views (the first part is tautological) but they establish the "anti-imperialist affidavit" for an essay concerned with the more parochial question of how to teach cultural studies in the US academy, and the fear that it will establish a new Orientalism:

> Colonial and postcolonial discourse studies can, at worst, allow the indigenous elite from other countries to claim marginality without any developed doctoral-level sense of the problematic of decolonized space and without any method of proper verification within the discipline. If this study is forever contained within English (or other metropolitan literatures), without expansion into a fully developed national culture studies, colonial and postcolonial discourse studies can also construct a canon of "Third World Literature (in translation)" that may lead to a "new

orientalism"... . We cannot fight imperialism by perpetrating a "new orientalism". (Ibid: 277)

No doubt this is an announcement of a new object of study for postcolonial theory. Just as beguiling is the unwarranted link between "fighting imperialism" and how, and in which languages, "Third World" literature should be taught in the American academy. More mysterious is the implication that a doctorate is necessary before a member of the "indigenous elite" from "other" (which?) countries can claim marginal status.

The politics of reason, culture and fundamentalism

In its most extreme critique of Western modernity and Enlightenment and in its onslaught against reason, humanism and historicism, postcolonial theory bears comparison with an altogether different contemporary critique of modernity from authoritarian religious "fundamentalist", "nativist" and obscurantist traditions. That the latter are apparently guarded against because of the catachresis that defines them has not in actual circumstance stopped them from loudly voicing abominable prejudices. Indeed, it may not *politically* matter if these prejudices can be traced back to the naturalism of Romanticism or to the sciences of Enlightenment, and hence to a condition defined by catachresis. Sometimes postcolonial theory, being unable easily to justify the "Western ideals" of cognition, reason and judgement, comes very close to assisting, or is immobilized when faced with, the standpoints of religious authoritarianism. Bhabha's view, in a discussion about fundamentalism, that "it is actually very difficult, even impossible and counterproductive, to try and fit together different forms of culture and to pretend that they can co-exist" is one such example, and its quite tragic universal ethical consequences need to be noted. Similarly (but paradoxically), in arguing that fundamentalism is already internally differentiated he comes very close to arguing that it will simply hybridize away (Bhabha 1988: 209, 214). Because of the cognitive, reflexive self-monitoring nature of all social systems, it would, in a sociological gaze, be extremely surprising if ambiguity, "hybridity" and ambivalence were not found in a bureaucratic formation (colonial administration) or political movement (fundamentalism). Nor are those moments of ambivalence unimportant or not worth investigating – the later chapters of this book demonstrate this kind of interest in small, transgressive moments. The methodological point is that deconstructionist methodology frequently institutes incomplete (uncomplicated) binaries that then have to be supplemented by complex devices such as ambivalence and hybridity.

The anti-materialist theories of culture in Bhabha's work are an interesting illustration of this process and are worth expanding upon here since they bear heavily on the broader discussions of ethnicity, religion and relativism that structure this book. In Bhabha's earlier work, the culture of the colonizer bore an ambivalent relation to that of the colonized. A strategy of pure domination was manifestly self-defeating, or was always subject to a contradictory process of both desire and disavowal. The colonized non-mimetically reproduced the dominant cultural form of the colonizer (such as in the Indian Civil Service) which turned its parodic gaze upon the colonizer. A hermetic strategy of power was internally subverted by the conditions of its existence – the conditions in which it had to learn about and know the subject of power, its partial incorporation of the subject into its own strategies of oppression, its appropriation of the other as a self that was always a deferred state of mimicry of the true self, and hence threatened its existence as self.

In his compounded concept of hybridity Bhabha expands these themes to present a theory of power and domination which, at least by implication, reaches well beyond the mechanism of colonial domination or racial oppression. The exercise of colonial authority requires a disclosure of its rules of recognition (the texts that elaborate knowledges of the colonized) just as the acknowledgement of authority depends upon the immediate visibility of its rules of recognition as a "necessity", a presence demanded by its utterance of historical inevitability, progress, modernity. However, according to Bhabha, colonial domination is achieved through a process of disavowal that is imbricated in the moment that it articulates the signs of cultural difference and integrates them within its systems of "hierarchy, normalization, marginalization". Domination has to disavow the chaos (illegitimacy) of its own intervention (oppression) by presenting its identity as necessitated by teleological evolutionism ("the civilizing mission"). Colonial authority must also represent all of the other (the country being dominated) by its partial self. This is another strategy of disavowal in which the dominated whole is able to be represented by a dominating illegitimate part. The process of knowing or representing the subject of discrimination itself incorporates within the strategy of discrimination itself the "denied knowledges" of the other. This opens an ambivalent space through which "resistance" to domination is a constant possibility. The production of these ambivalent spaces is "hybridity" – a reversal of the process of disavowal (rather than simply a native denial of knowledges of itself) that can turn its gaze onto the authority of power itself:

Hybridity is a problematic of colonial representation and individuation that reverses the effects of the colonialist disavowal so that other denied knowledges can enter upon the dominant discourse and estrange the basis of its authority – its rules of recognition. (Bhabha 1994: 114)

The presence of the hybrid thus makes the recognition of absolute cultural difference impossible – "differences of culture can no longer be identified or evaluated as objects of epistemological or moral contemplation: cultural differences are simply not there to be seen or appropriated"(Bhabha 1994: 114).

Bhabha employs Freud's discussion of fetishism and psychosis whereby the ego is split into two entities bearing contradictory relationships to the object – the realization of the object as the real object of knowledge, and the object as a product of desire that disavows its existence as the real object. These two psychical attitudes exist together without influencing each other. The colonialist gaze upon the hybrid, that which can no longer be differentiated as simply the other, turns into a paranoid gaze that must, but cannot, represent the colonized. The paranoid threat of the hybrid cannot be contained any more in dualisms of self and other, internal and external. Hybridity then, as an effect of colonial domination, radically subverts its authoritative condition of production. Hybridity is also not simply a site at which the colonized intervene in acts of anticolonial resistance: rather it constitutes that site of resistance itself.

This conception of hybridity in Bhabha appears to be a syncretism of several different theoretical gestures. One of these is

Bakhtin's reading of hybridity in *Little Dorrit* (Bakhtin 1981: 302):

> ... an utterance that belongs, by its grammatical (syntactic) and compositional markers, to a single speaker, but that actually contains mixed within it two utterances, two speech manners, two styles, two "languages", two semantic and axiological belief systems. (Ibid: 429)

This is combined with a psychoanalytic account of ego-splitting (*Spaltung*), a (Foucauldian) non-possessive conception of power and (what seems like) Ashis Nandy's elaboration of the ambivalence of colonial and postcolonial Indian identity (Nandy 1983). Bhabha's use of psychoanalysis is more than a form of reading: it is at least partially *explanatory*. However, even its use as a heuristic requires at least some methodological justification when applied in this universalist way. That aside, how is hybridity *particularly* relevant to the colonial situation, aside from its obvious racial-biological reference? Hybridity begs extension to any generalized master–slave type relations, all of which could be described as having some ambivalent property. Indeed, hybridity is such an expandable concept that it can be co-extensive with any micro- or macro-social relation.

In more recent work, Bhabha's conception of hybridity is extended to provide a different theory which contends that cultures not only meet at (or create) incommensurable sites and produce a "third" hybrid field, but that this meeting place is exactly the hybrid site through which "newness" enters the world. The problematic of cultural production, or more importantly the process of cultural translation, is linked to a theory of temporality, chronotope and performative agency (from speech–act theory). This concept of hybridity also expands to incorporate (what appear to be) aspects of Levinas's discussions of temporality and otherness, in particular the argument Levinas advances about the necessity of the meta-physical gaze of the other in registering, and creating the futures of the self:

> The instants do not link up with one another indifferently but extend from the Other unto me. The future does not come to me from a swarming of indistinguishable possibles which would flow toward my present and which I would

grasp; it comes to me across an absolute interval whose other shore the Other absolutely other – though he may be my son – is alone capable of marking, and of connecting with the past. But then the Other is alone capable of retaining from this past the former Desire that animated it, which the alterity of each face [the presentation of the other in excess of the idea of the other in me] increases and deepens ever more profoundly. (Levinas 1969: 283)

In Bhabha's elaboration of how newness enters the world, Levinas' other becomes identified as the migrant, or the others of colonialism. Bhabha privileges the migrant moment, and the migrant space (and "time") that exists in between two cultures.

Cultural globality is figured in the in-between spaces of double-frames: its historical originality marked by a cognitive obscurity; its decentered "subject" signified in the nervous temporality of the transitional, or the emergent provisionality of the "present" (Bhabha 1994: 216)

This emergent hybrid space is not a difference between two transcendental identities whose Hegelian realization is to be found either in the future or an invented past. Instead, these hybrid spaces are "opening out" and remaking the boundaries of any sign (such as race or gender) in performative actions that signify "neither one nor the other but something else besides, in between". This opening to a contingent future marks a "time" that is available to marginalized or minority identities to rehearse their performative agency.

The problem of this hybrid space is the problem of translation that itself "dramatizes the activity of culture's untranslatability" (ibid: 224). The hybrid moves beyond the simply plural, the assimilable or the racist – there is no "full transmissal of subject matter" between two cultures. The cultural modes of signification of *Brot* and *pain* cannot allow an identity completely congruent with bread. In each act of cultural translation, an agonistic supplement arising from the complementarity of language systems as systems of contestation and flux becomes the "seed of the untranslatable", the foreign element in the midst of the performance of cultural translation. This view of cultural incommensurability sits alongside a view of the hybrid that is able to transcend or bring into the open the untranslatability of cultures. But hybridity is also, in much of Bhabha's work, a type of syncretism, "a third space" that may not be either one or the other but is some partial combination of the two. Hybridity appears to signal both the possibility of cultural translation and the condition of its impossibility.

It should be apparent that Bhabha's chronotopic conception of hybridity is again universally assimilable. Each social act can be said to happen "hybridly" and each social act can be said to announce "the new", otherwise Bhabha would have to concede that only certain specified cultures have this property and that leads naturally to essentialism. Certainly this universal claim for hybridity is explicit in his writings – that all cultures are already "internally" and always hybrid(izing) before the artificial "moment" when they encounter another culture. So why should migrant and minority positions in the West be a special case of hybridity? Is it their *radical* alterity from dominant systems of signification? Is this a qualitatively different and more important type of hybridity that allows blacks, gays and women to interrupt the chronotope of modernity? What do these identities possess that, say, the maligned white working class do not? Is it something to do with their content? Surely religious fundamentalist identities also must announce "the new"? There is a suggestive way in which the privileging of the minority or migrant experience can slide into a form of essentialism in Bhabha's work that is battling with its other anti-essentialist, antihumanist, antihistoricist side. More generally, there is a deep tension in this work between an affiliation to the particularity of the migrant experience and a theory of space and time that is derived from it and then has to be universally applicable. If Bhabha's general theory of time, modernity, race and history can incorporate within itself both these perspectives – the absolutely marginal and the completely universal – does this not suggest something fundamentally misplaced about its own conception of the incommensurable? Similarly, in his conception of the compounded nature of hybridity itself, the methodologies of Freud, Lacan, Foucault, Levinas and Bakhtin, as well as perhaps Austin and Searle all co-exist. How is the translation across each of these radically different methodological positions possible in a singular concept of hybridity? (More problematically, how have *these* writers managed to provide the intellectual tools with which we can finally understand colonial domination?)

Bhabha is also extremely selective about the substance of the migrant's or colonial's experience itself. This is virtually entirely reduced to its designation as a race in modernity ("what do *blacks* want?"), and does not consider forms of identification among "migrants, slaves and ex-slaves" that evade race. (Needless to say, there is no acknowledgement of class.) This is part of a longer normative tradition of race-relations thinking that unwittingly reduces the experience of blacks to the parameters of race. In many ways, the thinkability of Bhabha's conception of hybridity has the normative discipline of race relations theory as its precondition, rather than the actual historical circumstances of ex-slaves and ex-colonials. It is also important to note the privilege given to the racial metaphor in his theory of Western modernity, time and culture. In some fundamental way for Bhabha, race seems to be almost a functionally necessary *a priori*, or precondition for the organization of Western capitalist modernity, its methods of temporality, space, culture, difference, newness, and its philosophy and epistemology. Why should *race* have the burden of this immense, rather transcendental role?

An important and common view of culture is reproduced in Bhabha's theory of hybridity: culture as equivalent to alterity which, given that in this methodology cultural difference is ultimately the difference between signifiers, reduces to a view of culture as originally incommensurable. This is one form of "naive incommensurability" that is extremely problematic. If one discovers an incommensurability between two cultures, then there cannot be an incommensurability there, or at the very least one has begun to translate one culture's meanings into the other. (If *Brot* and *pain* are incommensurable with bread, how is it that we can talk about this in English and indeed describe in English what this incommensurability is?) Bhabha may not deny that much of the content of two cultures is translatable but he would argue, however, that a core untranslatability remains. The status of this untranslatability appears to oscillate between an identity state of perfect translatability (two signifiers are identical and synchronic) and a state of core difference (two signifiers are different or non-synchronic). The circular aspect of this would be a necessary consequence of viewing culture as a synchronic system of signification and symbol.

However, this synchronic binarism is often complicated in many recent theoretical interventions, including Bhabha's, by inserting some kind of spatio-temporal iterativity. Difference is iteratively (re)cycled in a forward movement (the arrow of time), typically in a way that gives new meanings to those differences and their relations to "their" signifieds and referents through the act and the authority of repetition itself. (The view of culture as essentially arising from a binary methodology begs the question: how can culture be analyzable in such formally minimal diocratic Saussurian terms? Is this not, in its strongest sense, a disfigured philosophical rationalism?)

Something like the Sublime also makes its appearance in Bhabha's theory. Hybridity and "the third space" are ineffable concept-metaphors, like power/knowledge, that perform generative functions for Bhabha's theory. Hybridity is elaborated in Bhabha's work as existing in a kind of metaphysical "third space", an imaginary space–time that has some remarkable properties though we cannot exactly pin down its manifest mechanisms or its co-ordinates or even its existence. This imaginary space–time not only enables newness to enter the world but it also has the property of announcing the postcolonial's interruption of modernity's sense of time. The imaginary space–time also announces the time lag or "temporal caesura" (Levinas' discontinuity) that can form a basis for a different understanding of modernity. This space–time also appears to exist outside of the actual economic social constitution of differential times and spaces and, indeed, appears to be a functional condition for the latter. This suggests two possible explanations for why meanings, identities, cultures and so forth change, or indeed why change itself is possible: one is the banality of the arrow of real time; the more sensuous version is the hidden hand of the "excessive" imaginary hybrid or postcolonial space–time that is adjacent and exterior to the quotidian spaces and times that we live.

Conclusion

That the general forms of postcolonial and postmodern theory have distinctly metaphysical qualities may not in itself be problematic – some kind of pseudo-transcendental method seems to be a precondition for any form of rational or realist knowledge. However, the prominence of binarism complicated by a trinity, the work of the hidden hand, an absolute limit to the rationally knowable, some kind of transcendentalism, the privilege of some subject positions, sometimes combined with a unique and special incommensurability of some cultures or subjects, or the absolute decentreing of the subject in the presence of totality, infinity and ineffability all seem to be "religious" themes. What challenge can these theories, or the politics derived from them, pose for religious or racial authoritarianism?

Any critical assault on religious authoritarianism must start from the basis that there is nothing in those ideologies, or in the "cultures" that gave rise to them, that is beyond the analytic reach of reason, rationalities or the forms of knowledge that we have. Religious ideologies, political movements, societies, states, cultures and cultural practices, ethnicities, or forms of knowledge emanating from the "Third World" are not uniquely and distinctly closed, incommensurable, or shut to so-called "Western" forms of rationality and reason. There is no political or religious ideology that is epistemically special in relation to a putative universal critique. There can be no culture that has ontic privilege. In fact, the claim to dissimilarity, difference, closure and uniqueness is a foundational declaration of religious and racialist movements and it is this authority that they use to disavow critical assessment or political challenge. Versions of Spivak's argument that reason is necessarily Eurocentric (Spivak 1993b: 241) or Bhabha's arguments on foundational incommensurability are rehearsed by those same movements as legislative norms. Conversely, there can also be an intense disjunction between what postcolonial theory claims about its object of study and the latter's manifest activities. How does the "deconstructive case" that is the condition of postcoloniality lead to calls for the murder of a deconstructor? How does hybridity, catachresis, aporia or indeed "persistent critique" lead to Hindu Aryanism or global Islamic movements? How can newness lead to an obsession with oldness and antiquity? How does the subaltern silence of that theoretical gold standard, the "Third World woman", lead to the thunderous intolerance and bigotry of Hindu nationalist women?

A more complex double hermeneutic (Giddens 1979: 244) also comes into play between the analysis of these movements and the analytic methodology they themselves employ as a basis for political action. Arguments that differences are in some way radical, non-negotiable or untranslatable are at the core of authoritarian forms of Hinduism or Islam (or, indeed, Greater Serbian nationalism). Alterity is their prize. The methodology of difference employed by these movements is that distinguished signifier of cultural studies, the body and its uniforms of gender and masculinity. Indeed, both the analytics and the practice of semiology, and of cultural difference as sign, seem central to many religious movements. The special relation to modernity of the "Third World" subject that is analyzed by postcolonial or postmodern theorists becomes, for religious authoritarian movements, not simply an analysis of their condition but their manifesto for political action. The analytic privilege given to the colonial frontier in postcolonial theory is endlessly reproduced as a legitimating factor in ethnic and religious movements. The infinite, the sublime and mystic and mythic temporalities are not simply beliefs in Hindu nationalism but methodological objects from which forms of political agency are self-consciously derived.

If the theoretical concepts of postcolonial theory, such as hybridity or catachresis, are in some important way to be the tools for our critique of authoritarian movements, perhaps even in the engaged manner of *Ideologiekritik* by, say, exposing originary or nativist claims in authoritarian religious or culturalist movements, why have rationalism, humanism and realism been virtually the only effective critiques in actual circumstance? Authoritarian forms of Hinduism or Islam may demonstrate persistent critique, or even "persistent consolidation of claims to founding catachreses" but they seem infinitely more agitated when they are shown to be irrational, unwarranted and wrong.

CHAPTER 2

Authoritarian religious movements and modern civil societies

> ... more than once those who have the least defences against the violence of the powerful have dared to defy that power, dared to confront that violence with their own. And, more than once, those with the most meagre resources to resist oppression have won something important, as the result of that confrontation. And in every instance, it has never been *who is the leader* but rather *who are the people*. It has never been *what is the organisation* but *what is the crisis*.
> (June Jordan *Moving towards home*, p. 115, emphasis in original)

Introduction

The new social movements in the West have received much theoretical attention. Indeed, those movements around race, gender and sexuality can be seen as precursors to postmodern and postcolonial theory. However, relatively little sociological analysis has been focused on authoritarian religious movements and their modes of practical organization and political expression. Some of the discussions that do exist are made use of in this chapter and are linked to wider debates on civil society, social movements, globalization, space and new communications technology. Hence, this chapter presents a number of analytical themes that are important features of both progressive social movements and authoritarian religious movements, and implicit sociological comparisons are frequently made between them.

Globalization, time–space compression and the social totality

It is worth starting with the substantial problem about how we can explain events within, and the transient conditions of, the life-world during an anxious period in which postnational or global economic, political and cultural systems are in an unsettled and unpredictable state of reproduction and transformation. We can start with Laclau's Gödel-like critique of political sociology which states that "any structural system is surrounded by an 'excess of meaning' that it is unable to master and that, consequently, 'society' as a unitary and intelligible object which grounds its own partial processes is an impossibility" (Laclau 1990: 90).

Giddens' theory of structuration or Bhaskar's transformational model of social action, are useful sophisticated counterpoints to this discursive evaporation of society. Indeed, the burden seems to be on Laclau to explain how any social institutions manage to reproduce themselves at all, even if partially. However, there is an important argument made by Laclau that does not actually need to conflict with a critical realist political sociology (see, for example, Bhaskar 1986: 129–35, 1993: 124–6). We cannot know any discursive and formal system in its entirety without reference to an element of another discourse outside that system. The addition of a new discursive element creates a new system, which is also unknowable in its entirety without reference to yet a further discursive element outside the new system. This implies that political sociological explanations and descriptions are open-ended. However, it does not necessarily imply abandoning taxonomic and descriptive totalities and generalizations.

From a different position, Bauman says that the "organismic metaphor" for social totalities no longer has relevance and we must abandon systemic analogies (Bauman 1992: 190). Instead, political sociology "maps" the extreme self-reflexivity inherent in exceedingly complex social systems that create chaotic, indeterminate and open-ended political effects. Fredric Jameson has also usefully elaborated on the problem of mapping postmodern social totalities (Jameson 1991: 364–418). Postmodern space has made it virtually impossible for social and political actors to locate themselves, to organize their immediate surroundings perceptively and cognitively map their position in an overwhelmed, indeterminate external world. Jameson argues for a new politics and aesthetics centred on the "cognitive mapping" of the spatial that can create the basis for a new radical cultural politics in a postmodern period where "critical distance has been abolished". The central concern of cognitive mapping is to grasp the organization of capitalist totalities as holistic systems that create fragmentation and differentiation. The central tool of this process is narrative, not the re-assertion of grand narrative but the "non-mimetic" representation, or transcoding of "the lost unity of social life", to make connections between and to demonstrate how widely different elements can be contextualized within a broader framework outside which they are incomprehensible. He identifies "Third World literature" as one instance of the cognitive relational mapping of "nation", a position that has been criticized for its "Third Worldism" generalities (Ahmad 1992: 119, and ch. 3). Wallerstein's older "world systems" theory rejects a multiple society approach – the view that we can map and study one or more societies in isolation from their global historical, political and pre-eminently economic processes and the place of all of these in a postulated world system of nation-states, economies and, now, antisystemic oppositional movements (Wallerstein 1983, Arrighi et al. 1989). This approach frequently displays a sweeping economic reductionism and functionalism that considerably overprivileges economic processes over and above the autonomous political actions and relations of nation-states (Giddens 1985: 168). Notably, it fails to account for three aspects that have been identified with globalization (Harvey 1989: 272–4, 358; McGrew 1992: 92):

- The "contradictory" rise of both universalistic and particularistic tendencies as a result of globalization. The tendency of nation-states to have more influence in global affairs, including global fora while at the same time their legitimacy, competence, sovereignty and authority is diminished both internally within their boundaries and externally as a result of global economic or interstate constraints; the rise of regionalist, ethnic and religious movements within and across national-state boundaries and the rise of intense nationalism itself across and inside geographical nation-state boundaries. Of particular relevance in this context is the global political language of radical Islam compared with the severe constraints of nationalism, ethnicity and sect that it faces.

- The failure of global systems approaches to account for the non-economic cultural-political changes as well as "global" oppositional agency, most notably in the supersimilarity of social movement activities across nation-states. While recently the latter have been theorized within a world-systems approach, they have been essentially, and unconvincingly, visualized as anti-capitalist systems. Again, the supersimilar activities of both Islamic and Hindu global networks are important in this context.
- The consolidation of an autonomous realm of geomilitary global organization (Giddens 1985: 254, and ch. 9) under US hegemony that transcends the system of nation-states and is perhaps sociologically irreducible to "international politics" or the global economy.

However, the global-systems approach is useful in an indirect, but highly important sense. Its insistence from the outset for a holistic, global approach to parochial, local events and its attempt at integrating (typically in three-tiered fashion) the global, national and local as interdependent but globally determined systems does form one strand of a possible "cognitive map" with which we can understand translocal political phenomena. Wallerstein also introduces a dynamic conception of both global political processes and the organization of space, especially in its theorization of core, semiperipheral and peripheral processes within the world system.

The sociospatial dialectic and the imagination of time

Globalization, postmodernist theory, "Third World" feminism, human, urban and political geography have come together recently in new assessments of contemporary spatial and temporal processes. In earlier social theory, space was treated "as the dead, the fixed, the undialectical, the immobile" but time was dynamic and productive, the static Being against the dynamic Becoming, a placid Geography versus an energetic History (Harvey 1989: 273). Recent work has, however, given attention to space as a social construct that is both a condition for and an outcome of the dynamic social relations that transform it. The analytic use of "space" is often informed both by Lefebvre's distinction between three dimensions of spatial production and by Edward Soja's attempts at defining a sociospatial dialectic. Lefebvre distinguishes between:

- Material spatial practices – the physical and material flows and transfers that occur across space to ensure production and social reproduction.
- Representations of space that allow material spatial practices to be talked about and understood, whether in commonsense or academic jargon.
- Mental inventions (and their applications) that imagine new meanings or possibilities for spatial practices (Lefebvre 1991: 33, 38–9).

Soja is concerned to explicate a sociospatial dialectic that attempts to deal with the ontological fractures that the above schematic throws up. The relevant thrust of his argument is that

> Spatiality is a substantiated and recognisable social product, part of a "second nature" which incorporates as it socialises and transforms both physical and psychological spaces. [Furthermore] as a social product, spatiality is simultaneously the medium and outcome, presupposition and embodiment, of social action and relationship. (Soja 1989: 129)

Soja inserts the social production of space in the centre of the dialectic between real, physical space and our imagination of it. This view of space as a social practice and a social product forms a useful analytic for investigating the political activities of local communities and also "global" social movements. But while space has entered social science, its relation to political science proper is more elusive. There has been a considerable body of work done in the last decade that uses the *metaphor* of space – in the sense of Lefebvre's "psychological" or imaginative operation of space – to define or at least highlight a new cultural or oppositional politics. Spatial metaphors – nation, migration, homeland, borderlands, positionality, location, home, domesticity – abound in the writings of the black and women's movements and are strikingly visible in "Third World" feminist writing. Spatial metaphors as well as a forbidding emphasis on human geography are also central to the political epistemologies of religious authoritarianism, as we shall see.

Two central aspects of social movement activities are the relation between spatialization and identity, and the political configuration of the spaces of privacy and home. Both these concerns are directly related to the organization of spaces and places in which political communities are formed, public or private violence excluded, and politically intangible spaces for desire and pleasure created. This work, especially in "Third World" feminist writing, has considerably extended the ways in which spatialization has to be important for social movements and, in its complexity, forms a useful challenge to the view of those political activities as simply parochially inhabiting "place" (Harvey 1989: 302).

However, this use of space in oppositional movement discourse is frequently *symbolic* and frequently ignores the other social and material spaces that Lefebvre highlights. The expression of "positionality", for example, evokes position in relation to a matrix of discursive formations (such as "nation", "home") rather than position within a particular material or social space. From another direction, there have been different discussions around the political inhabitation and recreation of material and social spaces by radical social movements. The work of Castells on the formation of urban movements, and in particular his discussion of the political formation of gay communities in the Castro district of San Francisco is an exemplary argument on the relation between imagined space ("community-identity"), social spaces (the neighbourhood) and material spaces (the physical space of the urban/city) (Castells 1983, ch. 14).

The emphasis on space can also allow a different consideration of political identity. It is suggested that identity becomes less useful as a metaphor for social movement agency and that it is more productive to think in terms of the worlds that are created by that agency, literally the physical and the imagined worlds that agents negotiate. The combination of Cartesian-anthropomorphic identity with a binary methodology of signification paves the way for an analysis in which identity becomes so unstable and mutable that it acquires an arbitrary and random character in history and can vaporize easily. This does not easily lend itself to an assessment of why identities (and the conditions that create them) continue to persist or what happens when identities have to live physically in their or others' real worlds. Those worlds are enduring cultural-material sites that cannot be substituted with an analysis of signifiers. Identity also becomes more useful when the focus is placed more squarely on the manufacture of bodies that have to inhabit these spaces rather than simply the identities that preoccupy their minds.

Much recent theory deriving from the decentring of the subject in structuralist and poststructuralist work has elaborated on fractured identities and subjectivities, and extrapolated from this the notion of radical social "difference". Conversely, it has condensed the fractured nature of the social formation into the fractured sense of self in postmodernity. But this work has been unable to account for the problems encountered when apparently fractured subjectivities not only manifest themselves in the real world but do so as holistic and unfractured identities that interact with other wholesome subjects. Although identities manifest themselves across different (ontically "disjointed") social structures (ideology, agency, institution) and social spaces, this does not mean that those subjects necessarily have a sense of themselves as fractured across these spaces. Indeed, identity is the basis from which social movements elaborate knowledges that attempt to resolve the ontic fissures in the social formation and create "holistic" life-worlds.

The displacement of identity in favour of life-worlds is important because this is where identities manifest themselves in social spaces and create new social spaces. We need to apply Lefebvre's argument very strictly. Social movements produce new *physical* spaces, they create and transform *social* spaces and they *imagine* new spaces. All three spaces are constitutive of their life-world. At one level this is a banal observation since all social agency axiomatically takes place in and transforms space. But the importance for social movements is to undertake the transformation of space by valorizing their identity-bodies. There is an inextricable link between the production of identity, the manufacture of bodies and the transformation of the physical and social spaces of the life-world. The physical transformation of urban districts through the agency of black communities (Brixton, Southall) and gay communities (Earl's Court, Soho) has resulted in new social spaces that have to be negotiated by everyone. These are frequently contested sites, but the imagination of those spaces as symbolic communities of affirmation, resistance, pleasure and safety for the actual body becomes important for social and political theory.[1]

The glaring difference is the agency of women. There is rarely a women's realm in the sense of relatively segregated communities. However, the demands of the women's movement are related to the physical transformation of urban spaces, in particular the built environment, or the consequences for the latter of demands that are redistributive and gender-specific and that assess spaces for their safety and separateness, especially where this concerns specific services or arenas of pleasure and consumption. Similarly, home, domicility and community are influenced by the transformation of physical spaces in which women's domestic labour is organized and in which their safety from male violence is of consequence. The place of home, ideologically constituted as the reproductive domain of the private, personal and atomized, is disrupted by its politicization in women's liberation. Similarly, the space of home as an opportunistic location at which consumption is organized from the outside, and which promised the release of women in the West from the drudgery of domestic labour, itself became a site for a gendered critique of the relations of consumption and reproduction.

A broader spatial focus of this kind can ground some identities in their manifestly enduring cultural-material spaces. If we restrict attention to identity, social movements can be reduced to the production of signs. If the focus is on agency, this can lead to either a voluntarist or a redistributive conception of social movements (such as resource mobilization). While both signification and resource mobilization are necessary features of social movements,[2] neither of these explain fully the organic and historical processes that relate social movement identities to agency, persistent communities and urban spaces. A focus on social space (worlds) rather than identity also becomes important when political disputes between identities remain irresolvable at the level of ideological contestation and personal introspection. Finally, the manifestation of identities in worlds can perhaps begin the process by which we can examine both the dispersed and oppositional manifestation of identities. For example, a political strategy based on the identity of blacks that does not address how that identity has to live in worlds that also contain white (and other black) identities will be limited in its scope.

The recent assertion of space in postmodern theory, of course, ties in with another major focus of much intellectual activity: time–

space compression. The "annihilation of space through time" wrought by the revolution in new technologies, especially in air transport and electronic communications has been theorized in various ways and the consequent differential experience of time–space compression, the experience itself related to the level of technological development in a social formation, has meant the "relativization" of both space and time: "Each distinctive mode of production or social formation [will] embody a distinctive bundle of time and space practices and concepts" (Harvey 1989: 204).

Giddens had, earlier, theorized the concept of "time–space distanciation" or "time–space convergence" where different social formations created their own new "distanciated" time–space epistemologies that met at "time–space edges", usually edges between the "First" and the "Third" worlds (Giddens 1981: 91–7).

The effects of time–space compression need to be registered within the overall and overarching economic, military and geopolitical hegemony of the West. Time–space compression has its locus in Europe, the USA and Japan – the nation-states at the heart of "core" economic processes. This is what Doreen Massey has called the "power geometry" of time–space compression (Massey 1991). The Western geopolitical domination of space is a central aspect of this phenomenon and is frequently absent in discussions of time–space compression. (If the colonial relation was manifested in every Western cup of tea, neo-imperialist relations are etched on every processor chip that powers cyberspace.)

It seems important not to get caught up in the euphoric metaphors that time–space compression writings display. In one highly important sense, "time" has not collapsed and "space" has not been annihilated. The instant action-at-a-distance time compression experienced through electronic communications – the analogue and digital telephone, the Internet, e-mail, satellite, cable, radio and the fax – has become the metaphor for all time compression and "space destruction". However, mundane temporalities continue to exist alongside these instant times: the working day, the average life-span, the epochal half-life of nuclear waste, six years to build a dam, a year in a refugee camp, five years of civil war, a decade of Thatcherism – or perhaps the *longue durée* punctuated by Kondratieff cycles. While social activities have undoubtedly speeded up in a highly qualitative sense, only some aspects of them are "instant" and none of these are destructive of space, unless that space is imagined symbolically and socially rather than physically. Indeed, it could be argued that, in the main, older social spaces have been replaced or supplemented with newer and adjacent spaces, rather than "destroyed".

It seems more useful to think of a series of different, co-existing temporalities. These temporalities are not the time–space edges between "advanced" and "developing" social formations but exist, albeit differentially, in and across all social formations, all of which experience the uncertainty of different collective temporalities. It is the bundle of lived temporalities extending across different social formations, that more closely approximates to a "time–space edge" or "time–space epistemology", though both of these need to be taken in a weak sense. Similar parallels can be drawn with space. It seems more useful to think of several overlapping social (in Lefebvre's sense), "translocal" spaces – nation-state based and transnational military, economic and civil-society, community and home – each of which can represent distinct physical, social and imagined entities. Later in the book we will look at how new social spaces, complex composites of nation-states and life-worlds, are created as relatively enduring social structures through processes of globalization and social movement agency. Because social space is increasingly highly dynamic and because some spaces can be indeterminately bounded, the spaces that are inhabited and recreated by modern agents and institutions can seem collapsed in their imagined form. However, as Massey elaborates, this transformation of space is directly related to the geometry of global neo-imperialist power relations. The qualitative leap across physical space that is entailed in sending an e-mail from California to Frankfurt is different from the mass migration of postcolonial labour from India to Britain, or the massive migration of millions of refugees as a result of civil war or famine in Eritrea, Somalia, Mozambique or Uganda, though the latter may eventually involve the collective spanning by many more people of greater physical space (and consequently the creation of new social spaces – permanent refugee paths, camps and enclaves).

> Different social groups have distinct relationships to this . . . differentiated mobility: some people are more in charge of it than others; some initiate flows and movement, others don't; some are more on the receiving end of it than others; some are effectively imprisoned by it. (Massey 1991: 25)

We also need to note that while time–space compression appears to be dispersed in its manifestations and apparently universally accessible, at least in the West, the control of the modalities and technologies of time–space compression and electronic communications is, as Edward Said reminds us, in the hands of extremely few multinational corporations (Said 1993: 374). Massey is thus correct to identify the power geometry of global spatial production with Western capitalism and imperialism: it is the West that predominantly controls global spatial production, that controls how people move, that controls the technology through which space is "annihilated". However, as we shall see later, the political consequences of this are not determinate. Non-Western nation-states and civil societies frequently resist Western hegemony through the oppositional utilization of the same mechanisms of time–space compression in a manner that the West is unable to control or determine with any certainty.

A final problem is in defining the novel social and political relations that are generated in, around, and through electronic media and mass communications. There are three levels to this which fall into the following broad slots: mass print and electronic technology, mass interpersonal communications and interactive personal technologies. We need to distinguish between mass communications technology like print technology, radio, television, video, film, satellite and cable and other types of interpersonal communications like the telephone, e-mail and fax. These two areas need to be distinguished from a third area of computer networks, mass personal computing and interactive video-based or digital technology. The last area is the most unstable though certain technological developments (such as multimedia, optic-fibre software transmission and incorporation of computer software products into digital telephone communications systems) already highlight extraordinarily expansive tendencies. It is likely to breach and transform the spaces of mass and interpersonal communications and open up newer possibilities in that the distances between "passive" mass, interactive and interpersonal communications will disappear. The explosive rise of the Internet, and in particular the World Wide Web, together with its associated ephemeral multimedia software applications, and the growth of Usenet groups and Internet Relay Chat are part of this process. The electronic medium itself is already reconstituting a very different social field through and *in* which social and political interactions happen. This has been investigated as "cyberspace" and this concept informs some of the empirical studies in the book (Benedikt 1991). Cyberspace is central to the moment when a Muslim activist in Leicester faxed pages of *The satanic verses* to the Organisation of Islamic Conference in Riyadh and started a global political convulsion whose effects are still being felt. Similarly, it is impossible to understand Khomeini's near-divine emergence as Imam, or the mythical claims of Hindu nationalists without a sociological conception of relations created in and through electronic mass media.

Civil society, new social movements and the drift to absolutism

Social movements place extraordinary political emphasis on activism and organization within and across civil societies. However, much postmodern and postcolonial theory has a tendency to reduce this distinctive domain of praxis simply to the representation in discourse of practical activity. Against this epistemic fallacy it is necessary for sociological theory to re-assert the problem of agency, the moment where "things are done", where "doing" occurs. This does not simply constitute the Lukacsian field of reification and self-consciousness, nor is it simply the post-Althusserian space where ideology creates subjectivity (Althusser 1984), nor is it Gramscian common sense or "philosophy of life" (Hoare & Nowell Smith 1978: 196–200), though the latter constantly interferes with it. Older Marxist discussions of practical activity were dominated primarily with abstract discussions of labour, but these were not easily related to questions of organization and political agency.

However, the theorization of organized, disorganized, spontaneous or collective political agency, its relation to political representatives and its relation to the state has been an important strand in Marxist writing since its inception, even if in incomplete form.[3] The main tendencies in these early Marxist writings are the state-focused responses of Lenin, Kautsky and Bernstein as well as those more concerned with mass agency that is localized, relatively spontaneous and not necessarily or directly geared to the reformist or revolutionary seizure of state power (Luxemburg). This latter aspect was considerably developed in the writings of C.L.R. James and Raya Dunayevskaya and formed an important, rarely recognized, critique of Leninism, authoritarianism and antidemocratic Marxism (James 1980: 115–19; James et al. [1958] 1974: 86–105, 118–28). Their work also, significantly, took on board an assessment within modernity of the movements for "Negro" and women's emancipation when these issues were not fashionable (James et al. [1958] 1974: 73–6, 149–54). This tendency additionally looked at the implications of modernity itself. "Hegelian voluntarism", teleology, the critique of organization, the stress on self-activity, the delimited but important role of activists and the phasal sense of movement development that informed this tendency became part of the political practice of several Western and Caribbean organizations and added an important historicism to an analysis of their struggles. While there are immense problems with this approach, its value lies in the stress on "self-activity", organization, an innate suspicion of leadership and an uncompromising anti-vanguardism. Moreover, its "anti-state pro-internationalist" utopian thrust has considerable surface appeal. Some of the discussions of political organization and mobilization arising from these Marxist tendencies could usefully supplement social movement theory. In particular, there are gaps in the sociology of political organization of authoritarian religious movements in civil society. The emphasis on "organization, organization, organization" in the political activity of the far right-wing Hindu Rashtriya Swayamsevak Sangh (RSS) and the vast national and international infrastructures that such movements build around welfare projects, political activism, education, mobilization, rapid action and political violence need to be explored and described in greater depth, though some extremely important studies do exist (Gopal 1991, Basu et al. 1993, Andersen & Damle 1987). In particular, the relationships between activism, political leadership, political recruitment, mass mobilization and communal violence seem to be under-researched.

Gramsci's writings on the state, civil society and "ideology", despite their widely differing interpretations (compare, for example, Femia 1981 with Mouffe 1979), also have a bearing on these discussions. Gramsci's assessment of the state in advanced countries and its "gelatinous" but autonomous relation to a developed civil society has been of special significance in left analyses of the prospects and strategies for progressive social change in Western "liberal" democracies (Poulantzas 1980: 203–47, 251–65; Hall

49

1979, Hall & Jacques 1989, Laclau & Mouffe 1985). Within these neo-Marxist frameworks, the exemplary post-war models of progressive social and political action in Western civil society have often been the new social movements.

The rise of these movements, following the civil rights movements of the 1950s in the USA, has been linked to the development of post-Fordism or postindustrial society or changes in the mode of production in an informational or collective consumption-based direction (Castells 1983: xviii–xix). The new social movements have also been seen as empirical examples of the development of neo-Gramscian Marxism (Laclau & Mouffe 1982). Anthropological class has apparently lost its significance or capacity as an organizing identity for radical change (Gorz 1989). The new movements direct attention away from production and the labour process to forms of, broadly speaking, urban "consumption": the control over the processes of daily living, the human relations between individuals, and the re-organization of the social formation against what are seen as new modes of domination, inequality and terror. Social movements are not concerned with the long haul but demand instant, non-negotiable satisfaction of their demands (Gilroy 1987b: 226). Those demands are not simply of the state or the economy, or a desire to seize and control those institutions, but focus instead on the reorganization of urban civil society to create new, self-managed spaces or communities (Castells 1983: 138–63). Those movements' claim to "autonomy" from the state is their resolute political self-management and their political self-creation (ibid: 328). Furthermore, social movements share a fixation on the body (Melucci 1989: 122–5), and its relation to healing (ibid: 135–47), technology, spirituality, utopia (ibid: 82; Gilroy 1987b, ch. 5) or dystopia. Melucci's recent work examines how collective "action without actors" is fruitfully interpreted as the production of sign through the techniques of prophecy (the act of announcing based on personal experience), paradox (the reversal of dominant codes of meaning, and hence an exposure of their irrationality) and representation (a retransmission to the system of its own contradictions). These signals to dominant modes of information production and dissemination – symbolic orders – also mark out the different identities of the new social movements (Melucci 1989: 75–8). Much of this work, and its considerable development in Paul Gilroy's writings on diaspora and modernity, forms an important foundation for the analyses of social movements in later chapters (Gilroy 1987b chs 5 and 6).

However, some recent post-Gramscian interventions (Keane 1988a, 1988b) – with their imposing combination of democratically elected state power, extended democratization in civil society and a civil society seen primarily through its progressive social differences – are increasingly problematic. Indeed, the Rushdie affair can be seen as the metonymic dystopia that haunted this version of the radical social democratic project. There is first of all a striking difference between these *administrative-democratic socialist* analyses of social difference and the *utopian-ascetic* discourse of liberation and emancipation that informs the new social movements (Murphy 1992). To be sure, new social movements can incorporate administrative strategies for social change alongside their utopian demands. However, the commutopian strand, owing much to Rousseau, Saint-Simon and the Owenites, is also extremely important.

New social movements can construct demands of the social totality that are both radically unachievable and rhetorically essential. A major driving tension in many political movements is the manufacture of liberation discourse so that the latter is constantly changing, as some of its demands are negotiated and "met", so as never to let its demands be met. The utopian (or dystopian) realm is left changed but intact. This negative critique (dialectic) is a powerful engine for new critiques of the system as a whole. This indeed demonstrates how modernist utopian visions can form extremely strong critical theories of the social formation. This "negative dialectics" also reflects a general tension, immanent in all social movements, between the demands of utopian ideals and the necessity of administrative/systemic changes to negotiate some of those demands. Consequently, the utopian ideals have to be, strictly speaking, inexplicable in administrative terms and (hence) constantly revisable. The tensions in social movements between reform and revolution, systemic changes and piecemeal reforms, militant activism and bureaucratic leadership, liberation discourse and strategic political demands, liberation and rights/equality, bureaucratic co-option and mass movement are manifestations of this same political aporia.

Similarly, while new social movements develop sophisticated forms of mass organization and agency, they can demonstrate a profound neglect of democratic process. Considerations of democracy, which arguably are important as administrative processes, rather than simply constitutive of a political ideology, are often vitally absent from social movement analysis or practice. This absence is not simply a hangover of the Marxist or Third International critique of bourgeois democracy, of democracy as social fascism, or of the Hobbesian view of the state that can inform new social movement writings. Instead, consideration by many social movements of democratic administration, either of the state or in the organizational forms of activism, can be both incomplete and construed as immanent in an ideal form through an identification between democracy and the collective activity of the oppressed (the unelaborated mass presence). The mass movement, or mass activity is an immanent or ideal democracy of apparently direct mass participation that is assumed to be superior to the liberal institutions of formal democracy. The organization of democratic forms is assumed to arise naturally and inevitably from the experience of oppression and exploitation and from the collective or mass forms of resistance that are entailed.[4] There is of course no guarantee that formal democracy is such a Rousseauesque natural state. Consequently, social movements face a tension, often contained in the rubric of "authenticity", "authentic leadership" and "authentic representation", between the idealized imagined democracy of collective participation and the incomplete administration of democracy. A similar sociological tension manifests itself in authoritarian religious movements. In those movements, despite a formal dismissal of democracy and a centralized, undemocratic form of leadership, there is still an important discourse of collective, equal participation in mass activity. Indeed, the importance of mass and formally equal participation has resulted in complex apparatuses of gender-differentiated consultation, enfranchisement, selection and legitimation in the Iranian Islamic Republic, rather similar in some respects to the organic labour-state *nomenklatura* political system in the former Soviet Union. It is indeed difficult to know how any radical ideology that claims an affiliation with "the masses" can avoid these tensions.

Recent discussions of new social movements and civil societies have also demonstrated a different set of problems with contemporary liberal, progressive or socialist strategies that are based simply on the development of strong or developed civil societies as a safeguard against state authoritarianism or totalitarianism.[5] The re-assertion of social democracy through the newer language of hegemony, popular democracy and national popular struggles, while indicating a needed shift towards the institutions of civil society, still looks to civil society as a resource for essentially winning elected state power. The key underdevelopment in liberal and socialist political theory this highlights is: what political strategy can the left advocate when the adversary is not the state but (some of) the institutions of civil society? One defining characteristic of authoritarian religious movements is the importance of resolute, dogged political labour in civil society. Often, the focus is not the institutions of the state or even the desire to seize its institutions, but to control, re-organize, and hegemonize the private institutions of civil society, including the private spaces of home. Events in the early 1990s in India, Tunisia and Egypt created the situation that the state, often in highly authoritarian and repressive fashion, is the only guard against the "progressive desecularisation" (Vaniak 1990: 156–62) of an increasingly commanding and highly politicized civil society.

There are several other conceptual approaches that are also important to take into account. There is a striking similarity between the urban character of radical social movements, their conceptualization of authority, legitimacy, civil society, the body and spirituality and those of right-wing social movements, in particular the Christian right, anti-abortion and anti-gay movements in the USA (Diamond 1989) and neo-Nazi movements in Europe. All of these, in a schematic sense, integrate concerns of the body (and the tropes of family, gender and race) with political action in civil society influenced by utopian or dystopian visions. These visions are frequently channelled through virtually the same political language of liberation and emancipation that is used by the radical social movements. To be sure, much right-wing discourse has simply and disingenuously appropriated radical political language. However, the different character of the progressive social movements – the difference that makes a difference – needs to be marked out and explained.

This issue is further complicated by the relations between new social movements. The edges and intersections between the discourses of different social movements are frequently the site of highly authoritarian impulses which, aside from requiring explanation, are often far from concerned with the liberatory potential of social life. Both these areas point to another problem – the development of authoritarian discourse in the new social movements, virtually entirely marked by an obsession with cardinal difference, particularist distinction, separateness and distance. For example, multiculturalism and antiracism in the UK have created the space for religious and absolutist revival and the repression of women's interests (Sahgal & Yuval-Davis 1992, Southall Black Sisters 1990). Antiracism, black nationalism and black liberation discourse have sometimes resulted in some tendencies that range from crudely xenophobic "race logic" to race pseudosciences and metaphysical affiliations that are ventriloquisms of the classically fascist and Nazi. The development of repressive legislative radical feminist strategies around sexuality and pornography and several aspects of lesbian and gay "essentialism" are other markers. There appears to be a superficial link between these various positions that is based on the archaeological and anthropological absolutism they invoke to make claims for both liberation and purity. There is indeed a striking legislative anthropology of original difference in each of the radical social movements that can stipulate how to behave, what to consume, what to wear, who to affiliate with, and what rituals of membership and exclusion to enforce.

There is another major problem with the theorization of new social movements. The Western focus of much theory has obscured the rise of authoritarian religious movements in Western and non-Western countries. During the 1960s, authoritarian movements arose as modern mass religious movements in both Muslim and Hindu populated civil societies. One such movement instigated the only mass – indeed, Gramscian – revolution this century, and possibly since the French Revolution, which eventually led to the Islamic Republic of Iran. Many contemporary religious movements have the same characteristics identified by social movement theorists, especially Melucci, for new social movements in advanced, information-based capitalist societies. This of course begs the question: if new social movements arose in non-Western countries at roughly the same time and exhibited the same schematic characteristics as non-Western ones, what is *particularly* novel about the changes in Western social formations that occurred after the war, what is distinctive about the analyses of postindustrialism, urbanization and modes of information that produced these movements?

Several other areas indicate links between new social movements and newer dynamics in both Western and non-Western civil societies. Social movements manufacture an intelligible theory of the social formation that identifies the latter as a totality built up of simple monologic structures that *necessarily* create systemic forms of oppression for their functional survival (patriarchy, heterosexism, capitalism, the West, white people, men). Within this, a collective victim subjectivity is formed and a discourse of liberation is created that rests ultimately on the real or symbolic destruction of the totality. However, new social movements have a strong focus on *non-institutional non-systemic* forms of domination and terror arising from the life-world of civil society itself. This is not simply about changing relations among members in civil societies but appears to form a more expansive critique of civil society, in particular a critique of hostile civil domination, including domination by members of other new social movements. One important strand is the terror of violence to and murder of the body (such as racist, sexist or homophobic violence). However, this is just one strand within a general critique of civil society that exhibits an ambiguous fear of modern civil society itself. This integrates a vision in which the complexity and heterogeneity of the life-world makes the task of living within it and criticizing its symbolic orders an always necessary but always hostile battle, the latter assuming an enormous complexity that can never be resolved (Melucci 1989: 45–6). There is a strange logic to the political rehearsal of intelligible difference in complex societies. It becomes increasingly difficult to grasp differences from the complex social totality because it contains too many differentiations. New social movements rehearse this same complexity in their emphasis on constant differentiation. This has important progressive and syncretic possibilities. However, the task of criticizing a complex totality can be overwhelming and can result in dystopian closure. This powerful dystopian tendency has played itself out in a remarkable strand of slow genocide in each of the new social movements, whether this be the murder of women, or the genocide of blacks and gays.[6] Social movement identities oscillate between the will to desire (for liberation) and the fear of death (from violence) (West 1993a: 163–4), in particular acts of violence that offend or threaten the personal body. While this threat or the act is real and manifest, its rehearsal as a parameter for identity is considerably more complex and overdetermined by other political material. Fascist violence in antiracist discourse, genocide in black and gay liberation politics, and gynocide in radical feminism function as energetic, explanatory markers that constantly rehearse in potent form the threat of violent bodily destruction, the "daily onslaught" that is matched by the desire for personal or collective survival. The similar themes of "survival" and its associations with pain, suffering, endurance, terror and guilt are frequently rehearsed in new social movement writings, often out of the context of actual violence or its threat, as generalized discourses that compose victim subjectivity.[7]

This dystopian strand in new social movements is a gauge of both the indeterminate nature of power in civil society and the paradoxically systematic forms of authority, control, domination and repression that are emergent from within civil society in unsettled forms that have not been imagined before. These modes of domination could be elaborated in Weber's language of technical rationality and its transformed critique in the work of the Frankfurt School. However, they are not systematic and unfolding in the way that scientific rationality is and do not have a simple locus in the state or the economy or their bureaucratic institutions. These forms of domination also appear to be about continually disrupting rationalities and inserting new ones, or indeed shifting the ground all the time about the meaning and production of rationalities themselves. It is difficult to map these areas because they are emerging phenomena. Some of them may also represent progressive possibilities though they are sketched here as forms of domination and repression. However, it seems important to note the following strands:

The emergent social relationships created by new technologies in physics and biology. These elaborate a radically different association with machines and nature, with our bodies and the bodies of others (see especially Haraway 1991). This cyborg relation disrupts the Freudian body-of-itself that the baby initially discovers, but urges a reversion to an earlier state when the baby's sense of its body is universal and dogmatic but also completely dependent. In this cyborg form, our human agency and our re-socialization take place in and through technologically manifest relations that not only produce and reproduce our body but extend, control and dominate it. There can be a relative passivity of the human body when faced with the technological extensions of it through which it becomes active and manifest. However, the cyborg form can become politicized and, in combination with authoritarian ideologies, repressive if not quite genocidal.

The recreation of new pleasures of the body in spaces that are technical and electronic. The mutation of pleasure in electronic space, through audio-visual, mass or interactive technologies is an intimate social relation with technology that has never existed before, an affinity towards pleasurable association with machines rather than humans, or a pleasure-association with humans that is always mediated through technology. Unlike the Frankfurt School critique, which, in the Kantian sense, inserted the Aesthetic as the hope of emancipation between reason and technical domination, these new relations of pleasure in technology "deliver the Sublime" to the individual.

The appropriation and transformation of difference in technology as part of a general biopoliticization. The demand for difference in gender, race and sexuality is reified in technology and given back to the radical social movements as an obscene gift. The impact of the new social movements on biotechnology has been marked by detailed searches for biogenetic and physical difference, most importantly in the Human Genome (Diversity) Project. Some of these biopolitical technologies excavate difference (the differential sizes of brain cells in the hypothalamus of gay and heterosexual men, the length of the cortex cells in the brains of women, which explains their emotional as well as rational nature, the genetic propensity to HIV disease among blacks) and deftly confirm what some in the new social movements want to hear. This compression of the body to its genes is a related, though apparently reversed, part of the first point: the body is both extended in physical technology while the subject is compressed and reduced to its genes by the extension of biotechnologies into our deepest selves. There are already important political repercussions of this biogenetic logic, even though the technology is relatively new. Xq28, the alleged "gay gene" has been justified as grounds for selective abortion (*Gay Times*, September 1993: 15). The increasing incidence of femicide in India, and in South Asian communities in the UK, that has resulted from the deployment of ultrasound scans and other sex selection tests is one such example – a combining of religious orthodoxy or appeals to patriarchal "tradition" with new technologies of the body.

The disruption and substitution of rationalities through new transgressive "knowledges dressed up as reason". This is a complicated phenomenon that seems to have two important strands. The *technology of the emotions*, whereby the cathartic or melancholic play of emotions is gridded, marked out, contained and rationalized through technical knowledges and systematic, rational elaborations of the self. A wide range of disciplines ranging from psychotherapy (Melucci 1989: 141–5), counselling, encounter groups, new forms of management training, oppression awareness training, employment-related graphology right up to New Age and ascetic religions all demonstrate systematic methodologies for the rational elaboration of the self, and a rationalization of "emotional excess", while claiming that the latter is being freed or released. Much of this has its roots in late 1960s counterculture but its present form intrinsically elaborates the knowledges gained from the women's, gay and black movements: not "the personal is political", but the personal and emotional can be subjected to systematic discovery and manipulation through various rational discursive systems. Contrary to what many of these disciplines themselves state, namely that the emotions are being released and the authentic self is being discovered, it is more appropriate to view these as "mechanics of the soul" with their own systematic techniques of power/knowledge and practical domination.

The second strand, a "purity" urge, is the *terror of the self* elaborated through aphorisms of repression and transcended through mechanistic algorithms for personal change. Race, gender and sexuality awareness training, inner-child psychology, repressed memory accounts, Iron-John tribal masculinities, the Wild Woman, Afrocentricity, childhood repression, among numerous other knowledge regimes, elaborate a rationalized understanding of the self as constituted in and through modalities and systems of internal repression. These regimes are, in a strongly Foucauldian sense, procedures for mechanical elaboration and domination of the self. Both these strands seem to integrate the authentic search for the emancipated self with quite powerful themes of purity and primordial origin. In this sense, the search for the undominated inner self, an important progressive part of anticolonial and antislavery movements and other movements of the oppressed, now points to authoritarian tendencies. This terror of the artificial self, and its counterpart, the remoulding of a new primordial self, is a characteristic feature of new Hindu and Islamic movements.

The difficulty in applying moral archetypes of the good. The complexity and compounded nature of antagonistic events in the life-world make it difficult to assess and affiliate with an unambiguous good side of many real antagonisms. Binary narrative logics are frequently unavailable in modern antagonisms, including many civil wars. The nature of binary antagonism, a primary evil aggressor and a good victim is simple to comprehend in the case of the former Yugoslavia and in Greater Serbian ambitions. But consider the conflictual situations in Somalia, Quebec, Ethiopia, Lebanon, Uganda, Chechenya, Afghanistan, Karachi or Bihar.

The technical militarization of some civil societies and the desocialization of their public spaces, resulting from a dispersal of the legitimate use of the means of violence beyond the nation-state. This refers less to the violence of the nation-state in relation to its citizenry, (important as that is) than to another phenomenon present in some Western and non-Western countries – the legitimacy of (or the impossibility of halting) militia violence within civil society. This is substantially different from adventurism and "terrorism" but refers to a semi-permanent condition of belligerency enacted through armed conflict that the national security services are unable to contain. The presence of just a few dozen or a few hundred armed individuals is enough to permanently terrorize and control non-participant civilians and re-organize the public spaces of civil society. Similarly, the relative weakness of some nation-states, however repressive they may otherwise be, against armed garrisons that brutalize civilian populations can create a perpetual conflict (such as in Liberia, Uganda, Sri Lanka or Sierra Leone) which follows a contingent "logic" that is extremely difficult to comprehend in older binary narratives of political conflict or international relations.

The difficulties in enforcing a universal conception of human rights through just a critique of the state. One of the features of some civil societies is the inability or lack of warrant of the state in enforcing rights and protective practices for groups whose universal rights are violated by other groups within civil society. Human-rights discourse and practice have been traditionally intertwined with the responsibilities of the state. However, this can fail in some situations of civil conflict (such as interethnic or communal violence) where violations of universal rights are enacted by some sections of civil society against others and where legislative apparatuses are technically unable or unwilling to cope with civil violence. Translating universal rights, typically the rights of individuals, into community or group rights is itself problematized because it is through some claim to the latter that communal conflict itself arises. The general tension this reflects is between individual rights, communal rights and state power, legitimacy and competence.

The potential inability of the state to guarantee the universal and group rights demanded of it. This is a consequence of increasingly complex, and more chaotic and numerous demands for rights and recognition made from within civil society, sometimes against other groups in civil society. These claims while sometimes seeming to criticize the conception of universal rights, can actually legitimize them further. The demands for religious rights, or the instrumental critique by religious-political movements of Western "double standards" in human-rights issues paradoxically legitimize the idea of rights and democracy, even if those movements wish to deny them to others. For example, the Committee for the Defence of Legitimate Rights, a religious, and mainly authoritarian group that was formed by Muslim Brotherhood supporters to criticize the corrupt excesses of the Saudi dictatorship, but that wants a possibly harsher enforcement of Islam than currently exists in Saudi Arabia, still choose to rally around the banner of *rights.*

The apparent impossibility of postnational legislative warrants. The shape and condition of the life-world is related to many factors that are beyond the control of the nation-state or its civil society and which cannot be authorized or legitimized through the nation-based tropes of democratic accountability and law. In an unprecedented way, the life-world is increasingly dominated by extranational economic, political and cultural structures and forces for which there appears to be no possibility of legitimation, control or opposition through nationalized legislative warrants, or whose effects cannot be controlled or legitimized easily through existing national or extranational institutions. The idea of democratic accountability cannot be translated to these structures or their effects because there appears to be no possibility of administering their complexity and manifold nature. Paradoxically, transnational post-state associations between life-worlds appear to be equally part of this variegated and complicated traffic of ideas, products and translations of social, economic and cultural relations. However, while the latter suggests other important possibilities that are explored in later chapters, the overall effect is to diminish the relative areas of power of the life-world in comparison with the national and postnational political, economic, cultural and techno-logical structures that dominate it.

Space, time, totality and the body in authoritarian religious movements

Many of the themes discussed above become immediately applicable to analysis of authoritarian religious movements. Space works in a wide range of ways in guiding the political imaginary as well as the political activism of authoritarian religious movements. Each of the spaces of the global, transnational, national, urban city, local community, the domicile and the private are important. Virtually all contemporary Hindu and Islamic movements have a conceptual critique of the national space they inhabit. The space of the nation-state is disturbed, and sometimes evacuated of meaning and substituted with another imagined (and occasionally real) secular or sacred space of natural affiliation. In Hindu "nationalism", this mythic sacred space is "Bharat" or "Bharatmata" or "Mahabharat" ("Great Motherland"), now identified as geographically co-extensive with the current national borders of India, Pakistan, Bangladesh, Sri Lanka, Kashmir, Nepal, Tibet, Burma/Myanmar ("Brahmadesh"), Afghanistan, and nug-gets of several other countries. In Islamic movements, the transnational space varies but inevitably includes a spatial conception of *umma* that can be global or transnational in its imagination. The claims on geographical transnational spaces are manifest (Kashmir) or fictive (Burma). They can also be claims on symbolic spaces that re-organize the imaginary geography of the national space. For example, the recent importance of Ayodhya, and "Mumbai" (Bombay), Mathura and Benares rehearses a different symbolic map of national space in comparison with an older one (Delhi, Bombay, Madras, Calcutta, say).

In both Hindu and Islamic movements, the conception of transnational space has a conflicting nationalist aspect, often rehearsed through a critique of the West (another important spatial construction) or "imperialism". Both translocal and national aspects are important and reflect very precisely the tensions in globalization that were identified above. For example, Hindu nationalist movements can rehearse an intense and xenophobic Indian nationalism against Pakistan *and* can make a claim on Pakistani as being foundationally or originally "Hindu" and therefore part of "Bharat".

This tension between national space and imaginary transnationality has been subject to intense debate within and beyond these movements, especially with regard to the meanings and effects of claims to transnational space in Islamic movements. Some of the most intense theoretical critiques of Islamic movements have suggested that there is no possibility, given the economic and political circumstances, for Islamic movements to have any wide-ranging or significant impact beyond national borders. The Iranian revolution failed to be exported and the idea of "global Islam" has failed (Halliday 1994, Roy 1994). Even where Islam as a state ideology has been successful (Saudi Arabia, Iran, Sudan, Pakistan and, it seems, Afghanistan) it is secondary in importance to local, national and intranational tensions such as those of ethnicity, sect, "tribe" and other political allegiances. In other words, Islam has been overburdened with essentially secular problems of nation-formation, recognition of internal national differences, problems of constitutionality that undermine *shari'a*, severe economic problems that Islamicization has been unable to resolve and so forth. The main extranational power possible in this schema is ideological – the dissemination of propaganda, and its consequent impact on national Muslims and Muslims living in mainly Western civil societies, together with sponsorship of terrorist networks and factions (rather than movements) to pursue essentially national interests. Much of this is valid. However, this kind of analysis, because it is based on locating the influence of Islamic movements mostly within the matrix of economic and political power within the international arena, can elide the huge cultural impact of these movements in civil societies – in the restructuring of communal conflict, personal relationships, new forms of repression and conduct and so on. The impact on civil society and its cities can be monumental.

Spatial control, the urban environment and the community

Much analysis of authoritarian religious movements in relation to "the urban" has tended to reduce the issue to class factors. This is often based on a comparison with the period of the 1930s in western Europe. There can be some metaphoric value in an economistic reading that provides a sociological blueprint for authoritarian religious movements based on the equivalences found in Nazism around petty-bourgeois support, a disaffected intelligentsia, a disorganized working class, mass or permanent unemployment, economic collapse, youth mobilization, a dogmatic ideology of motherhood and family, a perceived internal threat and authoritarian charismatic leadership. However, this can ignore the substantive differences that new religious movements have thrown up in radically new global circumstances and the local circumstances of the modern city.

Authoritarian religious movements, with a few possible exceptions such as some of the *mujahideen* factions in Afghanistan, have been urban-based movements that are immediately geared to organizing control over public spaces in the modern city. The difference in their identities, and the identities of their others, are embedded in the local-territorial urban structure of city spaces. This does have some important demographic foundations that have been frequently linked to the rapid and growing presence of young, newly urbanized, unskilled and semi-skilled youth (usually unhelpfully catalogued as the *lumpenproletariat*) who are excluded from the city labour market, the housing-residential market and the employment bureaucracy of the state. However, the organization of identity-territories in the city is a much more complicated phenomenon. Enduring economic and residential segregation – and hence belonging – are key factors in organizing territorial communal spaces in the city for well-established classes. Similarly, student groups and established middle classes either unable to find employment or claiming insecurity in their class position against other economic groups have also been the backbone of urban religious movements. Several authoritarian religious movements have been explicitly backed by (mainly) industrial and finance classes.

A consideration of "space" rather than simply "class" allows for an analysis of city- or locality-based cross-class affiliations whose compounded nature is a distinctive feature of authoritarian religious mobilization. If analysis of the city is primarily determined by factors such as migrant labour power, class mobility, a segmented labour market, divisions between national and international or industrial and finance capital, and the labour process, then the impact of city space in creating the conditions for ethnic or religious confrontation can be missed. In his stimulating discussion of "world cities" and "colonial cities", Anthony King suggests that both these types of city

> provide the site for the confrontation and encounter between representatives and institutions of different nations, ethnicities, races, religions, and cultures. [The city provides opportunities] for the redefinition, transformation, and reconstitution of social, political, cultural, ethnic and biological categories. (King 1991: 44)

In much Marxist literature, these ethnic factors, which are reflexively integral to city-formation, can be ignored. For example, the lumpenproletariat (or "lumpen elements" in much South Asian literature) is a convenient reductionist shorthand for what is a highly complicated phenomenon that cannot be contained within an orthodox Marxist typology of classes. The "lumpenproletariat" can be all of the residents of local, caste- or sect-based shanty towns, student groups, adolescents, women, highly bureaucratic and territorial criminal organizations, paramilitary formations, participants in the permanent informal economy, the permanently unemployed, the "newly urbanized" youth and even religious leaders. If the "lumpenproletariat" organizes communally, it is through spatial symbolic organization in which these different class-fractions play a part. The "lumpenproletariat", in the form of settlement colonies and slums for example, also has an obvious political and symbolic significance that has been pointed out by Veena Das

> From the point of view of those who occupy the central spaces in Delhi, the peripheries are feared as slums. For the dwellers in these colonies, it is the city that is a landscape of fear. (Das 1992b: 13f.)

This can have momentous consequences that may be inaccessible in elementary class analysis. The presence of enduring so-called lumpenproletariat political formations can organize the real and symbolic boundaries, unity, identity and hierarchies of the city itself even as they are at its technical margins. The enormous impact on the organization and identity of Bombay by the agency of the Shiv Sena, a fascistic Hindu organization, has been described by several writers (see, for example, Heuzé 1995). The Sena was itself formed through a geographical slogan ("Maharashtra for the Maharashtrians", but now "Hindustan for the Hindus"), and its violent agency and extraordinary mass populist organization was pivotal in circumscribing some of the geographical and political limits and boundaries of the city of Bombay. While the Sena was marginal to official political culture, its presence and activities could also contain official urban politics, or more often set the agenda for them. Perhaps most symbolically, the Sena was responsible for the renaming of Bombay ("Good Bay" in Portuguese) to "Mumbai", a Marathi name for the Mother Goddess in Hinduism.

Similar parallels can be drawn around the activities of paramilitary political organizations in other cities. The rise of the Muhajir Quami Mahaz (MQM – Refugee People's Front) in Karachi in the 1980s is another example that highlights several of the issues discussed above. The MQM was formed initially as a breakaway group by younger members of the Pakistani Jamaat-i-Islami and has now virtually seized the support of the latter among urban migrant communities (Shaheed 1992). It declared that the radically ethnically diverse *muhajir* (refugee) groups in Pakistan (from 1947, following Partition, and others from Punjab, Bihar and Bangladesh in later years) constituted a nationality. This in itself is unprecedented – an "ethnogenesis" based on previous urban belonging and refugee experience. The intense armed conflict ("Kalashnikov culture") in Karachi from the mid-1980s to the present between *muhajirs*, including Biharis, and the Pathans, Afghan refugees and subsequently other Punjabi communities; the extraordinary impact of the Afghan civil war and its associated arms traffic; the control of urban territories and resources by organized crime; the massive impact of the global heroin trade in the organization of urban conflict and the urban economy; and the collapse of official state authority (itself re-appearing as another repressive armed combine) has utterly restructured the meaning and organization of the city and its public zones. What was a marginal, frequently "lumpenproletariat" conflict, entirely secondary to the Shia–Sunni and anti-

Ahmadi riots that structured religious conflict in the city, has now completely overwhelmed the centre.

This "communalization" of the city has obvious spatial consequences for the location, organization and formation of communities and some of these topics are discussed later in the book. However, of equal importance are the ambivalent interventions in the spaces of home, family and privacy. In an unprecedented way, private spaces are subject to reorganization and remapping by various authoritarian religious movements. The legislation of privacy is combined with detailed and intricate intervention in the activities of what constitutes the private and the familial. It is now virtually axiomatic that contemporary authoritarian religious movements, whether Christian, Hindu, Jewish or Islamic, are obsessed with redrawing the boundaries around how gender relations are lived and how family and sexual relations are organized. This has important spatial consequences. The domicile and the bed chamber as a private space of sex is subject to phenomenal and repressive external intervention in the name of national, communal or religious space. Consequently, sex, sexuality and family life are recreated in legislative interventions as public exhibition. The Offence of Zina (Enforcement of Hudood) Ordinance 1979 and the gender-differentiated laws of evidence and punishment in relation to adultery, rape and murder that were enacted under the Zia regime in Pakistan are such examples. These extremely repressive interventions paradoxically excavate the details of sexual narrative and practice for national popular consumption. They also advocate the right of both state apparatuses and civil society to constrain women's agency, action and freedom in private spaces (Mumtaz & Shaheed 1987).

Temporality, identity and agency

An important characteristic of progressive social movements has been to appropriate history, to attempt to insert themselves into the historical imagination of civil societies, nation-states and transnational communities. It has been said of black political agency that it aims to put blacks back into history (Gilroy 1987b: 12). The "innocent" use of the archives of history to pull the subaltern into the imagination of the present frequently depends on the construction of a monist chronology, a linear narrative and a phasal (but sometimes ruptured) entry into the modern, even if all of these are envisioned dialectically. This Hegelian historiography, so important to anthropological Marxism (Engels [1896] 1978), retains its stamp on both new and authoritarian social movements' imagination of the past in their present (and indeed, the Marxist-Leninist method can seem to be a virtual blueprint for the forms of political activism of authoritarian movements). The frequently used dialectic is one of presence–emergence, the emergence of the spirit (the subject, the oppressed, the identity) from the opposition between domination and the experience of being dominated and from which the arrow of time is punctuated by positive appearances of "liberation".

This necessary process of historical re-inscribing is, however, instantly troubled by two contesting tendencies. The historical writing is performed through the prism of a present political identity that desires to undertake the task of teleologically creating its legitimacy and its genealogy – it is truly a history of the present. However, that present identity is formed through, though frequently presented as the culmination of, an historical process and is, therefore, transient, contingent and liable to be supplanted. These two difficult processes of stasis and transience meet in a complex cultural-material field that works at its own elusive temporality. In "culture", identities continue to persist in some "naturalized", indifferent and glacial way even while they seem to be changing. There is a complicated traffic between the reified identities, political mobilization and history formation that emerge in religious activist writings, and the existence and endurance of these identities on a cultural plane. It is difficult to think of this relation as completed at some unspecified point between the poles of vanguardism or voluntarism. Similarly, while it is now more fashionable to deny the importance of formal activism, the relation between activism, the social movement and the wider cultural politics of community that envelop them is exceedingly complex. This is true even where activism manifests itself in blatantly vanguardist forms. The real as well as analytical divisions between "formal activism", the "social movement" and the "community" or "constituency" have broken down in celebrated periods of mass mobilization over the last decade in both authoritarian and progressive social movements. But, as social movement activism sheds older leftist heritages and assumes more variegated cultural forms that rely on an un-expected combination of mass audio-visual cultural communication

67

and local community initiatives, the relation between what is activism and what is cultural politics has become even more intangible and cannot easily be seen and understood in terms of the Blanquist–Jacobin heritage of the more socialist forms of activism of previous decades. The relative decline of the latter forms of activism does not signify the end of the "era of the masses" but, indeed, seems to confirm its expansion.

The sense of temporality in social movements is important, especially in the way social movements envision how they slot into the past and how they imagine their administrative, utopian or dystopian futures. There are important explanatory mechanisms by which social movements manage time. An Hegelian method is employed to explain the past, and anticipatory modes of explanation are used to engineer predictive strategies for future political action. These mechanisms are important in understanding the troubled present that all social movements inhabit. The demands for instant satisfaction, pleasure, equality and liberation within what appears to be a simple totality and the refusal of that totality to concede disrupts the Hegelian imaginary past of those movements and constantly recreate a frustrated present, itself a source of new identity, that iteratively threatens those movements' sense of themselves. This temporal dynamism is important for understanding why social movements cannot be reified either as agent-characters or, more simply, as signs. Their signal to dominant symbolic orders is never a unitary sign because it is always internally and externally threatened by new symbolic presences.

The political activities of authoritarian religious movements capture neatly many of these aspects. Both Islamic and Hindu authoritarian movements have a strong sense of elapsed or long gone utopia, a period of degeneration, dystopia, resistance and heroism against a conquering force, a dystopian present that is constantly emergent in intense action and activity and an inevitable future of redemptive utopia, permanent liberation and finally historical closure. This structure of time provides a reading of the historical process and of the present that the activists find themselves in. It also provides the content for their ethnogenetic projects. It is not a closed temporal system, as has often been said, especially about Islamic movements. The idea of inevitable historical closure, such as liberation, is part of the temporal imagination of agency in virtually all social movements, including those influenced by Marxism.

There are, of course, striking parallels between this imagination of the historical process and Hegelianism (or a form of Manichean-ism combined with history as process, totality and teleology). When combined with an ideology in which the social formation is seen as a simple reductive totality, this historical method provides impor-tant reasons for the anticipation of action, and for anticipatory and predictive strategies for political agency. The collapse of different temporal events into a single causal sequence, the elaboration of this sequence in relation to ideologies of power and domination, and the consequent formation of political strategies, is a universal method-ology in these movements. This Hegelian-"Marxist" method is not accidental to Islamic and Hindu movements. However anti-communist those religious movements are we cannot erase the influence of Marxist and communist inspired ideas on them, especially in the Middle East and South Asia.

The structure of time has been analyzed by Veena Das in the context of disorganized collective violence against another community. Das has shown how temporality works at several different levels in structuring both the meaning and the cause of particular actions. The temporal structure, direction and rhythm of particular social practices become constitutive of their meaning. For example, the origin of a riot may be impossible to find, but it leads to a sequence of events which, for both sides in the riot, provide "reasons" for what happened and why the participants acted as they did. These *alternative* interpretations of the temporal sequences of events provide the meaning for the violence for both protagonists. Other events – most notably repetitive annual or regular religious or ethnic festivals – themselves structure the reasons for and existence of collective violence (Das 1992b).

The social formation as a reductive totality

The expressive political ideologies of authoritarian religious movements, and consequently their forms of agency, are based on an *a priori* view (their "sociology") of the social formation as a reductive, elementary and intelligible totality composed of a small number of functionally dependent monological structures that, in the case of Western or secular social formations, necessarily create systemic forms of religious oppression for their functional survival. This physicalist–organicist view of the social formation seems to derive from Lamarckism or a crude Darwinism, such as that of Herbert Spencer. Indeed, in some important sense, it is Darwin and Newton (or perhaps Spencer and Laplace), rather than Hegel or Marx, who provide more accurate symbolic personalities for understanding some of the philosophical sediments in these movements. It is not surprising then that the political sociology manufactured by these movements is virtually entirely an elementary structural-functionalism combined with a reductive conception of social-Newtonian mechanical cause and effect. From one event we can explain a whole series of events automatically. Complexity, contingency and the compounded nature of social events are lost.

This uncomplicated systems approach is often combined with some kind of deeply embedded dysfunctionality at the core of the conflict or fissure in the social body. It is also here that the influence of a mutilated Darwinian evolutionism becomes evident. The dysfunctionality is a weakness in the social totality that needs to be eradicated. For Hindu revival, "the weak links in the great chain" of national pride are the Muslim and Christian minorities and the secularists of India. These weak others are also a moveable feast. In Pakistan, for example, the targets of official repression have been Shiites, Ahmadis, Hindus, communists and feminists.

Much of this "sociology" draws heavily on the metaphor of the human body. Indeed, the mapping of the human body onto the organismic social body is explicit in many authoritarian religious movement writings and is indeed central to their visceral forms of political mobilization. Partition, for example, is frequently illustrated in Hindu revivalist literature as the beheading of India; Muslim minorities are described as the "poison" in the blood of India and so forth. Clearly, the identification of an intelligible social totality within an organicist political ideology can lead to political strategies preoccupied with purity and pollution. The liberation of the social-body is inextricably linked with its purification. Both Hindu and Islamic authoritarian movements have traditional religious repertoires of pollution and purity that can be drawn on in political discourse.

The algorithmic personality and the masculine body in religious authoritarianism

A dramatic legislative anthropology is constitutive of the ideologies of Hindu and Islamic religious movements. At its centre is the incessant need to mould a new person in civil society. The Rashtriya Swayamsevak Sangh (RSS) has been explicit about this aim from its constitution in the 1920s, as indeed have most early Islamic movements such as the Muslim Brotherhood. The RSS' emphasis on "character building" and the creation of new persons in society, very literally the creation of a new Hindu man in both mind and body, has been at the core of its "cultural activities" and paramilitary organization. The RSS selectively recruits male children and adolescents, usually under the age of 15, who are obliged to attend *shakas* – compulsory rigorous daily physical exercise (variants of Indian martial arts and *lathi* (wooden staff) training) as well as education classes geared to person-building and nation-building. The aim is to instil the correct *samskars* ("impressions") in young minds through rote learning, discussions about selective and martial conceptions of Hinduism and gymnasia.

This *a priori* conception of personality and psychology is again strikingly functionalist. The mind is a *tabula rasa* and the correct inventory of ideas has to be scrawled onto it. This algorithm, once inserted, will lead, cybernetically, to the correct beliefs, reasons and actions. There is little room for doubt or disobedience. R. Hrair Dekmejian has usefully highlighted some typologies constitutive of the subject of fundamentalism that are important consequences of this algorithmic-functional method. He argues that the discovery of ideology and identity by the neophyte "produces a 'premature integrity' at an early age marked by extreme rigidity of beliefs and refusal to integrate new values into their ideological framework" (Dekmejian 1995:32–3).

This dogmatism, is, for Dekmejian, a result of social alienation, though it could be argued that the strategy of many modern ideological groups is to *produce* alienation and exteriority from the social body, to create self-professedly alienated individuals. Dekmejian highlights a number of consequent contradictory and unitary features in the psychology of the fundamentalist activist: inferiority–superiority, activism–aggressiveness, authoritarianism, intolerance, paranoia–projectivity, a conspiratorial worldview,

71

idealism, a sense of duty, austereness, conformity and obedience. These are ideal types that cannot all hold together in a single person or group.

The converse aspect of authoritarian religious movements is an intense and quite forbidding emphasis on the body, and in particular its masculine forms. The RSS' stress on daily physical activity and martial training is another cybernetic method. The authoritarian religious body is additionally highly stigmatized through its uniform, a conspicuous public marker of identity and difference. The RSS' uniform for *swayamsevaks* (volunteers) is a white shirt, khaki shorts, a *lathi* and a saffron flag. This uniform, invoking both the British colonial military authorities and the boy-scouts, is distinctive because it is modern and non-traditional. Aziz al-Azmeh has highlighted this in the context of culturalist Islam:

> ... Islamic 'culture' takes on the aspect of psychodrama, and the serious business of inventing a culture begins, primarily by the conjuration and proclamation of tokens (stigmata to others) of exoticism, particularly those which give a pronounced visual edge to the boundaries of exclusion/ inclusion. Basic and most plastic among these are dressing up, and exhibitionistic piety ... (al-Azmeh 1993:7)

This exhibitionism is a singular feature of RSS activities: huge outdoor *shakas*, bugle marches and parades, regimented displays of strength and difference. That the covering of the skin with a uniform – a new skin – is combined with visual difference seems to suggest something like a racial marker, or a racial metaphor of difference buried within the new fascination with uniforms.

The obsession with the purity of the body and its masculine, physical or ascetic forms has an alarming aspect when attention is focused on the body of the other. The emphasis on visceral degradation, carnage, butchery, massacre, gore, mutilation, dismemberment and the overarching metaphoric use of blood, fertility and pollution is a distinctive feature of the political language and activities of authoritarian Hindu and Islamic movements. The political languages of death, dying, revenge, martyrdom, purification or the murder of the other, and the visual impact of political material representing blood, traditional and modern weapons, and mutilated or dying bodies is a manipulative and cynical condensation of a social totality with the direct and immediate bodies one can have some control or power over: those of family, neighbours and oneself. The political languages created can be practically meaningless and ineffective ("Death to Amrika!") or they can be horrifying in their consequences for communal violence. The immediate control of the body has major relevance with regard to the gender absolutism that accompanies religious authoritarianism, and this is explored later.

The subject, the text and the good

There is a distinctive and selective way in which authoritarian religious movements remove moral and ethical considerations from questions of violence to or murder of another body. This is another aspect of the decentreing of the subject before God that has already been referred to. Religious discourse can provide two routes, one internal one external, for this "decentreing of the subject". One's actions, morals and thoughts, indeed one's regency, are rationally legitimized to oneself by an appeal to the wishes or laws of the Divine. The latter is typically a political ideology. Hence, it is simple to make dogmatic proclamations that disavow the subject. These are monotonous declarations of the form "In Islam this is forbidden ... " or "Hinduism says that ... " These statements manufacture a discursive Platonic ideal that does not (cannot) exist. The real world (often the West is compared to the religious ideal) is mapped against this imaginary perfection, which is never specified in detail, and of course will always be found wanting.

The other "decentreing" occurs through one's internal search for God, unity or the Ineffable which evaporates the ego in prelinguistic mystical experience. The importance of some variant of existentialist methodology for (the religious elites in) Hindu and Islamic revival has been apparent in the unsettled but strangely symbiotic relationship between mysticism and fundamentalism. In particular, the ambivalent and often tense relationships between sufism and rationalist Islamic revival (especially in Khomeini's work), and between the medieval mystical-ascetic traditions in Hinduism and rationalist Hindu nationalism are important reflections of this political dynamic.

The "decentring of the subject" in authoritarian religious movements does indicate an important difference from traditional religious orthodoxy which, typically, was concerned with careful exegesis of the sacred texts from which moral and ethical principles and ideas of good and evil were derived. In religious authoritarian movements, good and evil are just slogans that bear little or no relation to foundational ethical or moral considerations. Fairly typically, the good is defined through affiliation with an ideology or (which is pretty much the same thing) as doing what God said or intended. Evil is non-adherence to an ideology or (another version of the same thing) a rejection of or non-compliance with the way of God. In both cases, what is deemed good or evil is constructed as malleable. The philosophical structure that allows this kind of identity between one's beliefs and actions and the laws or desires of God was discussed in the previous chapter.

Importantly, in religious authoritarian movements, the decentring of the subject revolves around another key tension. The sacred text(s) are legislative. In this sense, for religious authoritarianism, nothing exists outside the text. But, at the same time, the text is not recuperable: it is too complicated, compounded, allusive and metaphorical, contradictory and plainly irrelevant or wrong. The only way in which the text can make sense is as a semiotic presence whose authority is immanent only in its utterance. Fundamentalism needs to create a considerable semiotic distance between itself and what the text may say. While this can also create spaces for progressive intervention, it also has the consequence that projects such as Hindu or Islamic "feminism", "Hindu science" or "Islamic democracy" are going to be inherently problematic. Fundamentalism, by turning text into sign, recreates the text as a completed, and usually simple totality. In this sense, authoritarian religious movements have to degrade the sacred texts, to translate them into intelligible, elementary political slogans. In revivalist Hinduism, this initially occurred through a clear and dogmatic substitution of numerous Vedic, post-Vedic and non-Vedic scriptures and traditions with one book, Tulsidas' popularized rendering of Valmiki's version of the *Ramayana* (Thapar 1991). This book, with its one principal God, Ram, fighting one principal enemy is easily reduced to a set of elementary political aphorisms for Hindu mobilization against Muslim minorities. To be sure, revivalist Hinduism is not entirely preoccupied with semitizing Hinduism, and other authoritarian possibilities also exist. However, in general a functional and cynical relation is created between a carelessly interpreted but complete text, the body and the body-social.

The sacred text, in both Hinduism and Islam, also has the new semiotic property of containing (all) knowledge and science. It is human failure not to recognize this. Both these aspects are important in examining the orientation of authoritarian religious movements towards science. In Hinduism, the impulse to *jnana* ("knowledge") can be both material and metaphysical, but both these are paths to God, or limited aspects of the Infinite that we may grasp, since we are fallible and imperfect. Islamic movements have similar constructions. These three totalities – the infinity of the world or God, the completeness of the texts and the imperfection of humans – while allowing cursory dismissal of the human sciences (except its own versions), also create an instrumentalist attitude towards the natural sciences. This results in an unusual alignment in which religious discourse can claim the fruits of natural science as its own while vigorously disputing the methodologies of natural science that discovered them, especially logical positivism and other variants of empiricism. There is, however, a powerful desire in religious movements to associate with "science", usually manifesting in synthetic and frequently obscurantist attempts to define a "Hindu science" or an "Islamic science". The Hindu fascination with electromagnetism in the last century and with special and general relativity, quantum mechanics and quantum cosmology in recent decades is one such example and is often combined with the belief that the *Rig Veda* and the *Upanishads*, or some of the *Puranas*, had already highlighted these discoveries. Some of the consequences of "religious science" are explored in the last chapter.

Conclusion

Authoritarian religious movements exhibit many of the same sociological features that the progressive social movements have been seen to have in social movement and postmodern theory. They are best viewed in a global framework, despite the severe national, economic and military limits to their political ambitions. Ideologically and culturally, authoritarian religious movements have the capacity to re-organize the formations of civil society, city, community and home in increasingly repressive ways. This is where they have been most effective. Authoritarian religious movements are

75

absorbed with the detail of the body and with the personification of their ideologies in the manufacture of new personalities and agents in civil society. Their rational political ideologies combine methodologies of time and space, subjectivity, science, utopia and liberation, body and gender, social totality and social purity. The next chapter examines how these themes relate to the modernity of authoritarian religious movements.

CHAPTER 3

The modernity of Islamic movements

And so, faced with the bestial hostility of the storm and the hurricane, the house's virtues of protection and resistance are transposed into human virtues. The house acquires the physical and moral energy of a human body. It braces itself to receive the downpour, it girds its loins. When forced to do so, it bends with the blast, confident that it will right itself again in time, while continuing to deny any temporary defeats. Such a house as this invites many to a kind of heroism of cosmic proportions. It is an instrument with which to confront the cosmos . . .
(Gaston Bachelard, *The poetics of space*, p. 46)

History [in political Islamism] takes place in two registers, one of which has a decided ontological distinction over the other: the authentic, and the inauthentic; that of the Islamic self, and that of its corruptions by otherness, such as non-Islamic people and religions, schisms, heresies and a manifold of enemies. The one is posited as original, hence necessary and in accord with nature, for Islam is a primeval religion (*din al-fitra*), and the other is poised as contingent, mere history, the passage of time as sheer succession and pure seriality, bereft of significance, and therefore of quality.
(Aziz al-Azmeh, *Islams and modernities*, p. 27)

Introduction

Many of the themes of the previous chapters become highly relevant to the main one explored in this chapter – the modernity of new Islamic movements. This discussion is continued into the next chapter which explores the related forms of political agency during the Rushdie affair. This chapter focuses on debates about the traditionality or modernity of radical Islam, and in particular the debates surrounding Khomeini's social and political thought. This area has been covered more competently and extensively by other writers. However, this chapter revisits some of these debates and discusses some themes that seem especially important to the theoretical concerns of this book. Two different terms will be used interchangeably with the problematic concept of "fundamentalism" in this and the next chapter: neofoundationalism (Smart 1992: 553) and neotradition (Hobsbawm & Ranger 1984, ch. 6). In addition, the term Islamism will also be used to describe Islamic fundamentalism. The first terms have the awkward task of describing the "newness" of religious identity formations, their original and foundational philosophical approaches and their re-invention of archaeological and anthropological traditions. The emphasis will be on their novelty and their original philosophical approaches, however much they themselves claim to derive from palpable traditions. Generally speaking, the indistinctness of the term "fundamentalism" in relation to other "traditional" religious formations is exactly what gives fundamentalism its important symbolic and political power, and thus it seems important not to become ensnared in the various hermeneutic circles that the concept can throw up. It is perhaps better to use a more historicized definition of "fundamentalist" to refer to modern movements that claim national-state political power or the repressive reorganization of civil societies on the basis of foundational concepts that are derived in the main from religion.

Modernity, tradition and radical Islam

The difficulty in classifying contemporary Islamic identities within the arrangement of modern–postmodern vocabulary emphasizes the partiality and Western focus of these debates. Conversely, many pro-Islamic discussions present preceding or contemporary Islams as finished edifices, pure formations, hermetically sealed from any contamination by the West. This view is reproduced by Western Islamophobic discourse, where Islam is constructed as monolithic, hermetic and therefore threatening. We need to avoid the now-instinctive tendency to classify every contemporary political manifestation as "new", as if this designation explains it, and to describe all novel ideological formations and all re-articulations of "tradition", including religious fundamentalism, as "postmodern", as if this explains them, whether these are manifest within or outside the West. But we also need to reject the view of religious ideologies as *particularly* traditional and static or exhibiting a unitary philosophy or history. Recent discussions on Islamic fundamentalism and modernity seem to be fixed within oppositional parameters in which Islam is seen either as an application of "traditional society" to modernity[1] or as a phenomenon that has leapt from a premodern existence to the postmodern and missed entirely the "stage" of modern Enlightenment.[2] We also cannot view new Islamic identities as "modern" simply because their champions use the technological products of modernization. Others seem to suggest that fundamentalist Islam is modern simply because it is contemporary (Bhabha 1990b: 215, 219). However, these views do not explain the exact affiliation or otherwise to the discourses of modernity that are contained in fundamentalist Islams.

This difficult area concerning the modernity of Islamic revival has been carefully discussed by several writers (Zubaida 1982, 1993, Abrahamian 1991, 1993, Rose 1983, Halliday & Alavi 1988, Halliday 1994, 1996, Keddie 1983, al-Azmeh 1993). I want to start with Aziz al-Azmeh's observation that

> Like all religions, Islam is neither above nor beyond history. For 1400 years, it has taken a bewildering variety of forms, each of which has proclaimed itself the most authentic .... The denial of this great diversity of Islamic traditions and of the reality of history does not convince the observer that a monolithic Islam is forming a society, but rather confirms the fact that religions do not constitute societies or histories but are rather constituted by them. (*The Guardian* 17 February 1989)

We can contrast this view with a contemporary "Orientalist" position, best represented in William Montgomery Watt's assessments of Islam and modernity (Watt 1988). Watt asserts that Islam, whatever historical forms it may have taken, has always had an image of itself that is totalizing, unchanging, self-sufficient, ahistorical and essentially medieval or traditional. Islam, in his view, has been virtually closed since the medieval period to external influences, especially the Enlightenment and contemporary Western social and natural scientific philosophy. Islam has no sense of history. Indeed, Islam cannot have a sense of historicity or progress, since that would entail recognizing its contingent nature rather than its self-view of totality, self-sufficiency and final revelation. (However, Watt does concede that Shiʿa Islam, because it has a strong Messianic component, does offer a teleology.) Consequently, its self-image is authoritarian – it can only deal with problems of contradiction, Western historical criticism, historical mistakes, real facts of history and modern sciences by closing off from them or suppressing them. Watt argues that, aside from a few uncharacteristic Western-influenced liberal Muslim tendencies, Islam has historically opted for a traditionalist inward-looking epistemology. This turn to essentially medieval juridical tradition is also a characteristic feature of fundamentalism. Furthermore, because Islam has closed itself off from Western Enlightenment influences, including developments in philosophy and science, it sees any Western assessments of it as attacks on it, whereas those assessments are simply applications of Western historical rationality and reason to religious texts and doctrines and not attacks on Islam as such. He also argues that Islamic jurisprudence and *shariʿa*[3] cannot be transported from essentially medieval nomadic desert communities to a complex and international modern world of diplomacy and negotiation, nor can Islamic countries desire Western technology and scientific education without taking on at least some of the baggage of Western philosophy.

We should note the importance of the contrasts between these two positions. For al-Azmeh, the critical or historical realist, Islam is patently historical and differentiated despite what traditionalist Muslims may say. Fundamentalism is one part of this historical change. For Watt, Islam is unchanging and is what traditionalists (and fundamentalists) say it is despite the monumental social and political changes in the histories of Muslim empires, communities and nations over 12 centuries. For the former position, to which we can fruitfully add Edward Said's view of "Islam" as an abstraction that acquires differential content in specific historical circumstances for different "communities of interpretation" (Said 1985: xv, 8–9, 41), the possibility is presented for a realist, critical and historical position that can disrupt traditionalist, "Orientalist" or fundamentalist views of a transcendental Islam.

This position logically cannot accept the view of any Islamic "self-image" as identical to the actual manifestation of Islam in history. More definitively, the Islamic social is not the same as "Islamic sociology" and neither of these are equivalent to the sociology of Islam. Indeed, this truth-claim of an identity between Islam as ideology, Islam as a social formation and Islam as a sociology is an original feature of Islamic fundamentalism. (Indeed, the discipline "sociology" is arbitrary and virtually any other human, and to some extent natural science, discipline could be substituted.) This *mise en abyme* is an essential strategy of fundamentalist political language that actively seeks to mystify these differences under some manufactured unity of ideology or God. (A distinctive argumentative style in fundamentalist political sociology, especially when faced with critique, is to shift ontic ground across, or claim an identity between, the individual, ideology, structure-institution and the social formation.) For the "Orientalist" position, however, those fundamentalist constructions of Islam are *validated*, since it accepts that Islam's contemporary "self-image" is identical to what Islam has always been (cf. al-Azmeh 1993). Islam is its unchanging nature.[4] Importantly, "Islam" in these "Orientalist" or "fundamentalist" constructions can act as a concept-metaphor, a character agent, a legislative Platonic ideal and a trope for the transcendental and sublime.

These two positions of al-Azmeh and Watt are ideal types that point to immense theoretical and political problems around the constitution of "tradition" in the modern world. Part of the methodological problem is in comparing just the political ideology and political language of fundamentalism with modernist, post-Enlightenment discourse separately from other economic, political, ideological and cultural features that have been identified as definitive of Western modernity. It is relatively straightforward to read religious fundamentalist political language and compare it with discourses of nationalism, the nation-state, liberation and so forth and hence deduce that fundamentalism is both modern and modernist and derives its key concepts in large part from Western political discourse. This is indeed a variant of postcolonial discourse methodology.

From another context, Sudipta Kaviraj warns against this kind of reductionism. He argues that some dominant strands in the Indian critique of colonialism were not just attempts to counter or criticize Western theories by the use of argumentative structures derived from Western theoretical discourse. Rather, these intellectual enterprises were attempted outside of Western orbits and asserted "the abstract possibility of other universes of theoretical reflection". Consequently,

> In writing the history of the discourses of the colonized, we must guard against the mistake of misrecognition, translating its concepts into its nearest European equivalents, like romanticism, socialism, bourgeois theory, etc. (Kaviraj 1993: 36)

This sounds eminently reasonable and to some extent plausible. However, the challenge is in defining the characteristics of an extra-Western intellectual universe that occurred in and against the period of colonization, was not bound by either "nativist" or "Enlightenment" strands, and could not be elaborated in relation to discourses of "the modern". This can lead to the kind of catachresis, or perhaps even aporia, that was discussed in Chapter 1. It reflects the problem of evaluation that remains mainly or solely within ideological formations or textual narratives. Another way of stating this problem reductively is by asking two related questions that seem to capture the main issues: whether any authentic nativist position is now possible after the fact of modernity; and whether the ideological claims of Western modernity as *telos* are indeed mirrored in the features of modernity inside or outside Western nation-states. In other words, it seems important not to separate historically the impact of modernity outside the West with the identified and claimed features of modernity in the West, but to consider both as part of a persisting and discontinuous set of global and historical transformations that have their own locally non-relativistically analyzable impacts and features. (Of course, the key historical problem is in describing what these transformations are.)

For our limited purposes, it seems important to acknowledge four broad factors:

- the complex interrelatedness of historical origins that defeats ideas of national, religious, ethnic, racial or (as is increasingly articulated) civilizational essence;
- the *absolute* global impact of Western "universalist" ideas and Western power in slavery, the colonial period, imperialism and global militarization, and in nation-state formation, science, humanities, industrialization, modernization and, broadly speaking, underdevelopment;
- the *unequivocal historicity* of the non-West (as well as the West) and its societies, its forms of economy and polity, its cultural, ideological, political and intellectual formations, whether prior to Western domination or during and after the colonial period;
- the asymmetric syncretism of Western and non-Western cultures, traditions, intellectual formations, ethnicities in which it is largely possible to identify Western, non-Western, anti-Western or traditionalist elements and influences through deeper hermeneutic study.

All these factors become important in discussing the "traditionality" or "modernity" of fundamentalist political ideology. Within the political ideologies of fundamentalism, it seems important to distinguish analytically:

- the articulation of traditional elements in contemporary discourse around modern problems of statecraft, civil society or war (for example, the trope of Husayn's martyrdom[5] in Shi'ism applied to thousands of young children who cleared modern Iraqi minefields for the Iranian Revolutionary Guard by walking through them);
- the syncretic application of tradition to modern problems (for example, Quranic "consensus of the community of believers" (*ijma'*) is transformed into the expansive pseudodemocratic structures of the Iranian Islamic state, which is faced for the first time ever with a key feature of modernity: the people);
- the creation of novel philosophies, constitutive of a significant break with (or an explicit attack on) tradition, which may or may not be subsequently legitimized by an appeal to tradition

83

(for example, Maududi's or Shariati's theory of an Islamic state (Maududi 1991, Akhavi 1983) or Khomeini's theory of Islamic government);

- the obscurantist re-assertion of tradition (for example, the truth of Islamic–Aristotelian logic and proof against natural scientific discovery or the human sciences);
- a new or non-contextual emphasis on some traditional elements that were not emphasized before, or may have been unimportant for long periods (for example, *jihad* against infidel polytheism translated to *jihad* against the USA, the Great Satan);
- the insertion of novel elements into an existing "traditional" discourse (for example, the new governmental role for the *fuqaha* (jurisconsult) that is urged in Khomeinism);
- the uncritical and unproblematic appropriation of modernist political ideas and discourse (for example, the constitutional framework of the Islamic Republic of Iran in which, paradoxically, *shari'a* is secondary to nation-state formation; or indeed the idea of political power itself, invested in the *fuqaha*).

It should be emphasized that all the above can occur together and are only analytically distinct factors. They stress the historicity of both Western and non-Western social formations. Moreover, they are amenable to sociological or political analysis. There is nothing extraordinarily obtuse or incommensurable about the essence of Khomeinism that prevents us *in principle* from comparing and contrasting its political language to the political languages of Bonapartism, dictatorship, totalitarianism, anti-imperialism or democracy – or to Shi'a intellectual traditions during the Safavid period, *usuli* jurisprudence, or, indeed, to discern the influence of sufi mysticism or gnosis (*'irfan*). It needs reiterating here that an important *a priori* claim of the discursive regimes, political languages and political projects of Islamic and Hindu authoritarian religious movements is their truth-claim about their ability to seal themselves against "external" comparative and historical analysis, usually by delegitimizing the latter through tropes of "authenticity". In this context, the perhaps more careful assessment of Orientalism by Edward Said becomes, for religious fundamentalists (including, interestingly, some Hindus ones), a mechanism for excluding critique.

This enclosure of religious political discourse is central to Islamist forms of political and emotional mobilization and activist rhetoric. It is also the (unfounded) source of the belief among some Western commentators that "Islam" has no conception of change or history. The latter also seems to be an example of the ontic fallacy discussed in Chapter 1: the knowledge-claim made about a complete and hermetic "Islam" by Islamists is identified as congruent with the actual manifestations of Islamic or Muslim history. Of course, the discursive closure is a rhetorical device that can be easily dismissed when one examines the content of fundamentalist discourse. Fundamentalism is by and large preoccupied with eminently unclosed political, economic and social problems, often in conceptual terms that are "Western". Put another way, the closure of discursive constructions is unsupportable (no discursive universe is closed) and is only effective through its dogmatic articulation as a closed system. It is another variant of the recovery of identity that occurs through its articulation rather than as a result of any essence it contains.

The authentic and the traditional

Much of the discussion around religious traditionality and modernity hinges around a third extraordinarily difficult concept: authenticity. Indeed, ideologies of authenticity can embrace quite neatly questions of authorship, origin, accuracy, representation, truth and reality, all of which can have clear religious undertones. The contemporary political importance of ideologies of the authentic in progressive and authoritarian social movements suggests further research (but see al-Azmeh 1993: 39–59). Importantly, one characteristic of religious revivalist political language is to detach "the authentic" from "the traditional". It may also be further argued that a feature of modernist ideologies was to undermine the closer premodern identity between authenticity and tradition.

The ambiguous late modern relationship between tradition and authenticity is vastly exploited in authoritarian religious movements. "Authenticity" has the important capacity to be both a claim on and a critique or rejection of "tradition". Tradition is evaluated against the measuring instrument of authenticity. To be sure, authenticity may be claimed by an appeal to an historical tradition.

However, political ideologies that claim to be based on tradition are important for this iterative claim, which may be more vital than the actual demonstration of traditional or historical content. Conversely, tradition may be criticized or rejected by higher claims to authenticity, as we shall shortly see. In both these ways actual historical traditions can be severely undermined by newer political claims to "authenticity" or "authentic representation". In its paradoxical way, the claim to authenticity in religious fundamentalism based on a return to originary positions (usually the sacred texts) is ruptural and can obliterate the more careful accumulation of historical tradition. The authentic becomes the novel. This announcement of the new that ignores the structures, institutions and ideologies that have accompanied the long development of societies and traditions can have difficult and dramatic political consequences.

Recent historiography has highlighted important issues about how "traditions are invented" (Hobsbawm & Ranger 1984). This work can be limited in its assessments of how *ethnicities* are recreated and how they relate to the invention of tradition or to "new" religions. However, this work is innovative in highlighting how history is re-inscribed and reclaimed. It is especially fascinating in describing how recent are many of the traditions we imagine. Eric Hobsbawm identifies invented traditions as belonging to three types: traditions acting to establish social cohesion, group membership or imagined communities; traditions as legitimizing social division and institutions of authority; and traditions as socialization systems which inculcate beliefs, values and conventions of behaviour. Generally, the inventing of traditions has been the preserve of status groups and elites, and concerns the recreation of hierarchy or the maintenance of the status quo by inventing new symbolic rituals of cohesion and adaptation. In addition, Hobsbawm highlights a connection that is used later between the need to establish tradition in a social formation through strong appeals to equality in such a way that the invented tradition generates or maintains considerable formal inequality and status differentiation.

However, the thesis of invented traditions raises other questions. Why is there the need now to invent traditions at all? Why are invented traditions now manifest as mass movements obsessed with both "liberation" and a post-fascist "purity"? ("Purity" being as much about the creation of an unpolluted personal identity as it is about inventing new symbols for elite identity.) Precisely why claims to authenticity or tradition should be so energetic is a key political problem. Why are ideologies that are formed in the present and gain their legitimation by an explicit claim to a "reversion" to the past and an apparent "revulsion at the future" so successful *today*? Why is the reversion to traditions that have never existed (such as Islamic government) and ethnicities that have never been (such the hegemonic assertion of *Ramabhakti* cults over a "unified Hinduism") so important *today*? Put another way, why have ethnogenesis and authenticity become so important in the political formations of late modernity?

Several themes seem to be important in addressing this very difficult issue. One central aspect of colonial modernity was to remove the epistemology of history from the colonial populations it encountered and subjugated. The classificatory urge in modernity appropriated, reified and put into stasis the histories of its subjected populations even as that history was being changed by modernity itself. The freezing of colonial or "Third World" populations and social formations in time is an important contemporary metaphor that still commonly locates those populations as existing at the *frontier* between European modernity and their aboriginal static histories. (The "Asiatic mode of production" in classical Marxism is one instance.) While colonization lasted for centuries and decolonization is only a few decades old, the impact of modernity and the new and complex indigenous non-Western histories it created are frequently erased in popular memory by the overarching presence of the colonial frontier. This is also often true for nations that were not formally colonized.

Frontier reasoning is an important element in understanding the insertion of "tradition" into contemporary Western or non-Western political discourse. The present, and in some cases extremely recent resonances of the Crusades, slavery, colonial domination, colonial massacres, slave and anticolonial revolts, colonial sexual subjugation and its associated motifs of black sexual prowess or exoticism, are importantly dependent on frontier metaphors, on "the original encounter". Contemporary political discourse frequently recreates this frontier. Perhaps definitive of much contemporary political discourse is the constant interrogation it faces regarding the authenticity of its origins "in the West" or "outside the West". In this sense, frontier reasoning, and especially the colonial frontier are

87

energetic sources of new tradition. Every one of the apparently traditional Islamic or Hindu ideological sects or political formations that either intervened during the Rushdie affair or make up current Hindu revivalism can be traced back to a formative period during either the 1850s (in struggles against colonialism) or the early to middle part of this century (the phase of decolonization and nation-state formation). That frontier, in its form of twentieth-century US economic imperialism and earlier British–Russian economic colonialism, has been extremely important for Iranian Shi'a revivalism. In this condition of Western economic colonization, elements of Shi'ism acquired importance as a result of their translation and transformation into a modern anticolonial anti-imperialist discourse. In some densely interesting way, the religious revival seen in Islamic and Hindu movements is a product of colonialism.

Another tentative argument is also relevant. It is not simply that in the nineteenth and twentieth centuries buried traditions in colonized countries asserted themselves against modernity but that the idea of "Third World" tradition was itself a modernist creation emphasized most directly in the colonial frontier itself, just as the idea of traditional societies in the West could not have been conceptualized outside modernity. Modern sociology itself arose through that major symbolic opposition it constructed between *Gemeinschaft* and *Gesellschaft*. Similarly, few "Third World" social formations can be seen as purely "traditional" in the sense that they remained untouched or untransformed by the impact of colonization or (mercantile) capitalism and then by (peripheral-Fordist) industrialization, urbanization and technological modernization in this century and (towards the end of) the last century. The impact of Western colonialism and capitalism involved differential changes in many "Third World" social formations in which an assemblage of rural and urban modes and relations of production, labour organization, colonial "native" administration, state, army and police formation, enforced modernization and enforced stagnation and new organizations of civil society all co-existed. These changes in many "Third World" social formations as a result of capitalist penetration and colonization can be seen as radically differential when compared with nation-state formation, the separation of polity and economy, the formation of an "undominated" market, industrialization, the organization of nuclear family forms and domestic labour and the relations of production through the selling of formally free labour power that occurred in the capitalist West (though even that is now changing).

This persisting *bricolage* of "modes" and relations of production in "Third World" social formations is an extremely strong critique of teleological economic determinism, including Marxian, Smithian and Fabian political economy. Each of these ideologies also has conceptualizations of traditional (premodern) society and, importantly, *the natural state* that is necessarily transcended in modernity but still acts as a supplementary marker for the utopias these ideologies offer. But the other side of political economy – broadly developmental theories of the nation-state and civil society – are also strongly criticized by the actual political and social formations that have arisen in the Third World. There is, for example, no simple language of *Western* teleological modernity that can describe contemporary economic, political or social formations such as those of Saudi Arabia, Nigeria, India or Sri Lanka. These countries can rely variously on different combinations of state nationalization, modernized and "traditional" rural methods of production, factory-based free wage labour as well as massive modernization projects that can be dependent on indigenous or migrant bonded and "serf" labour. They can provide free-trade zones and tax benefits for Western multinational corporations in which formally-free labour power is superexploited and trade unionization is organized in ethnic and religious modalities or is heavily corporatized. Political government may take the form of formal democracy, a single party dictatorship or a modernized religious absolutist state administered by a gigantic oligarchic bureaucracy whose functioning depends on an essential social system of corruption. Furthermore, the economic fortunes of these nations (gross domestic and national product) vary, either enabling them to compete globally or condemning them to failure.

The social formations of Western modernity can have identified sociological features, such as the nation-state, constitutionality and nationalism, capitalist industrialization and finance capital, a globalized system of nation-states, urbanization, bureaucratic organization, informational surveillance and militarization, together with various organizations of civil society, popular enfranchisement and the nuclear family form. However, in some way or another, at least some of these features can also be identified in virtually every contemporary social formation, however "traditional" it may outwardly appear. Modernity, if envisaged as a global system of dominance, exploitation and capitalist (and communist) expansion, radically transformed non-Western so-called "traditional societies" into forms that had not previously existed. These social formations are often inexpressible in the vocabulary of Western modern versus Western traditional societies because they do not fit into the universalist *telos* that accompanies the theorization of Western modernity. In this sense, it does not help to call these formations non-modern, antimodern, "outside the modern" or "outside of Western modernity", or even contra-modern, even if we qualify all these by stating that those formations are not premodern either, since that evades the impact of modernity, the idea of a modern society and the actual practices of modernization. This emphasizes again that the *meaning* of modernity in the West and the *impact* of modernity outside the West are artificial separations and are better seen as different aspects of a related phenomenon.

Some of this is reflected in the way new traditional ideologies in some "Third World" countries can be a rejection of Western *modernity*, but almost always undertaken using the explicit content of *modern* discourse, especially around nationalism, liberty and political government. This is not a new phenomenon but was integral to the formation and critique of modernity and Enlightenment from its inception: the "Black Jacobins" of San Domingo in 1791 refracted the French revolution and demanded its products from the perspective of the slaves and colonized. Anticolonial liberation movements illustrated this problem differently. Those movements demanded rights and freedom from colonial domination, expressly using the content of Enlightenment discourse against its representatives, for a nation-state and a nationalism that itself was a creation of modernity and may not have existed in that geographical boundary or ethnic content prior to colonization.

These two themes of the transnational and nationalism are old ones that recur frequently in new traditional or fundamentalist discourse but can take highly ambiguous forms, mirroring the contradictions in the West between transnational systems and the nation-state. They can also allow for a different discussion of tradition. New "traditional" ideologies are frequently concerned with explaining the extremely difficult disjunction between a nationalism that was invented and an internationalism that is dominated by the West. Both the new traditions examined in this and the following chapters rehearse a complex critique of "impure" secular postcolonial nationalism and a critique of the West's iniquitous domination of the global. They can be both deeply nationalistic and have a global methodology. In this sense, it is tempting to see new traditional ideologies as functionally nationalistic, despite their critique of the nationalism they inhabit. Whatever they may claim otherwise in criticizing nationalism, they are essentially geared to creating a new nationalism. New "traditional" ideologies in "Third World" countries can also appear to be "functional" in this sense because they can be read as aiming for "national development" and integration, usually into a capitalist world market and global political system that is dominated by the West, while simultaneously articulating what appears as a regression to premodern certainties through an appeal to "tradition". In this sense, however religious a state may be it cannot possibly escape the condition of its secularity. This is a general issue that haunts Western as well as non-Western societies and is probably best expressed here as a tension between Enlightenment secular rational nation-statecraft and the content of modern nationalism, which can be seen as a Romantic product. Put differently, it highlights the problem of how secular rationality can be co-extensive with mystically defined nationalism, a problem currently at the heart of contemporary Western European politics.

However, some new traditional ideologies also contain important transnational strands (such as pan-Islamic revival) that disrupt the idea of simply forming a new national identity, in particular an identity based on ethnic nationalism. Indeed, the critique of ethnic nationalism is explicit in many forms of Islamic and Hindu fundamentalism. This suggests a displacement of ethnic nationalist identity by a new religious-political identity that need not be based on ethnic history and tradition. This can be a complex discourse that renews an often-imposed postcolonial nationalism while at the same time attacking the foundation of Western modernity from which nationalism itself arose. In this way, new traditional ideologies can discursively transcend rather than simply accommodate to the nation-state and can consequently aim for "economically dysfunctional" physical and military expansion. The demands of some Hindu "nationalists", for example, for the restoration of an ancient Hindu empire that actually never existed or the combination of Iranian nationalism with pan-Islamism exhibit this same contradiction, and their manifest activities may involve "economically dysfunctional" assistance outside their own national borders (for example, in Lebanon).

The Khomeinist assault on tradition

It is necessary to continue by examining one particular brand of revolutionary Islam that forcefully intervened in the Rushdie affair. Khomeinism, as embodied in the early writings of Ruhollah Khomeini during the 1960s and in the political practice of Shi'a Islam in Iran after 1979, represents a major epistemological break with both orthodox and reformist-secular views of Islam as strictly a religious ideology that only subsequently intervenes in the political process, if at all. To align with this kind of assessment implies an explicit criticism of Western discourses that have constructed radical Islam as "medieval" and Judeo-Christian discourses that concerned themselves with viewing the Rushdie affair with strictly religious accents, using in particular the themes of blasphemy and multifaith tolerance (Commission for Racial Equality 1990a, Ruthven 1990, Weldon 1989).

Khomeini's social and political thought creates an important distance from earlier conceptions of the role of Islam in social and political processes, though it also mirrors other developments in twentieth-century Islamic social and political thought. While "anti-imperialist" or anticolonialist Islam had existed since at least the 1920s and while a view of Islam as a manifesto for Muslim political activism had existed for much longer, the critical aspects of Khomeinism were to recast Islam as an explicitly "anti-imperialist" movement of the oppressed that was simultaneously a legitimating ideology for active mass politics and a radically new system of political government, state formation and civil society. For Khomeini,

> Islam is the religion of militant individuals who are committed to truth and justice. It is the religion of those who desire freedom and independence. It is the religion of those who struggle against imperialism. But the servants of imperialism have presented Islam in a totally different light. They have created in men's minds a false notion of Islam. The *defective* version of Islam, which they have presented

in the religious teaching institution, is intended to deprive
Islam of its vital, revolutionary character. (Khomeini 1981:
28, emphases added)

We should note Khomeini's characterization of the traditional
religious institution as actively promoting a false, "imperialist"
version of Islam. Centrally important for Khomeini and for many
fundamentalist movements was the view that, because of Western
imperialism and colonialism, the conception of Islam that exists is
false, defective, corrupted, impure or polluted and that it must be
returned to an originary or pristine state of beauty, truth, unity,
justice and militancy. Consequently, he proposed a radically new
personal, pure, non-privatized Muslim identity. Islam had to be
displaced from being an orthodox religious-legal and moral tradition that could govern the small-scale affairs of Muslim communities into being a revolutionary political ideology. The importance
of revolution in Khomeinism is itself an Enlightenment strand.
Khomeini was also explicitly opposed to the "traditional" practice
of religion in Islam, and the elements of faith, prayer and scripture
were of relatively little consequence for him. Instead, Islam should
actively constitute and mobilize Muslims in civil society. Its purpose
is not to make subjects more religious but more political (Ja'far &
Tabari 1984). This has momentous consequences. It means an
active conception of civil society in which legislation can be
administered by its members outside of, but with the authority of,
the institutions of the state. This is not just an extension of the state
into civil society (as existed under the Shah's totalitarian regime) but
a conception of the latter having its own authoritative and autonomous forms of discipline and punishment.

The group who should undertake the task of reformulating
Muslim identity are the *fuqaha*. Central to Khomeini's philosophy
is the unorthodox reconstruction of the governance or guardianship
(*velayat*) of the jurisconsult (*faqih*). In Shi'ism, the *faqih*

> ... is learned in matters pertaining to the function of a
> judge, since the term *faqih* is applied to one who is learned
> not only in the laws and judicial procedures of Islam, but
> also in the doctrines, institutions, and ethics of the faith –
> the *faqih* is, in short, a religious expert in the full sense of
> the word. (Khomeini 1981: 60)

The *faqih*, for Khomeini, must also possess two other characteristics besides knowledge of law: justice ("excellence in beliefs and morals") and leadership. Khomeini also states that "knowledge of the nature of angels, or of the attributes of the Creator, Exalted and Almighty is of no relevance to the question of leadership" and nor is knowledge of the natural sciences (ibid: 59). The necessary qualities that he identifies combine to make the *fuqaha* suitable to assume political governance over the Muslim community. Khomeini's view of the *fuqaha* as a "distant" group of knowledgeable, just leaders who are morally pure and incorruptible and whose only concern is the well-being of Islam and the Muslims, is a neo-Platonic strand.

How did Khomeini theologically justify Shi'a clerics assuming the secular role of executive, juridical and legislative leadership of the Muslim community in a new Islamic state? Khomeini argued that this is demanded by "tradition":

> ... [the Divine ordinances] of Islam are not limited with respect to time and place; they are permanent and must be enacted until the end of time. They were not revealed merely for the time of the Prophet merely to be abandoned thereafter.... Since the enactment of laws, then, is necessary after the departure of the Prophet from this world, and indeed, will remain so until the end of time, the formation of a government and the establishment of executive and administrative organs are also necessary. (Ibid: 42)

This transcendentalist conception of Islam supplies a highly abstracted epistemology of history that ignores the struggles for power and control in the early histories of both Sunni and Shi'a Islam. The theory of history is linked by Khomeini to a conception of political and bureaucratic power embodied in the modern nation-state. In an important way, history (represented as a transcendental abstraction) is completed in its combination with a perfect state. This is itself an extremely common, almost definitive strand in post-Enlightenment political philosophy (though it has traditional and ancient precedents in both Western and non-Western thought). There was, according to Khomeini, only disagreement about who should head the state after Muhammad's death. But,

The nature and character of Islamic law and the divine ordinances of the shari'a furnish ... proof of the necessity of establishing government, for they indicate that the laws were laid down for the purpose of creating a state and administering the political, economic and cultural affairs of society. (Ibid: 43)

Khomeini referred to verses of the Qur'an, the Sunna and other commentaries as well as the practice of, for example, Islamic taxation to provide the ("Aristotelian") proof that "tradition" demands an Islamic state. Furthermore, the *fuqaha* have to directly assume something approaching the *divine* role of the prophets and the Imams of Shi'ism. Khomeini did not simply say that the *fuqaha* must act as deputies until the occulted Twelfth Imam returns. He traced a direct line of authority and, importantly, some form of spiritual transcendence from the prophets and Imams to the current *fuqaha*. Indeed, the *fuqaha* are "the proofs to the people" and "the proof of the Imam":

All the affairs of the Muslims have been entrusted to them. God will advance proof and argument against anyone who disobeys them in anything concerning government, the conduct of Muslim affairs, or the gathering and expenditure of public funds. (Ibid: 87)

In making this totalitarian claim, Khomeini is quite explicit that its traditionality is ambiguous. It is possible, he says, to have certain reservations about its chain of transmission through tradition. However, once the claim is established, the *fuqaha* have to not only approximate to the kinds of guidance that the Imams and prophets provided, they have to fulfil the *complete* functions of the Imams and the prophets. This, he argued, is also demanded by tradition: after all how can the *fuqaha* only fulfil *some* of the traditional functions laid out in the Qur'an and *hadiths* (teachings of the Prophet)? For Khomeini, only the *fuqaha* have this role – orthodox religious scholars, scribes and exegetes are not good enough. "Traditionalists who have not attained the level of *ijtihad* and who merely transmit *hadith*" cannot know how to apply religious ordinances in their generality or specificity (ibid: 70).

The concept of *ijtihad* rather than *taqlid* ("imitation" of earlier ordinances) is extremely important in Islamic fundamentalism. *Ijtihad* is essentially about innovation and re-interpretation, about forming new opinions and extrapolations that are apparently in line with the sacred text. Many Islamic fundamentalists question the whole basis of Islamic jurisprudence and its various schools, all of which have historically evolved over many centuries from applications and interpretations of the texts. Their fundamentalism resides in displacing the validity and legitimacy of the history of Islamic jurisprudence and urging an authentic, though semiotic, reversion to the original text of the Qur'an (and the Sunna and Hadith) to interpret it anew without the baggage of its history and development (Zakaria 1989 provides examples of the consequences of ignoring that history of development).

Finally, Khomeini says that the *fuqaha* have an obligation to assume political responsibility because it is their divine duty to protect Islam. These are quite astonishing founding claims that directly contradict most Shi'a traditions. In the latter, no human political authority is legitimate after the Occultation of the Twelfth Imam and that authority can only be re-established on his return. Among Shi'a authorities, it is traditional that some form of *velayat-e-faqih* is exercised over three areas of Muslim activity: over people who are victimized, such as widows or orphans, and their property; over the property and activities on which the religious life of the community depends, such as mosques; and finally over the general welfare of the Muslim community, such as advocating on behalf of the oppressed, condemning sinners and issuing *fatwas* (opinions) on juridical matters (Rose 1983). However, some Shi'a scholars had earlier made a fourth claim that extended *velayat* to the exercise of some direct authority by the *faqih*. In the absence of the Twelfth Imam, the 'ulama (religious judges-scholars-leaders) gradually assumed the authority to act on behalf of the Divine Imam and assumed various religious functions such as giving judgements on religious law, collecting religious taxes and leading Friday prayers. But,

> Until the advent of Khomeini . . . none of the leading *ulama* formally laid claim to the right to deputise for the political authority of the Imam. This political authority was either held to have lapsed with the occultation of the Imam or . . . the *ulama* would sometimes advance arguments to justify

the interim derivative authority of the secular political authorities. (Momen 1989: 64).

There is some debate over the extent to which Khomeini's claim represents an absolute rupture within Shi'ism or whether it can be situated as a relative advancement of political tendencies already existing within Shi'a juridical traditions. However, while previous Shi'a authorities did generate "an extensive speculative literature describing an ideal imamic government",

> any *velayat-e-faqih* in political matters is extremely limited in Shi'i tradition. With the exception of the eighteenth century[6] CE, in no period has direct political authority been claimed for jurisprudents by any significant number of Shi'i authorities. Rather, the appropriate political *velayat* of jurisprudents was defined in terms of occasional intervention into political affairs to redress grievous wrongs and safeguard the religious and moral standards of Muslim society. (Rose 1983: 176)

Khomeini not only extended the parameters of political *velayat* but engaged in a caustic critique (and, later, violent suppression) of *fuqaha* who saw their duty as falling outside of their formal involvement in political authority:

> The agents of imperialism, together with the educational, propaganda and government apparatuses of the anti-national puppet governments they have installed, have been spreading poison for centuries and corrupting the minds and morals of the people ... sometimes I see people who sit in the centers of the religious institution saying to each other, "These matters are beyond us; what business are they of ours? All we are supposed to do is offer our prayers and give our opinions on questions of religious law." Ideas like this are the result of several centuries of malicious propaganda on the part of imperialists, penetrating deep into the very heart of [religious centres] causing apathy, depression and laziness to appear, and preventing people from maturing ... (Khomeini 1981: 136)

THE MODERNITY OF ISLAMIC MOVEMENTS

Here the process by which the colonial frontier energizes a new tradition is illustrated. Khomeini inserted the colonial frontier into his claim against Shi'a religious orthodoxy and on this basis expounded his new tradition of *velayat-e-faqih*. However, Khomeini went much further than just asserting the divine right over political guardianship of the *fuqaha*. That right had to be exercised through a modern system of Islamic government (*hokumat-e-Islami*). The Islamic state was essential not only because of the need to protect Islam and Muslims from "imperialist corruption" but because Islamic government was demanded by Quranic and Sunna *tradition*. In justifying Islamic government, Khomeini again used the colonial frontier as the basis from which to criticize religious orthodoxy and insert his new interpretation that the religious texts patently demanded an Islamic state. *Hokumat-e-Islami* was his second major epistemic break, though Khomeini barely spells out in detail what the government would actually be like and what it would do except that it would necessarily be undemocratic, would install *shari'a* and collect the appropriate taxes. The "knowledgeable and just" *fuqaha*, as of divine right, would be the only group who could control the government-state and one of their major roles was to encode *shari'a* into the heart of the new Islamic state and civil society.

Several Arab Muslim countries had institutionalized (versions of) *shari'a* to differing extents and for different political reasons. For Khomeini, these states were compliant client-states of British and especially American imperialism, equally responsible for the oppression of Muslim masses. In opposition to this, Khomeini's project was the reconstruction of Muslim identity afresh in direct opposition to "Western imperialism" and the "Westoxication" that had previously corrupted it in Iran and elsewhere. This insertion of anticolonialism and "anti-imperialism" as a constitutive aspect of his discourse owed to the national liberation struggles of colonized countries, the important influence of communism in Iran prior to the 1979 revolution and the struggles of Palestinians. "Anti-imperialism" also highlights a global concern within Khomeini's new tradition. His political language of contemporary anti-imperialism was based for its external referents on the realist economic colonization of Iran by the USA and skilfully utilized the language of colonial liberation movements. However, "anti-imperialism" for Khomeini was translated into an attack on the

West, and especially "the Great Satan" (USA), for spreading "corruption on Earth" and the "corruption of democracy". ("Corruption on Earth", among other such "corruptions", are traditional Shi'a tropes that became extremely important for Khomeini in "purifying" Iranian civil society.) Similarly, translated Iranian Marxist oppositions between "the oppressor" (*mostakberin*, "the mighty") and "the oppressed" (*mostazafin*, "the meek"), as well as the irreducibly Marxist conceptions of "imperialism" and "exploitation" were used consistently by Khomeini (and in other Islamic movements). These extremely important symbols were initially manufactured within the logic of left anti-imperialism and appropriated (and translated) into a regional revolutionary Islamic ideology. (Suggestively, if the often small amount of formally religious rhetoric is removed from the political language of many Islamic movements, the bulk that is left is "Marxism".) However, the critique of the West[7] in Khomeinism was not just of its economic/military domination and exploitation but more its ethical, moral, political and social manifestations, including its "philosophy", its organization of gender-sexual relations, its "materialism", its forms and relations of consumption, its "democracy", its "modernism", its Zionism, and its desire to destroy Islam. The *fuqaha* and *umma* were presented as permanent victims of the West. A picture of the West was reconstructed in which the Great Satan was singularly motivated by the desire to extinguish Islam, the Islamic state and especially the divine clergy.

In his conceptions of *velayat-e-faqih*, *hokumat-e-Islami* and "anti-imperialism", Khomeini breaks definitively with "tradition" and the custom of gender-differentiated "equality" in Islam, in particular the tradition of Islam as a non-clerical, non-hierarchical religious practice. His is an invented tradition that pits itself against older traditional elements and customs in (Shi'a or other) Islam, especially the popular or mass practices of Islam. (In this sense, both Islamic and Hindu fundamentalism represent "high" ideologies that can be dismissive of vernacular religious traditions.) This, of course, makes the application of the popular concept of "fundamentalism" to, say Khomeinism, immediately problematic, especially as the latter is a major and definitive break with orthodox scripturalism. Khomeinism instead attempted to recreate a new foundational basis for its politics based on a new conception of purity and liberation, a theory of political government and a global conceptual method.

Importantly, this type of neofoundationalism can also break with the claim to the ownership of tradition. The latter is not displaced by other claims of tradition but the idea of tradition is itself attacked as backward and regressive. This type of attack is a striking feature of many of Khomeini's writings. This can distance the actual content of the text and consequently displaces the contradictions in the texts that orthodox tradition may have tried to resolve by careful exegesis.

Within Khomeini's invented tradition, there is an extremely important tension between the demand for liberation for the oppressed masses and the necessity of creating the power and privilege of an authoritarian status elite (the *fuqaha*) over the masses. The *mostazafin* (the meek, the downtrodden) are a rhetorically essential and completely unelaborated energetic presence in Khomeinist discourse. This need to create an invented tradition that apparently embraces the oppressed while privileging the power of a totalitarian elite over them is an important aspect of the modernity of fundamentalism.

Khomeinism, fundamentalism and modernity

If the non-traditionality of fundamentalism is relatively easy to demonstrate, its substantive *modernity* can be much more difficult to grasp. It is worth starting with a discussion of fundamentalism, which poses the same issues in a different way. Youssef Choueiri makes a useful distinction between "revivalist" Islam (an eighteenth- and nineteenth-century phenomenon, whose contemporary product is modern Wahhabism and the Saudi state), "reformist" Islam (an urban intellectual movement vigorously opposed to Islamic tradition that tried to accommodate Islam with Western philosophies and cultures) and his conception of "radical Islam", a twentieth-century phenomenon that grew in direct reaction to the nation-state and that "does not revive or reform [but] creates a new world and invents its own dystopia" (Choueiri 1990: 10). Choueiri argues that *all* these movements can be accurately described as fundamentalist since they all start from the premise of revealed truth and apply, to greater or lesser extent, exegesis of the Qur'an to legitimize their ideologies.

We have already noted that neofoundationalism institutes a strategic relation to the sacred text which is not simply hermeneutic but semiotic and concerned to re-present an eclectic, inattentive and careless semiology of the text. It can refute from the start the careful orthodox textual concerns with ethical and moral issues. Ethics, morals, sin, good, evil, the good life, the good society, right and wrong are semiotic products whose meanings are permanently deferred. They are barely interrogated in fundamentalism and rarely explicated. This of course constitutes its considerable danger. Fundamentalism is based on little ethical or moral foundationalism and that can make its ordering as a postmodern phenomenon so tempting. But it does have a type of foundationalism that is concerned with bodily purity, purity of action, civil purity and state power and this is what makes its further metaphoric association with, for example, neo-ethnic movements of the far-right attractive.

Central to this discursive strategy in fundamentalism is the necessity of generating indistinctness. In several important ways, the various aporias in Khomeinism seem definitive in addressing the question of their modernity. Importantly, Khomeinism like much Islamic revivalist ideology, has extraordinarily little to say about its key founding concepts. In Khomeini's writings the practice of government is barely elaborated. There is no theory, and very little non-rhetorical discussion, about the structures, systems, causes, functions and nature of oppression or exploitation (the latter is either a result of the West or reduces to essentially social-welfare conceptions that may involve widows and orphans, the disabled and the poor.) Indeed, in fundamentalist political language in general there is virtually no foundational basis for its otherwise energetic conceptions of oppression and exploitation. These are literally tokens derived from the sacred text. Similarly, there is virtually no conceptual discussion about "the masses" or "the people", the social formation or its civil society, even though these are essential to Khomeinist forms of mobilization. Even "Zionism" and "anti-imperialism", both central aspects of its discourse, are barely elaborated and can essentially be reduced to politically effective antisemitic and xenophobic tropes. In important ways, many of the political symbols that complement Khomeini's theory of guardianship and government, or indeed fill in its gaps, are dependent on nineteenth and twentieth century modernist discourses of liberalism, communism and fascism. Do they demonstrate its modernity?

Much of the modernity of Khomeinism has been subject to

extended discussion in a number of stimulating interventions. An extremely important early argument about the modernity and novelty of Khomeinism, and by extension Islamic fundamentalist movements, was put forward by Sami Zubaida (1982) and, in a different form, by Gregory Rose (1983). Khomeini's *velayat-e-faqih* is in essence an unsophisticated claim relying on relatively straight-forward interpretations from canonical "tradition". Zubaida asks, "If it is so simple, why, one wonders, is it so novel, why does the idea ... not have a more secure ancestry in Islamic jurisprudence?" (Zubaida 1993: 18).

Zubaida argues that the novelty of the new interpretation of *velayat-e-faqih* is that its "credibility and thinkability are facilitated by the conditions of the modern state and politics". Moreover, crucial to the plausibility of Khomeinism is the idea of the people as a political force, a completely modernist strand. This last aspect is also central to Ervand Abrahamian's thesis of Khomeinism as a populism not entirely dissimilar to Latin American totalitarian-populist movements. Similar ideas are elaborated in Fred Halliday's discussions that, as distinctive as the Iranian revolution was, it is essentially intelligible and explained in terms such as populism, the will to power by certain social and economic groups and classes and so forth. For Halliday, Khomeini's "traditionalism" is not inherited unproblematically from the past but is novel and modern. Khomeini's originality lies in the combination and interaction of (claims to) "tradition" and modernity (Halliday & Alavi 1988, Halliday 1994).

These discussions are substantially accurate and have guided the discussions in this book. Generally speaking they rely on three methods to demonstrate the modernity (rather than just anti-traditionality or novelty) of Khomeinism:

• the modernist preconditions of ideology, state, nation, people and globalization that Khomeini either inherited without acknowledgement or that formed the objective conditions for his theory;

• the gaps and aporias in his theory of guardianship and government that were filled with either essentially modernist political language or essentially modernist administrative, coer-cive and bureaucratic principles either by his followers or in the actual Islamic Republic of Iran;

- the translation of Khomeini's concepts of guardianship and government into broadly Western modernist political theory (of, for example, totalitarianism or nationalism).

However, it is worth inverting these methods: if Khomeinism is essentially modernist why did it not claim to be so, why did it not secure its foundations in or against more explicitly recognizable modernist debates? Importantly, Khomeini, despite whichever communist or socialist strands he may have tacitly appropriated, virtually entirely ignores Western political debates in his *Islamic government*. Khomeinism also contains immense "excesses" that take it beyond what we might call modernist political ideologies. Conversely, why is the modernity of Khomeinism most easily demonstrated either by filling in its gaps and discontinuities with modernist content or by illustrating its *a priori* modern preconditions?

This can raise difficult and politically important questions. For if the modernity of Khomeini's political ideology is most easily exposed because of its preconditions or subsequent translation into and comparison with Western political theory, then this can be reduced to a view of modernity as "the contemporary". It also suggests that any reactionary or totalitarian ideology – whatever its substantive, elementary, unformulated or confused content – can be reified as a modernist discourse because of its preconditions of existence. Put differently, new traditional ideologies, born in modern political and economic conditions of existence, can have the capacity to be turned relatively easily into effective political projects, however confused, derivative, non-originary, non foundational or senseless their substantive ideologies may appear. The obvious sociological comparison is with Aryan National Socialism of the 1930s whose originary foundational claims very quickly disappear into eclectic, relatively recent borrowings of antisemitic ideologies, strands of eugenics and scientific racism and various mythical political symbols from which a modernist political project is derived.

Clearly, it can be difficult to easily characterize Khomeinist ideology within a *Western* telos of modernity. However, there is less difficulty in demonstrating the modernity of the Islamic Republic of Iran (IRI). "Actually existing Islam", especially the modern "secular" constitutional nature of the IRI, its integration into a global

103

system of nation-states and capitalist economies, its "separation" of state and civil society, some form of universal "enfranchisement", consultation, consensus and "democracy", a war economy, and so forth have been used by writers to demonstrate the modernity of fundamentalist Islam. It seems important to register the *a priori* bureaucratic methodology and procedural rationality of the Islamic state, and its preconditional orientation around the translation of modernist political concepts and political theories into Islamic terms. A key feature of the Islamic state is its republican constitutionality and the separation of legislative, executive and judicial powers. This derives neither from Islamic principles nor Islamic history but from the American and French revolutions (*The Constitution of the Islamic Republic of Iran*, articles 57–61). Importantly, *shari'a* is secondary to the Constitution, and the roles, duties, functions and powers of the *fuqaha* are defined by the Constitution and not the other way around (see *The Constitution of the Islamic Republic of Iran*, "General principles", and the powers defined in chs 6,7,8,9 & 11). It has been argued by Olivier Roy that this essentially makes the Iranian state "secular" (Roy 1994: 177). This has been most strongly emphasized by Fred Halliday in a discussion of one of Khomeini's last major acts. In an exchange with President Khamenei, who had announced the primacy of *shari'a* over other laws, Khomeini introduced a new concept of "absolute vice-regency" (*velayat-e mutlaq-e faqih*) legitimized by the importance of constitutionality and the national and people's interest over and above Islam itself.

> Islamic government, which stems from the absolute guardianship of the Prophet Muhammad, is one of the primary injunctions in Islam, taking precedence over all subsidiary precepts, even praying, fasting, and performing the Hajj. (Khomeini, quoted in Moin 1994: 93)

The interests of the people, as arbitrarily defined by the *fuqaha*, could be used to override any Islamic injunctions (Halliday 1994: 100–1). Halliday also argues that the implementation of this concept could resolve the Rushdie affair, as indeed could the death of Khomeini which brings into question the "legitimacy" of his *fatwa*. While this can be seen as a definitive break with the concept of *velayat-e-faqih*, it still leaves aside the question of the religious form of state and civil society in the IRI. Of particular interest is the question asked by Baqer Moin (1994: 93) about the relation between absolute vice-regency and Khomeini's mysticism, a relation between politics and the numinous that is explored in Chapters 5 and 6:

> Was it Khomeini the jurisprudent who was extending his absolute rule to all paths of life in order to preserve the Islamic government, or was it Khomeini the mystic who was fusing *Velayat-e Motlaqa-y Erfani*, or absolute gnostic rule, with politics? (Moin 1994: 93)

It is perhaps here, in the dense relationship between mysticism and political rationality, that important modern totalitarian themes are most relevant and at their most ambiguous. Many of the features of Khomeinism and the IRI are emblematic of modernity while other features suggest neither modernity nor premodernity. The creation of the Islamic state is a very modern reformation of nationalism and the nation-state but it is opposed to modernist secularism (or conversely, it exhibits the emblematically modern tension between secularism and the content of nationalism). Its organization as a bureaucratic-rational structure, especially in its formation of soviet-like *shuras* and Islamic *komitehs* (workers' councils and Revolutionary Guard structures) is a modernist enterprise. The highly elaborate mechanisms of mass participation in civil society, based on a translation of the Quranic *shura* are equally modernist. The IRI's ferocious and expansive apparatuses of repression invoke totalitarian forms of modernity. The construction of a monumental military war machine is also a modernist venture.

The recreation of urban, rural and indeed global Muslim identities acutely aware of their place in opposition to the West and secularism suggests a phenomenon ineffable in Western conceptions of the modern. However, Khomeini's classic stress on both the nation-state and the transnational Muslim community (the *umma*) is an embodiment of late modernity. A prominent consequence of this last element is the attempt by contemporary Islamic movements to recover pan-Islamic ideological ground. Khomeinism was an attempt at a modern reconstruction of a global pan-Islamic community whose symbolic allegiance traversed and superseded political and citizenship obligations to any one nation-state or ethnic affiliations to any one national community. This new pan-Islamic identity itself suggests the tendency towards globalization in modernity in which the nation-state is diminished in importance. Both the Constitution of the IRI and Khomeini's writings embody this transnational essence:

> We see . . . that together, the imperialists and the tyrannical self-seeking rulers have *divided the Islamic homeland*. They have separated the various segments of the Islamic *umma* from each other and *artificially* created separate nations. (Khomeini 1981: 48–9, emphases added)

We finally need to note a couple of other aspects of Khomeinism and related political ideologies. They are irrealist critical theories of the world system. Realism, which necessarily means some affiliation with materialism and an implicit critique of strong anthropomorphism, is explicitly rejected for the special, chosen nature and importance of humans over any material circumstance. Similarly, the explicit agency of humans cannot be subjected to critique if it is assumed to have been authorized by God, though that agency is patently human. At its worst, any group claims the authority of God to engage in arbitrary acts, displacing its own evident agency by mobilizing Godly inspiration. We have noted that this is a "decentring of the subject" in which the subject is constituted through (religious) discourse existing beyond it. From a critical realist perspective, the coupling of human self-importance and a denial of responsibility for human agency is a dangerous anthropomorphic self-deception that recurs in strikingly similar forms in Christian, Zionist, Islamic and Hindu fundamentalist movements.

Khomeinism explicitly aims for both *liberation* and *purity*, in particular purity of culture, ideology, *umma*, nation, civil society and the body. In Iran, Pakistan, Sudan and Saudi Arabia and in every nation where fundamentalist movements have demanded Islamicization and the installation of legal codes based on *shari'a*, the most energetic demands and the areas of greatest controversy have concerned the Muslim gendered body and the Muslim gendered self, but not necessarily issues such as Islamic taxation, economic laws, land and property codes, or even criminal codes or *hudud*. In Islamism, as in other neofoundationalist ideologies, the personal is political. Though the new Islamic subject is "decentred", the body is still the proof by which Islamicization is measured. It is the surface on which new traditions undertake their cathartic obsessions with purity. This purity urge, which need not have any basis in the traditional text, forms an important technical method by which civil society is disciplined and purified, the surfaces and territories of the Muslim body are marked out and new Muslim bodies, including deceased bodies,[8] are created. This combination of liberation and purity, in which the *umma* both needs to be liberated and is also impure and contaminated ("corrupted") by un-Islamic influences, constitutes a powerful strand of *permanent dystopia*. A logical consequence of this is that Khomeinism explicitly refuses a place for formal democracy, nor can it or will it guarantee the rights or freedom of any common individual or collective unless it is the chosen clergy.

> Anyone who rules over the Muslims, or over human society in general, must always take into consideration the public welfare and interest, and ignore personal feelings and interests. Islam is prepared to subordinate individuals to the collective interest of society and has rooted out numerous groups that were a source of corruption and harm to human society. (Khomeini 1981: 89)

The denial of individual human or minority rights is coupled with autonomous legislative structures in civil society that possess the legitimate use of the means of violence. This has meant the violent suppression of political, ethnic, women's and religious rights and the explicit distance between itself and conceptions of human rights and civil liberties. The *fatwa* against Salman Rushdie was one tyrannical act among thousands of executions, incarcerations, acts of torture and murder enacted in Iran against writers, intellectuals, dissidents, feminists, homosexuals, communists, Kurds, Bahais, socialists, religious moderates and Islamic political opponents of Khomeinism, including the Mojahedin of Iran and the supporters of Ali Shariati. It is a political system that has allure and appeal for some in London and in Bradford.

CHAPTER 4

The Rushdie affair and the deceptive critique of imperialism

The elite do not understand the dynamics of mass communication – how reports spread and how rumours, sometimes exaggerated and wild, fly and take possession of the minds of men.
(Syed Shahabuddin MP, *Times of India*, 13 October 1988)

The traditional politics of the subject assumes that there is one group of humans whose strategic position uniquely entitles them to represent the plurality. The philosophy of the subject always searches for a particular group – be it the proletariat, women, the avant-garde, Third World revolutionaries, or the Party – whose particularity represents universality as such. The politics of empowerment, by contrast, proceeds from the assumption that there is no single spot in the social structure that privileges those who occupy it with a vision of the social totality. This is so not only because late-capitalist societies and their grievances generate a pluralization of social victims, their objectives, and their modes of struggle, but also because the experience of difference that cannot be co-opted in imposed identity is liberatory.
(Seyla Benhabib, *Critique, norm and utopia*, 1986: 352)

Introduction

Many of the initiating elements of the last chapter are highly relevant to an assessment of political agency during the Rushdie affair. It will be argued that the creation of new modern spaces through the mobilization of electronic communications corresponds with the analytical limitations of the space of community and of "race" in British national space. The local spaces of community and nation are importantly transgressed during the affair by Muslim social movements. However, the political framing of these subjectivities in relation to the "bigger" social spaces implied in ethnicity, religion, postcoloniality, diaspora and anti-imperialism also need to be questioned. The Rushdie affair threw up transnational social spaces that were not altogether diasporic, since they involved affiliations between life-worlds from different national spaces that had nothing in particular to do with earlier national or continental origins. Nor were these ties logically mappable in terms of older religious or ethnic affiliations or even the most elementary of historical links between different communities, since many of these were created anew during the affair (for example, Shi'a political "hegemony" over Sunni Muslims).

The new social spaces created during the affair were *relatively enduring* non-contiguous communities that enveloped life-worlds across different nation-states *and* the institutions of some nation-states in self-similar social and political actions. These spaces were ideologically articulated through the trope of *umma* (the Muslim community under Muhammad, now translated as "the global Muslim community"). These articulations failed to create *umma* as an enduring social space and it persisted primarily as a powerful imagined space. However, during (and prior) to the affair, new physical links of identity were created between sections of different Muslim communities across the world and in this sense we can speak of some *umma*-type social spaces that embraced sections of some Muslim communities. *Umma* was the identity trope that gave unity and meaning to (ontically) different life-worlds and institutions. The creation and reproduction of novel, enduring social, physical and imagined spaces that sit unevenly across nations, civil societies and communities is one explicit project of Islamic and Hindu fundamentalism.

As one consequence of this the epistemology of "race" can be easily transgressed by some contemporary black agents. This should not be taken as an abandonment of "race", either as an analytical tool or as an endogenous signifier within actual political processes. The suggestion advanced is that we need to contemplate "race" as one constitutive signifier among several concerned with the creation of black political subjectivities. The latter are, however, also dependent on elements that can transcend "race" but also appear to transcend or rework "religion", "tradition" and "ethnicity" as well as "community" and "nation". Jameson and Bauman have used the terms "neo-ethnicity" and "neotribes" respectively to describe similar identity formations in Western social movements (Jameson 1991: 341; Bauman 1991: 136–7). Harvey describes social movement activity as focused on creating "place", whereas capitalist accumulation is about expanding and transforming space (Harvey 1989: 302, but see Harvey 1993: 24). Both these positions will be implicitly argued against.

Narrating the Rushdie affair is a problematic undertaking because of the vast number of discourses that intervened in and created it. The Rushdie affair represented an extremely complex "contemporary archaeology" of political practice. It seized upon and exposed the contradictions in virtually every modernist political discourse: the tension between ethical universalism versus group particularism, the rights of minorities, the articulation of novel political identities, the character of mass movements, the repressive reconstruction of "race" in the Western nation-states and the modern future for the black minorities in those nations. It also played out against a violent historical backdrop of Western economic, political and military domination of non-Western nation states.

Particularly important among these historical influences was the demonization of Islam and Muslims by the West and Israel, the 1982 Israeli invasion of Lebanon and the Israeli-sponsored massacre by Lebanese Christians of Palestinians at Sabra and Chatila refugee camps in 1982, the continuing Israeli bombardment and occupation of southern Lebanon and its repressive military occupation of the West Bank and Gaza strip. The US bombing of Iraq and Libya and the fate of Bosnians are parcelled in this same trajectory. Hence the theme of "imperialism", which has been a pivotal concern of Islamism, is especially pertinent. However, Islamism has no qualms about the forms of property, labour and financial relations defined in Western capitalism and imperialism, though it rhetorically opposes "usury" and can articulate social tax-like mechanisms for some redistribution of wealth. (Traditional Islamic laws and customs include taxes on land, wealth and military expenditure, different taxes for protected minorities (usually Jews and Christians) and charitable taxes (*zakat*). There are traditional Islamic injunctions against lending money at a fixed rate of interest, hoarding money or creating monopolies.) Islamism is committed to capitalist economic relations (private appropriation, extraction of surplus value from systems of socialized production, disparities in wealth and power) and to specific forms of technological development (military, agricultural and industrial, and selectively communicational) and is not inherently opposed to economic expansionism. Nevertheless, Islamism represents a critique of Western (and communist) political power and a critique of "Western" social formation, including formal democracy, "Western" philosophy and "Western" culture, especially its relations of gender and organizations of sexuality. In this it has been an especially effective political ideology.

A lobbying affair

The Rushdie affair first arose as a relatively mild phenomenon within British public culture following the publication of *The satanic verses* by Viking/Penguin in September 1988 and after its shortlisting for the Booker Prize. It was not, however, until mid-January of 1989 that the infamous book-burning incident was staged in Bradford. The time gap between publication and the forthright British Muslim protests against the book contained a number of important events that prefigured the incidents that were to follow.

Critical to the affair were a number of events within India itself. Reviews of the *Verses* in Indian magazines and newspapers, together with the publication of two interviews with Rushdie in *India Today* and *Sunday* resulted in Syed Shahabuddin, a Muslim MP from the then opposition Janata Party, starting a vociferous campaign to have the book banned by the Indian Government (*The Sunday Times* 19 February 1989). Following lobbying by Shahabuddin and others, the Finance Ministry of the Indian Government banned the *Verses* on 5 October 1988 under the Indian Customs Act. Rushdie, in turn, wrote an open letter to the then prime minister, Rajiv Gandhi, that identified the ban as arising from opportunistic actions by the government to win Muslim support (for the November 1989 general election). Shahabuddin's rhetoric against Rushdie, in an article that referred to both "literary colonialism" and "religious pornography", contained many of the threads of protest that were later made by British Muslims against the book:

> You depict the Prophet whose name the practising Muslim recites five times a day, whom he loves, whom he considers the model for mankind, as an impostor and you expect us to applaud you. You had the nerve to situate the wives of the Prophet, whom we Muslims regard as the mothers of the community, in a brothel, and you expect the Muslims to praise your power of imagination? ... No your act is not unintentional or a careless slip of the pen. It was deliberate and consciously planned with devilish forethought, with an eye to your market. (*Times of India* 13 October 1988)

The structure of this rhetoric is important for several reasons. First, the debate around *The satanic verses* is immediately symbolized in the personage of Rushdie himself against an unelaborated united Muslim presence in which, consequently, the intellectual and political themes of the book are evaded. Secondly, the rhetoric reproduces the blasphemy – it says what Rushdie has been forbidden to say. Thirdly, it asserts the importance of a sexual narrative in the offence that was caused and highlights the centrality of the protection of Islam and the Muslim body against sexual pollution. Many of the blasphemies contained in *The satanic verses* were insulting because they were sexual and unambiguously referred to prostitution, sodomy, sexual licentiousness, illegitimacy and the polymorphous perversities of the body. Many Muslims also repeatedly referred to Rushdie's use of sexual expletives throughout the book. Finally, Shahabuddin's article begins the construction, in the language of conspiracy, of a manifest intentional assault by the West against an Islam that needs to be protected:

> Rushdie "the Islamic scholar, the man who studied Islam at university" has to brag about his Islamic credentials, so that he can convincingly vend his Islamic wares in the West,

which has not yet laid the ghost of the crusades to rest, but given it a new cultural wrapping which explains why writers like you are so wanted and pampered ... tell your British champions and advisors that India shall not permit "literary colonialism" nor what may be called religious pornography. Not even in the name of freedom and democracy, not even under the deafening and superb orchestration of your liberal band. (*Times of India* 13 October 1988)

Rushdie is situated outside of the colonized masses, Indians, the Muslims, the Third World. He is "an overrated Eurasian writer", an agent of the "colonial" or "the Western". Rushdie is not of India but of "the West" and this depiction refers us to much more than his place of residence: Shahabuddin is stating that because of his attacks on Islam, Rushdie's identity *cannot but be* Western and all that the latter entails. As important to Shahabuddin's rhetoric is the signification that demarcates Muslim inclusion within and exclusion from the *umma*, a process that is semiotically completed in Khomeini's *fatwa*. Here, Shahabuddin identifies, positions and encloses Rushdie in relation to the frontier signification of both the Crusades and Western colonialism. The extremely recent importance of the Crusades in energizing a precolonial frontier is a distinctive reductionist method that was increasingly articulated as the affair developed. The trope of the "Crusades" is one method by which the West (or often any defence of Rushdie) becomes simply a contraction to "Christian". At the same time, it could be argued that the secular or atheistic West had lost all sense of the sacred. This refractive, doubling and splitting nature of the historical signs and symbols generated during the affair by Muslim and non-Muslim commentators has a deeper significance which is explored later.

The *Sunday Times* (19 February 1989) reported a direct link between events in India and the start of the protests in Britain. The political importance of these links has often been missed in assessments of the Rushdie affair and highlights the extensive global activities of the Jamaat-i-Islami. The Jamaat-i-Islami (JI) was one of the most important Islamic fundamentalist organizations to have developed in this century and was until recently the dominant fundamentalist party in Pakistan. It was founded in 1941 by Abul a'la Maududi, formerly an Indian journalist, who is often described as the founder of modern Islamic fundamentalism. Maududi's writings are especially important for having outlined, prior to Khomeini, a theory of the Islamic state and of an activist non-privatized Islamic identity through which it could be achieved. Maududi's work was extremely influential across the Middle East and North Africa and considerably influenced Sayyid Qutb of the Muslim Brotherhood in Egypt. Today, various sections of the worldwide JI network are active in Pakistan (and Afghanistan), India, Bangladesh, the UK, Malaysia and South Africa.

The JI has acquired important political influence in the UK, though it has no mass support among British Muslims. It is represented by several organizations, of which the Leicester Islamic Foundation, the UK Islamic Mission, the Young Muslims UK and the Bangladeshi Dawat ul-Islam are the most important. The Islamic Foundation, formed in the 1970s, describes itself as "an educational and research organization devoted to developing a better under-standing of Islam among all the people of the world, Muslim and non-Muslim". The Foundation is affluent and is a major publishing and dissemination house for Jamaati materials, including translations of many of Maududi's writings. The director general of the Islamic Foundation was Khurram Jah Murad, an engineer, and deputy *amir* of the Jamaat-i-Islami in Pakistan. Its chair is Khurshid Ahmad, an economist, also a deputy *amir* of the Pakistani Jamaat-i-Islami. Both Murad and Ahmad were politically close to Maududi and together with the *amir* of the Pakistani Jamaat-i-Islami, Qazi Husain Ahmad, are the best representatives of the Maududist tradition. Both were also supreme heads (*nazim-i-ala*) of the affiliated Islami Jami'at-i-Tulabah (IJT), an extremely violent anti-left mainly student movement in Pakistan. The IJT, which functions relatively autonomously from the JI, and which has at times been difficult for the JI to discipline, has been seen as responsible for much of the turn to violence and gun culture in Pakistani cities. Both the JI and the IJT have played a momentous role in the repressive Islamicization of Pakistani civil society and institutions, especially under the Zia dictatorship, which they considerably influenced and with which they were closely affiliated (Nasr 1994). The UK Islamic Mission, established in the early 1960s by JI activists has been important for its educational and *dawa* ("call", invitation to Islam) activities, especially among younger Muslims, and in its work in

115

influencing social policy and local authority initiatives for ethnic minorities. It has about 20 centres and mosques in the UK. Its youth wings, The Young Muslims UK (YMUK) and the Young Muslims' Women's section, are influential among Muslim students at universities and colleges. YMUK activities include a magazine (*Trends*), *dawa* activities, political education, conferences, seminars and youth summer camps (Lewis 1994).

The Leicester Islamic Foundation has published a large and wide-ranging number of books and pamphlets on subjects ranging from support for Hassan Turabi's Islamist dictatorship in Sudan to social policy guides for statutory and voluntary sector professionals in the UK. One of the Foundation's publications, *The Muslim guide* (McDermott & Ahsan, second revised edition, 1993), is endorsed by David Lane MP, the former chairperson of the Commission for Racial Equality. The inexplicable way that religious authoritarian Hindu and Muslim organizations have become entangled with and empowered by the formally secular institutions of British multiculturalism is explored in the last chapter. The Jamaat-i-Islami has also established a presence in Bangladeshi communities through the (relatively autonomous) Dawat ul-Islam. The Bangladeshi Jamaat-i-Islami, and its affiliates in the UK became embroiled in an important political difficulty following a Channel 4 *Dispatches* report in May 1995 on the war crimes atrocities committed by Jamaat-i-Islami supporters in East Pakistan in opposition to the Bangladeshi nationalist movement that fought for separation from (then West) Pakistan. This tension between Bangladeshi nationalism and a pan-Islamism fostered by a mainly Pakistani group is likely seriously to affect the JI's impact on Bangladeshi communities in the UK.

The Jamaat-i-Islami is extensively dependent on Saudi funding, especially through the *Rabita* (World Muslim League). The JI and its related groups constitute one of two main Saudi-financed international networks (the other broadly directed by the Egyptian Muslim Brotherhood), though since the second Gulf War several local alliances nominally controlled by the Jamaat-i-Islami and, especially, the Muslim Brotherhood have been severely disrupted. The importance of the Jamaat-i-Islami during the Rushdie affair highlights the enduring influence of Saudi–axis organizations in structuring the political representation of Muslim interests in various nation-states and civil societies and controverts the view, enunciated often enough, that the protests against Rushdie were simply a manifestation of grassroots hurt or offence. Similarly, a common assertion by many Muslims during the affair was that the Saudi dictatorship had been slow to respond to the affair. This may or may not be the case, but the networks under Saudi patronage were virtually entirely responsible for initiating the early stages of the Rushdie affair.

According to the *Sunday Times*, Aslam Ejaz of the Islamic Foundation in Madras had written to a Faiyazuddin Ahmad of the Islamic Foundation in Leicester in early October 1988 urging him to start a similar campaign against *The satanic verses* in Britain. The Islamic Foundation in Leicester sent a letter on 3 October 1988 to Muslim organizations, mosques, leaders and ambassadors of Muslim countries in Britain setting out the blasphemies and urging action against Viking/Penguin (Ahsan & Kidwai 1991: 315–16). The letter was sent exactly one week after the book was first published, illustrating the rapidity of the Jamaati response. Virtually every paragraph of this letter from Leicester is, astonishingly, reproduced word for word as "a thorough investigation into the matter" in the South African government's banning order of 24 November 1988 under its 1974 Publications Act (Appignanesi & Maitland 1989: 63–4, Ruthven 1990: 95). The complex traffic in information that resulted in the views of a Jamaat-i-Islami organization in Leicester being reproduced in the South African government's order in Johannesburg highlights the importance of transnational activism during this initial phase of the affair. For example, the value of electronic communications in campaigns against the book was underlined in an address by Khurshid Ahmad of the Jamaat-i-Islami, representing the Islamic Council of Europe, to the 18th Islamic Foreign Minister's Conference held at Riyadh on 12 March 1989, where it was urged that "positive efforts be made at all levels to project the true message of Islam through the latest technology available" (Ahsan & Kidwai 1991: 192).

The Leicester organization also sent photocopies of the offending pages from *The satanic verses* to the 45 embassies in Britain of the member countries of the Organisation of Islamic Conference (OIC) in October 1988. Ahmad also flew to Jeddah, Saudi Arabia, and lobbied the leadership of the OIC which then telexed member countries, urging a ban of the book. Syed Pasha, secretary of the Union of Muslim Organisations in Britain (also set up under the

117

auspices of the *Rabita*) called a meeting of the union's 19 council members on 15 October (which was also attended by Sher Azam of the Bradford Council of Mosques), where it was decided to start a campaign in Britain to get the book banned for its blasphemy and for its insult to Muslims. Pasha wrote to Penguin and also to Margaret Thatcher, the Lord Chancellor and the Home Office in an attempt to get the book banned. A third British campaign was also organized, from November 1988, through the Central London Mosque in Regent's Park, during which the mosque leadership made representations to the Home Office.

There are several important aspects about these initial activist responses to the book. Virtually all the initial responses to the affair resulted from Saudi-financed or influenced networks. The Jamaat-i-Islami in India was first off the mark in bringing *The satanic verses* to the attention of mosques and Muslim organizations across Britain. Its British representatives were directly involved in initiating both the Leicester campaign and the activity of the Central London Mosque. The three main organizations that launched campaigns (the Islamic Foundation, the Union of Muslim Organisations and the Central London Mosque) all received Saudi patronage. These Saudi-axis organizations were all elite groups. Importantly, they did not organizationally involve the larger network of Barelwi community mosques, though several Deobandi groups were represented in a subsequent Action Committee that was formed by the Saudi-axis organizations at the Central London Mosque.

The sect differences between Deobandi and Barelwi communities are worth briefly highlighting, though it is important not to see the Rushdie affair as determined by these differences. Both the Barelwi and Deobandi movements grew from the 1850s during the period of British colonial rule in India (Robinson 1988). In Britain, the Barelwi sect is the largest, followed by the Deobandi. The Deobandi sects are historically based on the teachings of the Islamic seminary at Deoband in northern India which was founded in the 1860s. Deobandi organizations are widely represented in the UK and include the important seminaries (*dar ul-ulum*) in Bury and especially Dewsbury, the Jamiat-i Ulama Britannia (an organization of Deobandi *'ulama*), and the Jama'at al-Tabligh (an offshoot movement of the Deobandis, based in Dewsbury, that emphasizes revivalism through preaching and by example through personal conduct) as well as numerous other mosques and organizations in the north, the Midlands and London. The Barelwis are a sect of essentially sufi-inspired devotional Islam which was consolidated in Bareilly, northern India, again in the second half of the last century. The Barelwi sects in Britain follow mainly the Chisti, Naqshabandi and Qadiri sufi orders and, like most South Asian Sunnis, the Hanafi legal school. In Barelwi teaching, mystical experience and intercession by minor saints and spiritual teachers (*pirs*) between believer and God are acceptable, but go sharply against Deobandi and Wahhabi (Saudi) Islamic orthodoxy. Particularly relevant for understanding Barelwi involvement in the Rushdie affair is the devotional love for Muhammad that the sect emphasizes, and that bears comparison with Hindu devotionalism. The Barelwi sect is widely represented in Britain through a large number of (usually impoverished community) mosques and through the World Islamic Mission (created in opposition to the Saudi *Rabita*) and the Jami'at-i Tabligh al-Islam, both formed by Maroof Hussain Shah, an extraordinarily influential *pir* in Barelwi activities in the UK (Lewis 1994: 81–3).

Differences in belief between Barelwis and Deobandis have been seen as the main source of religious conflict within South Asian Muslim communities. The Barelwi sect is usually imagined to be the most politically liberal in comparison with the Deobandi/Jamaat-i-Tablighi, Ahl-i-Hadith and Jamaat-i-Islami sects or groups in Britain (Robinson 1988). However, the devotional aspect of the Barelwi sect, in which the prophet is almost deified, has led some commentators to suggest that this devotional idiom resulted in the "liberal" and flexible Barelwis being the most militant protesters against *The satanic verses* (Modood 1990). However, others viewed the Rushdie affair as explained by the puritanical nature of the Deobandi sect. To be sure, sect conflicts can be extremely important. For example, the Deobandi and Ahl-i-Hadith sects (and the Jamaat-i-Islami) are often (ritually) referred to in pejorative terms by Barelwi organizations and are seen by many Barelwis to represent (or be indistinguishable from) Wahhabi doctrines and Saudi political interests. However, intra-sect differences can be far more important, as can conflicts arising from *pir*, organizational, nationalist, ethnic or linguistic loyalties.

The initial elite campaigns against *The satanic verses* were based on defining a global parameter to their scope of political action, manifested in using the most important mechanisms of time–space compression: the air corridor and electronic interpersonal communications. The focus of activism was both the British nation-state (especially Mrs Thatcher's government) and other nation-states and civil societies. The calls to protest against the book were done by endlessly reproducing the blasphemy (by photocopying) and sending it electronically by fax and telex to sites of transnational Muslim representation. The blasphemy was selected for electronic reproduction and transmission as if it in itself was evidently sufficient in mobilizing Muslims and their hurt and offence. These initial elite-group protests did not succeed in organizing a mass base amongst the Asian Muslim communities in Britain (though other community groups did, such as the Whitechapel Islamic Defence Council's protest rally on 10 October 1988) and were more directly concerned with representing and lobbying on behalf of an imperceptible Muslim community.

In late October, a UK Action Committee on Islamic Affairs was formed. The Action Committee represented the Saudi-axis organizations in the UK and was chaired by Mughram al Ghamdi, the director of the Regent's Park Mosque and a Saudi diplomat. The Action Committee included the Islamic Foundation and the UK Islamic Mission (both Jamaat-i-Islami organizations), the Dar ul-Ulum (the Dewsbury Deobandi seminary), the Ahl-i-Hadith organization (the main representative in Britain of the puritanical Ahl-i-Hadith movement, formed in India in the 1850s, which is based on teaching the centrality of Qur'an and Hadith only) and the Council of Mosques and the Union of Muslim Organisations (both of which were formed in Britain through Saudi influence). The Action Committee sent a wide appeal to British mosques and Muslim organizations:

> Recently, an Action Committee has been formed in London to stand against this sacrilege in a united and responsible way. It was not possible to invite all organizations and mosques at a very short notice especially those who are outside London. May we therefore request you to kindly form your own local action committee comprising as many organisations as possible and demand at least three things:-
>
> 1. To immediately withdraw and pulp all copies of the above mentioned title as well as to undertake not to

INTRODUCTION

allow to be published any future editions of this sacrilege.
2. To tender an unqualified public apology to the world Muslim community for the enormous injury to the feelings and sensibilities of the Muslim Community.
3. To pay adequate damages to an agreed Islamic charity in Britain.

The Action Committee also urged various kinds of activism:

> Please also launch a signature campaign through the mosques and organize telephone calls to the publishers to register your protest demanding the above three things. Please liaise with the Action Committee in London and keep us informed of your action. We are contacting the Muslim Ambassadors to seek their help in blacklisting Penguin books and banning its publication in Muslim countries. We are also exploring to take all possible legal action. We will insha'Allah, keep you informed of all developments. Please do try to approach your local MP's and police chiefs and tell them that the publication of this book has angered and outraged Muslims enormously and they should take up the matter with Scotland Yard to prosecute the publisher/author under criminal law, ie Public Order Act or Race Relations Act.[1]

This appeal did not call for a mass demonstration or pickets. It did not hint at the forms of protest that have typified Asian community mobilization since the 1960s. Instead, it was more concerned with the coordination of lobbying activities, putting pressure on statutory and private bodies and adopting legalistic measures against the book, its author and its publishers. This itself suggests that the committee did not organically represent grassroots Asian (particularly youth) organizations. However, its invocation of the "world Muslim community" is an extremely important translocal signifier: the *umma*, though an unelaborated presence, was a legitimate structure for political action. The *umma* was constructed as a global presence that was unitary and universally, monologically hurt and offended by the book. This is an important

121

substitutionism that structures much of the Muslim activist discourse during the Rushdie affair. It is a key aspect of the disciplinary strategies used in more self-avowedly fundamentalist contributions in which new articulations of Muslim identity were both constituted and constrained (Butler 1993: 93). Another theme in many such identity-claims was to assert an enumeration of the *umma* – "1 Billion Muslims" – an incomprehensible number, even for its articulators, that stressed the curious legitimacy of statistical or scientific method in making such an absolute claim.

Impact International, a Jamaat-i-Islami influenced Islamic journal, continued the *umma* identity theme in an editorial (28 October 1988):

> ... it is time now for the Ummah to stand up for the honour and dignity of its faith, of its Beloved Messenger of God (peace and blessings of God be upon him) and of his family and companions (may God be pleased with them all). If they do not, then they should be prepared to receive more Rushdies and more Penguins. We have never made an editorial appeal like this, but we are asking readers to pursue these demands both with the publishers and Muslim authorities through telegrams, letters, telephones, personal representations and through all civilised and legitimate means. But please leave Mr Salman Rushdie all to himself and to his charmed circle of "literary critics". We have to say this because we also sense a milling anger about the outrage committed by him. (Quoted in Appignanesi & Maitland 1989: 61)

This statement gives notice to the *umma* about the possible consequences of its failure to act against the book. It is inventing a tradition of a *global umma* that has never existed and could not have existed prior to the technological advances engendered by modernity. This leads to several tentative observations. If a global Muslim *umma* does exist, it can only do so as a social relation if it is defined in and by networks of electronic and print communications technology. It is through these essentially mass media relations – social relations that take place in, through and because of the existence of mass and interpersonal electronic audio-visual communications relations – that the idea of *umma* acquires a symbolic homogeneity and a real status as an imagined transnational community. Mass media relations substantiate the imagined space of global Muslim community. Outside these relations *umma* has limited tangible existence or manifest synthesis if we are to view it as a coherent global social community. In this sense, *umma* is avowedly constructed as a "hyper-real" community and its motifs of solidarity, affinity and identity exist in their reproduction through electronic and print imagery. It is important to stress that mass media is not simply a representational form, whereby an existing *umma* is simply depicted. It is a productive form whereby community is created through relations between social agents that are articulated in communications technology. Mass global media creates the possibility of enduring, temporally equivalent but geographically non-contiguous communities. Conversely, the reproduction of communities is not completely determined by local position but relies on non-local material. Similarly, that electronic medium is neither determining of *umma* nor ever separable from it. While outside of the mass media relation we can only speak of local communities with their specific histories and differential national, regional, ethnic affiliations, the *umma* created in mass media impacts on these communities just as their local activities reproduce it. The traffic is not simply into mass media relations but the latter has reproductive consequences outside its electronic medium.

There is a complicated relationship between the existence of *umma* as an imagined global community and its actual impact on particular Muslim communities. We need to apply Doreen Massey's observation that some groups are more in charge of the mobility of time–space compression, others follow or are effectively imprisoned by it. In the initial Muslim response to the Rushdie affair, those that initiated "the flows" were Muslim umbrella and elite organizations, many of which had already established agendas for the place of a revivalist Islam. In Britain these were initially rival Maududist, Deobandi and Khomeinist[2] organizations as well as more elite Muslim organizations like the Council of the Regent's Park Mosque, the Council of Mosques in the UK and Eire[3] and the Council of Imams and Mosques.[4] While the larger "organic" sector of community mosques (many of which were also aligned to these different tendencies but not determined by them and had other, including Barelwi sect, affiliations) did discuss the issue of *The satanic verses* during this initial phase, South Asian community mass mobilization came later. The importance of these explicitly politicized tendencies during the early stages of the affair was in establishing the overall scope of their activism both locally (in Britain) and transnationally and in initiating the flows by which Muslim identity was re-articulated through a new conception of *umma*. Identity-claims synthesize and make homogeneous for their subjects the various ontically different structures within the social formation. This lends itself to further extrapolation because mass media relations do the same thing. The medium of electronic communications, dissolves the differences between culture, institution, agency and space. It forms the perfect modern medium through which differential identities can symbolically coagulate and rehearse their unity. We should also note that it has the potential to displace the sociology of community, civil society and nation-state, the politics of race, ethnicity and nationalism and the historical narrative of colonialism, migration and diaspora.

Islam in Albion: the community leadership–youth movement axis

From January 1990, a very different activist response emerged in public culture, one that was organized and mobilized through the British Asian Muslim communities and the network of community mosques rather than the formally political organizations. It was an important and definitive phase of Muslim social movement that managed to articulate the mass offence, hurt and anger that was felt by Muslim communities in the UK. The activities of Muslim organizations in Bradford were symbolically pivotal within this phase of the protest (though they were hardly the only or sometimes even the main source of Muslim community activism – for example, in October 1989 a leaflet produced in Blackburn urged mosques to organize petitions at Friday prayers and urged mass pickets of bookshops stocking the *Verses*). During November and December 1989, a series of meetings were held in Bradford organized by the Bradford Council of Mosques (BCM),[5] the Barelwi Jami'at Tabligh al-Islam mosque and various other organizations. Indeed, every mosque in Bradford had discussed, or was urged to discuss the issue of *The satanic verses* at Friday prayers during this period of mobilization.

The network of community mosques across Britain is one of two highly dynamic institutional forms through which Muslim social movements are organized, and displaces a view of those communities as either simply antiracist or ethnically carved. An important process was taking place during the mid-1970s and especially in the 1980s in terms of the reorganization of Muslim political agency and affiliation in relation to the nation-state, the local state structures and policy-making bodies and towards overseas funding states and funding bodies in the Gulf as well as Pakistan and Bangladesh.[6] The relationships between elite Muslim political organizations in Britain with the funding states (Saudi Arabia, Libya, Iraq among others) as well as their sect, party, movement and national affiliations within Pakistan, India, Bangladesh and the Middle East, and between all these generally elite institutions, the network of community mosques across Britain and the local Muslim communities form an extremely complex and dynamic set of political structures. The community mosques and various Pakistani, Gujarati Muslim and Bangladeshi welfare organizations are also a fixture in the political and organizational traditions of the voluntary sector and the home-grown institutions of multiculturalism, where, generally, Asian organizations were thought to constitute either an ethnic or antiracist presence. Many Muslim (and black generally) institutions received significant political patronage from the Labour Party (and in some cases the Conservative Party) and received some funding from left-Labour authorities, often having a gelatinous relationship with the latter. This relation with the local state is important not for its funding arrangements (which were usually minimal for community mosques) but because of its importance in legitimizing the political representation of the local community. These factors are highly dynamic and acquire the capacity for creating and enabling novel symbolic sites of struggle in Britain's black communities that have been habitually overlooked in race relations writing and antiracist activism.

The struggles for the control of prestigious or community mosques by different Muslim factions during the 1980s were demonstrated in quite severe ideological and sometimes physical battles. The battles were frequently seen as simply between Deobandi and Barelwi sects or between Saudi-influenced organizations and others. However, they were far more complicated and could not be reducible to these differences. Typically, many of these local processes were heightened by the benefaction of funds by overseas bodies or by application for funds or representation on local state bodies by particular mosques or Muslim organizations, which then constituted a site of struggle for local representation of different Muslim interests. Those interests could be based on caste, clan, nationalist, religious sect or subsect or communal affiliation, *pir* loyalty, allegiance to political organizations and parties overseas, or personal rivalries and managerial, financial and administrative issues. The policies and activities of the local state in this dynamic can become important. The local state (or other funding bodies) usually demanded appropriate (or selective) elections through mass (or private) meetings for the governing body or trustees of a mosque or the creation, again through community elections, of a single representative body that could represent all local Muslim interests (a very similar dynamic occurred in the local representation of Hindu and Sikh interests). The procedural tasks contained in these activities – the nomination of embassy or high commission representatives and funding administrators, the registration and nomination of organizations, the selection of legitimate organizations, the nomination of individual representatives, the allocation of seats, the holding of private or community elections and so on – could each become symbolic sites of struggle for representation and leadership. The community mosque election process became, in numerous towns and cities, an important local stage where the struggle for the legitimate representation of Islam was fought out, often dramatically and sometimes violently and corruptly (through the mobilization of non-existent or non-local "members" of an organization). The importance of these processes for community, race and identity formation and for the legitimation of selective and non-secular representations of "community" should not be underestimated. Here, it is not being argued that the local state "creates" the Muslim community or that the activities of overseas funding bodies and their representatives and administrators in Britain are unequivocally determining. Indeed, the latter are less important for the small and poor but more numerous community mosques. However, the substantial historical divisions within Muslim communities formed one important background to the mobilization during the Rushdie affair.

The second important development concerned the transitional period from the mid-1970s to the mid-1980s within which various discourses of "black youth" were constructed and negotiated within public culture, social policy and within the Asian and Caribbean communities. Youth politics became an important hegemonic focus for much Asian political energy. Asian youth "found their strength" in this period and, at first, they negotiated a distance between their cultural institutions and those of religious and community leaders and local authority race relations functionaries, though the subsequent political enmeshing of these institutions calls into question the degree of "secular" remoteness youth organizations achieved from the traditional institutions of community formation and discipline. During the 1980s, there was an alignment of institutions of political legitimation almost exclusively along the community leadership–youth movement axis. This represented an exceedingly complex, often unstable set of structures. However, there are important affinities between the concerns of these institutions, especially where these denote the selective control and disciplining of Asian women, the regulation of sexuality and the establishment of domains of "home" and privacy. The rise of the Asian youth movements in Bradford, Sheffield, Dewsbury, Manchester, Bolton, Southall, Newham and in other towns and cities during the late 1970s and early 1980s illustrates some of these characteristics. After the decline of these organizations, primarily through local authority racial equality or multiculturalist policies in the early 1980s, an interesting development was their replacement, especially in London and the northern towns, by explicitly Muslim-identified youth groups, student *dawa* associations and Islamic students' associations, and in London and Birmingham by Sikh and, later, Hindu counterparts. Youth organizations that were primarily formed in response to racial violence and policing were replaced by organizations primarily identified by ethnic-religious, sect or national affiliations. This desecularization of Asian youth politics is extremely important and has syncretically influenced other progressive and secular Asian youth cultural activities. Much rests on the future relationship between these religious and secular forms of Asian youth cultural politics.

The mobilization against *The satanic verses* in Britain's Asian Muslim communities took place against this background of kinetic community and youth activity. Those communities were not politically inactive before the Rushdie affair. The stereotype of Asian passivity informed much of the lascivious shock and surprise felt by left and liberal commentators as the Rushdie affair unfolded. However, in 1981–2 Bradford (and indeed, Britain) had seen a pivotal youth and community campaign in defence of 12 young Asian men (of Muslim, Hindu and Sikh origins) who had (allegedly) made petrol bombs during the 1981 riots in the city. The erasure of this historic and irreducibly secular campaign in much recent discussion about Bradford is of interest. During the 1980s, Bradford had also witnessed effective campaigns for halal meals in schools and for the resignation of Ray Honeyford, (a headteacher who severely and disparagingly criticized black and Asian cultures in the pages of the neoconservative journal, *The Salisbury Review*), as well as campaigns for separate Muslim schools.

The intervention of the Bradford Council of Mosques, roughly equally representing local Deobandi and Barelwi and other sect mosques, was an important legitimating factor within the Muslim communities that could not have been achieved by the elite political organizations or the Arabic Muslim organizations in London that had intervened in the very early stages of the affair. Sher Azam, chairperson of the Bradford Council of Mosques wrote to Margaret Thatcher in the following terms:

> Honourable Madam,
> The Muslims of Bradford and all over the world are shocked to hear about the Novel called 'SATANIC VERSES' in which the writer Salman [Rushdie] has attacked our beloved Prophet Mohammed (PBUH) and his wives [by using a] dirty language that [Muslims cannot] tolerate . . . . We [as] Muslims will never allow or ignore such rubbish words used by a person who is either mad or thinks he is ruling the whole world in which there are Millions of Muslims. We [were] very much distressed when we came to know about the author living in Great Britain and the publishers too. As citizens of this great country, we have expressed our very ill feelings about such [a] harmful novel and its publishers and state that the novel should be banned [immediately] . . . (Quoted in Ruthven 1990: 97–8)

Azam's letter is important for its globalization of the real distress felt by Muslims and of Rushdie's apparent sense of his own power, invoking both the metaphor of conspiracy and the view of a co-ordinated attack on Islam personified in the Westernized symbol of Rushdie himself. Its further importance lies in its ambivalence towards British national belonging. The letter instantly invokes a global, extranational Muslim identity (a contemporary *umma*) which at once displaces "racial" or ethnic identification with Asians and supersedes affiliation to British nationhood. However, a claim to the latter is subsequently asserted in a manner that again displaces explicit racial identification by ignoring the racialization of British greatness. But finally, "race" is obliquely implanted by the need to stake a claim to British citizenship at all. In this sense, race is constitutive of the imaginary *space* in which Muslims are to be disciplined in their inhabitation of British national identity. This aspect of the Rushdie affair, the claim to British national citizenship and the subsequent reworking and minimizing of British belonging in favour of a greater allegiance to global Islam and the *umma* was as consequential to new right discourse as it was to pro-Khomeini Muslims, such as Kalim Siddique of the Muslim Institute for Research and Planning. The anxieties of the right centred around its inability to situate Muslims as a race within the British nation when Muslims firmly and politely declined to be mobilized by the resonant symbols of British race formation and nationalism. We should also note that the race emplacement of the Muslim communities by both the British right and the left during the Rushdie affair was tangential to the discourse being created inside the Muslim communities themselves.

This indeterminate positionality in relation to nation is an imaginary and a social *spatial* fluctuation in which several life-worlds, rather then identities, collide. The "Muslim community" is scattered in geographical Britain, an "intolerant medieval race" in British political discourse, an excluded element in the British nation, a "displaced peasantry" that had migrated from the periphery to the centre of multinational capitalism, a component of Britain's modern disintegrating labour force, an oppressed subject of racism and an antiracist agent. However, it was also symbolically part of the world Muslim community, even if that community was being created as it was being articulated, and it historically belonged to the (mainly) Asian diaspora. In several important ways, demonstration of secular Asian diaspora identity was already subverted from the start through the extremely bitter experience of decolonization and partition and the present

THE RUSHDIE AFFAIR

circumstance of Kashmir. But diasporic identification was further mutilated by the idea of *umma* itself, which was not ostensibly based on original affiliation, national allegiance or ethnic identity.

Leaving aside its evident consequences for black identity, this new identification through *umma* constituted an erasure of British *Asian* identity, a secular construction that had earlier dominated political discourse around race, ethnicity and national belonging. That some of the black left could only comprehend this new identity by comparisons with "ethnicity", "fundamentalism", "tradition", "nationalism", "black nationalism" or "cultural nationalism" emphasizes the unavailability of a political language that could describe any of *these* formations satisfactorily let alone grasp them as manifestations of a single phenomenon affecting different black communities. The evident problem was in explaining new translocal phenomena using the sociological deposits of nationalism, ethnicity and community and an historical narrative of colonialism, migration and diaspora, all of which had previous utility and value in giving meaning to black political agency. It was dependence on this sociohistory that ensnared feminists, secular Muslims and much of the left in binary oppositions between fundamentalism and liberalism, racism and censorship, multiculturalism and intolerance, pluralism and universality, "religious intolerance and moral void", Enlightenment and tradition, which they kept claiming rendered them silent and unable to act.[7] These miscellaneous rocks and hard places do refer to important political problems that transcend their binary framing. But it was the overwhelming presence of a symbolic transnational *umma* that silenced progressive opposition by virtue of its multiple and globally disparate presences and highly energetic representatives, not many of whom could easily be opposed by secular Muslims.

In this new conception of *umma* we see sketches of existential and social location that can be buried in the single social space ("community", "civil society" or "nation") and the single historical narrative (colonialism, migration, diaspora) but can also overlap or surpass these. Importantly, the social referent implied in *umma* is none of these sociological spaces. However, neither is *umma* an entirely imaginative space with no particular social referents and no material manifestation. It has multiple social referents in several civil societies, several social movements, some nation-states and some transnational organizations, which acquire meaning, gain momentum, and are accumulated together in electronic media relations. It also locates an important problem about how political actions by social movements in one civil society generate actions in other civil societies without the mediation of any *national*-state.

The burning of the book

How fragile civilisation is; how easily, how merrily a book burns!
(Salman Rushdie, *The Observer* 22 January 1989)

[The Muslim's] campaign to have the book banned, on the grounds that it blasphemes Islam, led to a demonstration over the weekend in Bradford in which, following the example of the Inquisition and Hitler's National Socialists, a large crowd of Muslims burnt some copies of the book. (*The Independent* 16 January 1989)

[On 11 December 1989] about 500 Muslims in Bradford gathered to listen to the offending passages from *The Satanic Verses* .... Though I took great care to censor some of the more profane suggestions, I was physically prevented from reading even some of the censored materials by a number of outraged Muslims in the audience – one of whom fainted with anger. It became rapidly clear to the Bradford Council of Mosques that only a dramatic ritual would ease the frustration and vent the profound anger of the believing community. Accordingly it was resolved that a copy of *The Satanic Verses* be burnt publicly in front of the Bradford City Hall. (Akhtar 1989: 42–3)

The symbolic gesture of Muslim activists in Bradford in burning copies of *The satanic verses* in Bradford city centre on 14 January 1989 was the first major event that brought the mounting controversy around the book into British public culture. This book-burning incident received extensive coverage in the media and became a subject for parliament. A number of political themes emerged following this incident. The book-burning was quickly identified in public discourse with Nazism. Muslims were easily portrayed as an intolerant, irrational minority. The associated imagery was that of medievalism and backwardness versus freedom of speech, rights and liberties, civilization and Enlightenment.

The incident rapidly brought to the political surface an existing tension between the presence of blacks in Britain and what British national belonging now means. This appeared as two sides of an *extremely* problematic triangle: between multiculturalism and British nationalism, and between multiculturalism and secularism. (The third problematic side concerns the content of British nationalism and its relation to secularism. These tensions appear in virtually the same way in contemporary debates about national belonging, secularism and multiculturalism in India, and indeed reflect a much longer debate that British multiculturalism could learn from.) Multiculturalism came under considerable attack for different reasons by conservatives, liberals and black and white feminists (from different positions inside the triangle, as it were). Protest, though not a formal right under British law, is a negatively sanctioned liberal democratic "freedom". Months before the Bradford incident, Labour MPs had ceremoniously burnt copies of the government's new immigration rules. A major plank of the anti-Poll Tax campaign, which was occurring during that time, was the public burning of incomplete poll tax forms (almost certainly an illegal act). It seemed, however, that a symbolic protest by a black minority, an act completely within their "rights" to perform, instantly called into question the conditions of their presence within Britain and brought forth prose and invective which made them symbolically un-British:

> The Muslim minority has contributed much to the nation's commerce and entrepreneurial spirit. Its members have been notably law-abiding, and their devotion to family values, hard work and personal integrity are rightly admired. It is important that their spiritual values should be respected, and that they should be spared from racial discrimination in all its forms. They in turn, however, must not seek to impose their values either on their fellow Britons of other faiths or on the majority that acknowledge no faith at all. (*The Independent* 16 January 1989)

This editorial from the *Independent*, entitled "Islamic Intolerance", is important in highlighting many of the liberal anxieties regarding multiculturalism and national belonging that subsequently gained momentum following the *fatwa* and seemed to involve a shift in the meaning of British liberalism itself. The editorial explicitly recognizes – through interpellations such as "their fellow Britons" – that Muslims are British in some way. But, in a subtle manner that is immanent in the editorial as a whole rather than explicitly stated, and by questioning the right of Muslims to protest at all, to "impose their values", the editorial marks Muslims out of Britishness. The editorial needs to qualify that Muslims are hard-working and law-abiding, as if the latter works in favour of British belonging. Suppose they were not? Would an editorial advising the National Association of Viewers and Listeners speak of the Protestant ethic that might inform outraged upper middle-class families in the Shires? Would it question their national belonging? Surely their eccentric protests would be envisaged as peculiarly wholesome and English? Would such an editorial oppose their right to protest *at all*?

An important transformation was occurring in this liberal attempt to grapple with the tensions between multiculturalism and British national belonging. In the case of the *Independent*'s editorial, it was not simply a racist response, a reworking of Powellism, or even of the "new racism" that it informed. It was a representation of the symbols of Britishness in which the British tradition was identified with freedom and democracy, both a real and an invented tradition from which Muslims, by virtue of their protests, had deliberately excluded themselves, not because of their "cultural difference" – the *Independent* generally fell on the side of the need to respect Muslim spiritual and cultural values – but by their *irrational* political discourse. This liberal response attempted to construct a difference between Muslims and Britishness that was not explained by the cultural difference thesis of "new racism", though cultural difference was an important marker, but neither was it explicitly maintained by "racial" difference. Difference and exclusion from national identity rested on non-adherence to Western reason and Enlightenment. Muslim "race formation" appeared to be occurring somewhere between the poles of Western superior reason and Muslim subaltern superstition.

This can be compared to how the black left represented the

Muslim protest. Bernie Grant, Labour MP for Tottenham constituency, sponsored an amendment to an Early Day Motion in parliament which initially expressed "regret" at the publication of *The satanic verses*. Grant's amendment argued for the extension of the blasphemy laws to non-Christian faiths. This repressive act by a secular left-wing black politician was justified on the basis of "antiracism". It exemplified an extraordinarily naïve algorithm used by much of the black left that the demands of any "black community" are equivalent to "black-political" demands and thus are to be supported. Strangely enough, antiracist and black nationalist rhetoric was used to justify "non-black, non-racial", anti-secular claims. Keith Vaz MP, a Catholic Black Sections colleague of Grant's, was later to identify himself explicitly with, and indeed lead, Muslim protests against the book, which included, among other things, the burning of an effigy of Rushdie. Vaz's cynical particularist alliance with "fundamentalist" rather than secular Muslim sensibilities was strikingly similar to the way secular MPs in India play with Hindu and Muslim communal fire. It also highlighted important issues about representing the universal interests of an electoral constituency as a Member of Parliament. This tension, though rarely discussed, was integral to the Black Sections campaign: how is a particularist tendency to represent a universal, and indeed national interest, as Black Sections were committed to doing in the environment of the Labour Party and British parliamentary democracy? Additionally, both these black left interventions were primarily informed by a racialization of Muslims, a response which was different to that of the *Independent*.

The Bradford book-burning incident was followed, on 27 January 1989, by a national demonstration organized in central London by the Islamic Defence Council, an *ad hoc* group based in east London. Both the book-burning incident (in fact, by the end of January there had been numerous public book-burnings, mainly in northern towns) and the London demonstration upstaged the letter-writing and lobbying campaigns organized through the Central London Mosque and the UK Action Committee on Islamic Affairs. Indeed, the book-burnings and mass protests, based in the South Asian communities, seemed to have disturbed the elite committee-based and lobbying organizations, including the Jamaat-i-Islami. Some of these organizations appeared to be frightened by the momentum of mass Asian Muslim protests and either backed away from these protests or explicitly warned against them. The Islamic Society for the Promotion of Religious Tolerance, one of the first organizations to protest against the book, began to warn of the "sleeping demons of racialism" being awakened as a consequence of the protests and began to take an increasingly "moderate" line.

The London demonstration attracted several thousand Muslims, and petitions were presented to Downing Street and to Penguin:

> Memorandum of Request
> From: The Muslim Community in Britain
> To: The Owners of Penguin Books Limited
>
> The issue is plain and simple .... That no individual much less a whole world community can accept to be abused and insulted in the filthy way that this "novel" work has sought to do; and no "serious publisher" can take shelter behind the undisputed right of freedom of expression in order to publish such dirty work .... We wish we did not have to repeat it again and again that it is neither honourable nor acceptable to publish insult. We are not objecting to anyone writing critically or irreverently about Islam or Muslims. Hundreds of such works have been published in the past and hundreds more are going to be published in the future ... Islam stands on its own merits and we have no tradition of burning and banning such works. (Quoted in Appignanesi & Maitland 1989: 78–80)

The letter urges Penguin to pulp all remaining copies of the book, undertake not to publish any future editions and offer an unqualified apology to the world Muslim community. The letter also repeats the blasphemies contained in the book. The argument of the Muslims who organized the demonstration (and who referred to themselves as the "Muslim Community in Britain") is that *The satanic verses* insulted them as Muslims, insulted their faith or beliefs, or insulted the "world Muslim community". Additionally, it is said that the book was an insult to Islam, or to the Prophet, or his wives, or the Archangel Gabriel. It is then said that Islam is strong enough to withstand these attacks upon it, and that it is not in the tradition of Islam to ban books. It then urges that the books be pulped.

It is clear that *The satanic verses* greatly hurt and offended many

Muslims by insulting their beliefs. However, at this stage it was far from clear whether the "hurt" and "offence" could have sustained the momentum of the campaign. "Hurt" and "offence" had a limited potential for political mobilization. They echoed discursively manufactured feelings but presented no clear political goals except for banning the book and appeals for multiculturalism. There were some competing views about the extension of blasphemy laws among Muslims, since some Muslims argued that blasphemy laws had failed to protect Christianity against secularism.[8] There is a much deeper problem, that will continue to recur, about the Muslim argument for the extension of blasphemy laws since the latter currently only recognize blasphemy against Christianity and are therefore unfair. The logic of this argument, which is foundationally based on a universalist claim for equal treatment for all religions, also applies to Judaism, Vaishnava, Shaiva and Shakti Hinduism and its subsects, Sikhism, Buddhism, Shi'as, the Ismaili sect, the Qadiani Ahmmaddiyas (one of two Ahmaddiya sects, and virtually universally hated by other Muslims), Rastafarianism, charismatic, evangelical or fundamentalist Christian sects and so forth. Virtually all of these "blaspheme" against each other, with Hinduism probably having the greatest capacity to be seen to implicitly "blaspheme" any semitic or monotheistic religion.

"America and Israel are enemies of Islam": the *fatwa*

> In the name of God Almighty . . . I would like to inform all the intrepid Muslims in the world that the author of the book entitled *The Satanic Verses*, which has been compiled, printed and published in opposition to Islam, the Prophet and the Koran, as well as those publishers who were aware of its contents, have been sentenced to death. I call on all zealous Muslims to execute them quickly, wherever they find them, so that no one will dare to insult the Islamic sanctions. Whoever is killed on this path will be regarded as a martyr, God willing. In addition, anyone who has access to the author of the book but does not possess the power to execute him should refer him to the people so that he may be punished for his actions. May God's blessings be on you all. (*The Observer* 19 February 1989)

On 12 February 1989, police in Islamabad, Pakistan, opened fire on a mass protest against *The satanic verses* during which several people were killed and dozens injured. During the clashes, police officers used semi-automatic and pump-action shotguns against over 2,000 demonstrators. The demonstration, organized by Jamaat-i-Islami activists, was not only against *The satanic verses* (and also demanded the death of Rushdie) but was a protest against the United States. Demonstrators smashed windows of the US Information Centre in Islamabad and burnt the American flag. Effigies representing the United States and Rushdie were also burnt. The following day, a similar protest in Kashmir ended in one death and over a hundred people were injured.

The Islamabad demonstration has been noted by many observers as the moment that triggered Khomeini's *fatwa* against Salman Rushdie. The argument is that Khomeini did not wish to see Iran falling behind in the demonstrations against the book and needed to engineer internal blocks against the influence of reformists in Iran who wanted explicit political accommodation with the West. However, the demonstrations in Pakistan are important in themselves in a far deeper, even more Khomeinist sense. These were the first demonstrations that explicitly linked the theme of the book with US imperialism, US support for Israel, Israel's occupation of Palestine and Western anti-Islamism. The demonstrators weaved the protest against the book into existing political discourses against US imperialism, Zionism and the modern capacity of a politicized Islam, the agenda for which had been previously set by Khomeinism. The background to the demonstrations was, of course, the election of Benazir Bhutto and there was no doubt that the organization of these demonstrations was explicitly linked to opposition to her and to the reformist policies of the Pakistan People's Party.[9]

Hence, the demonstrations in Pakistan represent an important expansion of the political discourses that informed the Rushdie affair: Pakistani anti-Rushdie protesters chose to destroy an American agency and were then shot at and killed by functionaries of a reformist regime that had replaced an Islamist military dictatorship. From here on, the affair is not simply an issue of "offence" to Islam, though this continues to resonate strongly in all the Muslim discourses. Nor is it a simple reflection of Muslim grievances against "the West". Rather, it explicitly encodes concerns about the book into modern Muslim political concerns about the role of the West and the US in the "Third World", the policies of Israel and the struggles of Palestinians, the models of democratization in non-Western countries and the crises of legitimation of radical Islamic political regimes.

Khomeini's *fatwa* needs to be viewed within this wider, contingent political context, which was shaping the affair but was also influenced indirectly by the rearticulation of Islamic subjectivity since the Iranian revolution. The demonstrations in Pakistan utilized themes that ostensibly shared the same discursive space as Khomeinism (despite the ideological differences between Khomeini's brand of Shi'ism and the Jamaat-i-Islami). They represented a diffusion of Khomeinist epistemology about the role of Islam in the modern *global* political process. The fact the Muslims were demonstrating against Bhutto, US imperialism, Zionism and a book and its author is testimony to this newer repertoire of Islamic concerns.

Similarly, Khomeini's *fatwa* and the subsequent statements by (now President) Hashemi Rafsanjani and (then President) Khamenei made explicit political links between the book, the external context of the Iranian revolution (American imperialism) and the internal threat to the power of the clergy in Iran. Rafsanjani explains the publication of the book thus:

> Following the blows they [the US, Zionists, Satanic people] received from Iran after the Islamic revolution, as well as following the might of Islam that they saw in Lebanon and Afghanistan and the dynamism and awareness they saw of Muslims all over the world, they arrived at the conclusion, in their analysis, that all this stems from the holiness which covers everything which is sacred in Islam. This keeps the minds of the Muslims clean and gives dynamism and happiness to the world of Islam. Materialism and all kinds of political forces failed to break such a holiness. So they chose this method of action – choosing a person who seemingly comes from India, apparently is separate from the Western world and who has a misleading name. They begin their work in this fashion. Money has been given to that person, in advance, as royalties. They appoint guards for him, in advance, as they knew they were going to do. One notes that Zionist publishers are involved and that

translations have already been prepared in countries like
America [*sic*] and Italy. (BBC Summary of World Broadcasts
17 February 1989, quoted in Appignanesi & Maitland
1989: 84–6)

The conspiracy theme, itself a reduction of political forces to the
personal, is glaring. It also rehearses anti-Zionist themes that are
indistinguishable from antisemitism. Many responses to the publication of the Rushdie affair reiterated the theme of anti-Zionism
but from a new political tradition that owed more to the *Protocols
of the Learned Elders of Zion* than to the secular concerns about
Palestine, southern Lebanon, the tyrannical policies of Israel
towards Arabs or, indeed, to the actual history of the Zionist
movement. Antisemitism in some responses to *The satanic verses*
was often the most prominent singular theme and received virtually
no published rebuttals from other Muslims.[10]

Khomeini, in a subsequent message, also makes explicit to his
listeners that the book is an attempt to destroy the radical *'ulama* in
Iran and that the manifest political and economic problems in Iran
are the fault of the West and the US:

> Truly, if anyone thinks that colonialism has not and does
> not persecute the clergy which has so much greatness,
> honour and influence, is that not naive? The issue of the
> book *The Satanic Verses* is that it is a calculated move
> aimed at rooting out religion and religiousness and above
> all Islam and its clergy. Certainly if the world devourers [US]
> could, they would have burnt the roots and the title of the
> clergy .... Today, 10 years after the Islamic revolution, I
> admit – as in the past – that some of the decisions of the
> early stages of the revolution in entrusting important
> positions and affairs to those who did not have pure and
> real faith in the pure Mohammadan Islam were a mistake.
> Although even at that time I was not personally in favour
> of their taking such positions, I accepted it through
> consultation and the advice of friends. Even now I strongly
> believe that they do not think about anything but diverting
> the revolution and directing it towards the world-devourer
> America .... God wanted the blasphemous book of *The
> Satanic Verses* to be published now, so that the world of

conceit, arrogance and barbarism would bare its face in its long-held enmity to Islam; to bring us out of our simplicity and *to prevent us from attributing everything to blunder, bad management and lack of experience; to realise fully that this issue is not our mistake, but that it is the world devourers' effort to annihilate Islam, and Muslims*; otherwise, the issue of Salman Rushdie would not be so important to them as to place the entire Zionism and arrogance behind it. (BBC Summary of World Broadcasts 24 February 1989, quoted in Appignanesi & Maitland 1989: 90–91, emphases added)

It should be clear from this just how important the Rushdie affair was in Iran in providing the radical *fuqaha* with the repertoire for cynically attempting to secure their political legitimation and to externalize their political and economic failures. This has been read by many commentators as an incorrect use of Islam by the Iranian leadership. A *fatwa* is traditionally an opinion from a selected authority (a *mujtahid* in Shiʿa, or a *mufti* in Sunni Islam) and is not a judgement (which can only traditionally happen after a formal trial in a *shariʿa* court in a Muslim country) and furthermore its applicability cannot spatially transcend the *dar al Islam* (House of Islam, or a Muslim nation-state) (*The Independent*, 22 February 1989.) However, this is precisely where the reconstructed spatial capacity of Islam represented in Khomeinism makes its use in this manner entirely legitimate. Islam, in Khomeinism, has acquired an indeterminate spatial and global capacity. Khomeinism does not represent a set of medieval religious injunctions but is a political ideology that shares a concern with global events with the same force as any other modern ideology. The *fatwa* was not exceptional to Khomeinism but was its logical product. It perhaps demonstrated how far radical Islam had travelled from "tradition".

Consequently, understanding the *fatwa* requires another paradigmatic shift. The *fatwa* could not have transpired or had any bearing outside of a modern technocratic and multinational political context. The *fatwa* was designed for national and global reception. The importance of the *fatwa* against Salman Rushdie was precisely related to the fact that it was not issued in, nor could it have had any commensurable meaning in a premodern Muslim empire, town or village. This introduces sharply the importance of absolutist control over the means of mass electronic communications in rehearsing totalitarian neotraditions. Fatima Mernissi argues that, in the history of Sunni Islam, the *imam* (the male religious guide or leader) was a permanently and knowingly vulnerable figure since he was scared of God in case he made an unjust decision in God's eyes and he feared the masses, in case his decisions led to his assassination (Mernissi 1993: 23–4). Mernissi argues that the modern "media *imam*" does not have these vulnerabilities. The traditional *imam* could always be argued with and reasoned with. The "media *imam*" cannot, since the political control over the means of mass electronic communication prevents this. We can extend this argument further. The mass electronic media create a relationship between the *imam* and his followers that drastically and permanently transforms the meaning of faith, obedience and spiritual teaching in ways that are untraditional and, in strictly traditional terms, often "blasphemous". It is axiomatic in Islam that human (or animal) representation is forbidden since Islam was formed explicitly against idolatrous worship, though Khomeini's regime depended virtually entirely on cultivating a visual cult of personality. In both Sunni and Shi'a Islamic thought, political authority resides with God[11] and political leaders can have only a limited or derivative authority, if that. Furthermore, in Shi'a Islam, no political authority on Earth is legitimate until the Twelfth Imam returns. However, the Iranian Islamic regime vigorously promoted the televisual cult of personality of Khomeini. His entry into global mass media relations was equivalent to claiming an identity for "the modern *imam*". The office of "Ayatollah" was itself a nineteenth-century invention and that of the Supreme ('Uzma) Ayatollah was invented in the twentieth century (Mernissi 1993: 24). But media relations also allowed Khomeini to accumulate more than human identity. While he never explicitly claimed to be the Twelfth Imam, his followers widely cultivated an ambiguous view. The designation *Imam* Khomeini has two very different meanings, one completely mundane and vulnerable, the other approaching the Divine and Absolute. This simulacrum of a Divine Imam is an absolutist media symbol that erased, for a while, the theological and political contradictions within Shi'a traditions.

The immediate aftermath of Khomeini's *fatwa* in February 1989 brought fierce international reaction and forthright defence of

141

Rushdie and *The satanic verses* from Western governments and liberals. Equally, the *fatwa* galvanized and mobilized numerous groups of Muslims across the globe against the book and its author, as indeed it explicitly intended to do. Uniquely, in comparison with other contemporary political events, the Rushdie affair was carried through an immense range of political institutions, including Western and non-Western democratic nation-states (Britain, India), exceptional non-Western nation-states (Iran, Pakistan), world governmental bodies (United Nations) and non-governmental organizations, pan-Arabic (Organisation of Arab Unity) and pan-Islamic transnational institutions (Organisation of Islamic Conference), voluntary bodies, research groups, terrorist organizations, commercial and economic institutions, the institutions of global communications, national networks of community organizations, social movements and civil societies. The affair also demonstrated a variety of different *forms* of political agency (institutional, collective and individual) and the deployment of numerous cultural symbols. The importance of cultural mobilization – essentially political action against what were seen as Western cultural and political formations – was made explicit by President Khamenei:

> The method which received more attention from the start, and which was considered more effective for [World arrogance] was the *cultural method*. We Muslims should be as wary of the enemy's cultural front as we are of the enemy's military front. As the enemy's attack on our frontiers brings us into action, the enemy's attack on our cultural frontiers should evoke a reaction from us at least to the same degree, if not more. (BBC Summary of World Broadcasts 20 February 1989, quoted in Appignanesi & Maitland 1989: 87, emphasis added)

Indeed, it is this cultural methodology, whether arising from the West or outside it, that elaborates the new frontier between the West and the "Third World" from which new traditions were created (see Table 1).

The *fatwa* was the semiotic completion of this frontier space through which the *umma* and the West were imagined. The West's frontier symbolism was resurrected primarily through its discourses of freedom, rights, free speech, liberty, tolerance and Enlightenment

Table 1 Frontier symbolism in the Rushdie affair

'Liberal democracy'	Islamic government
Formal democracy, freedom	Consultation, consensus, clerical totalitarianism
West	Third World, Orient
Global world system, US hegemony	Imperialism, neocolonialism
Modern, modernity, archetypal modernization	Medievalism, "mutilated modernity", failed modernization
Judeo-Christian	Islam
Murder	Execution
Death	Martyrdom
Book burning	Protest, hurt, offence
Text	Scripture
Fiction	Fact
Science	Revelation
Truth (rational)	Truth (revealed)
Secular	Sacred, holy
Tolerance	Defiance
Nation state – civil society	*Fuqaha – umma*
Mullah, mad mullah	The modern *imam*, the "media *imam*"
Individual	Collective
Reason, enlightenment, rational	Superstition, fanaticism, emotional

which were threatened by the Orient, the barbarian and the medieval: modernity was threatened by its past. But the frontier symbolism invoked in radical Islam through tropes like "the Great Satan", "corruption on Earth", democracy, "evil", conspiracy, Zionism, martyr, apostate and blasphemer, was temporally located in the present. Great Satan, the "corruption of democracy", and "World Devourer" all "translate" US global domination, imperialism, the military aggression of Israel and the plight of Palestinians. Martyr, apostate and blasphemer have important meanings in traditional Shi'ism (but do not necessarily have the same, if any, meanings in the Sunni traditions). But these were put into practice as translocal or global symbols against the modernist phenomenon of the mass production and consumption of a Novel written by an Author.

There are thus important disparities in the temporal readings of the affair by Western and Islamic commentators. Radical Islam's temporal epistemology was focused on the present and the future

143

(its time had come), the West's seemed focused on its past. Especially important for the latter was the imagination of Oriental torpidity that existed before the arrival of modernity's colonial frontier. Many Western responses imagined this as the premodern frontier that "Third World" social formations always return to following their repeated failures to modernize, democratize, nationalize. Conversely, "Oriental despotism" (an important Enlightenment strand) is the absolute essence of non-Western political formations and, in Western eyes, there is no difference between Khomeini or Fahd or Saddam Hussein.

It is of considerable interest that many Western commentators repeatedly recreated the Rushdie affair in terms of the past the West left behind. This is suggestive of fears of the present that evade actually existing Western societies and their relationship to minorities, women, political censorship, liberty, equality and Christian and Jewish fundamentalism. Many Muslim commentators recreated the affair as the corruption of Western modern imperialist society which Islam has either actually transcended (as in Iran) or metaphorically transcended in its utopian forms of belief, faith and the ideal Islamic community. In these deliberations Western society is frequently compared to a utopian Islam but the latter is rarely compared to "actually existing" Islamic or Muslim societies and the latter are rarely criticized for their formations of state, civil society and gender relations. Distinctively, utopian Islam is compared to contemporary Western societies rather than contemporary Islamic ones. The abstracted concept-metaphor that "Islam" becomes in these interventions is always extratemporal and extraspatial. These differential temporalities are significant because their clash framed virtually all interventions and analyses of the Rushdie affair. Muslims could easily point out the hypocrisy, "double standards", corruption and deceit of the West and the latter could easily point to the repression, intolerance and "backwardness" of Islam; both parties had substantial material with which to do so. This does not suggest that there existed a Habermasian space in which the affair was resolvable. Instead, temporal positioning and spatial organization were important in establishing and rehearsing the various incommensurabilities that each side relished. Incommensurabilities were not just "there"; they were actively made. Western modernity recreated Islam as regressive, premodern in time and locally manifest in space and it was not any of these. Its relationship to "cultural" way through traditions that have never had any historical, geographical, national, ethnic or, arguably, religious affiliation. It was also through this new cultural method that the indeterminacy of Western spatial authority was demonstrated. The West may command the mechanisms of time–space compression but its authority is not final or complete. "Third World" formations utilized exactly these mechanisms to compress space and time in their own way.

These issues considerably complicate understandings of physical, social and imagined local communities residing inside the national space. They result in a kind of aporia that is exactly manifest in the view that the vast majority of Muslims in Britain did not support the death sentence on Rushdie and the views of other writers that they probably did. It re-appears again in the absence of any denunciation by any significant Muslim leaders in Britain of Khomeini's *fatwa* and the brutal assassination of a Belgian *imam* who did. In an important way, the imagination of a unified translocal *umma* and its representative mass media form acted very powerfully to discipline secular Muslims, to silence those who would object to the considerable attention given to authoritarian Muslim strands.

The authoritarian Muslim *umma*-identity that was heavily promoted during the affair did, however, soon collapse. One of the very first actions by British Muslims at the start of the affair was the burning of *The satanic verses* in Blackburn. In July 1992 another event occurred in that town. For several nights Asian youths numbering in their thousands engaged in pitched battles against each other followed by "an epilogue of full-blooded attack" on the Lancashire police who were attempting to separate them (*The Independent* 24 July 1992). The youths, the overwhelming majority of whom were born in Blackburn, "as British as fish and chips", were fighting each other as rival Indians and Pakistanis, after the former had accused the latter of harassing Indian women and organizing the local economy of drugs, prostitution and petty crime. The gang formations in those events were identified by recent nationalist identities (as Indians or Pakistanis), their "difference" constituted not just through ethnic identification as Gujeratis or Punjabis but also from historical grievances over differential access to the resources of the local state and economy. However, those youths who battled each other so fiercely had previously marched together in the city under the solidarity and celebration of another

conceptions of Western modernity was indescribable and its location in space was translocal and indeterminate. Radical Islam created Western modernity as a spatially-globally organized threat but disputed its conception of its past and its universal claim on the present or the future. The most important theme was that of an overarching, ahistorical, essential conflict that bore little relation to the actual conflicts that the West has historically engaged in (Halliday 1994: 91–3).

Conclusion: complex translocal communities and the aporia of *umma*

These issues of temporality have related spatial aspects. It is worth briefly comparing some political imaginations of the space of *umma* as a conclusion to this chapter. Both Tariq Modood's and Bhiku Parekh's explanations of the British Muslim response to *The satanic verses* relied essentially on combining an ethnicity-based paradigm of considerable religious conviction and evident ethnic traditions with an environmentalist approach that highlighted the manifest economic poverty, racial discrimination and Islamophobia faced by Muslims in Britain (Modood 1992, Parekh 1990). Both these factors led to the protests that started the whole affair. Their assessment is essentially local and empirical. Both writers distinguish sharply between the anguish of an insecure community in Britain identified primarily through a religious identity, and the *fatwa* and the revolutionary Islam rhetoric of some Muslim representatives and organizations. This tendency recognizes the real hurt and anguish felt by Muslims and is critical both of Muslim leaders who failed to speak out against the *fatwa* and the comforting refuge of racism and nationalism that many liberals turned to. This tendency concedes that revelation is as real and frequently far more important than race for the faithful. Others such as Kalim Siddique of the Muslim Institute have, like representatives of all social movements, discursively shrunk the world to their size and focused on the creation of a global Muslim presence:

> ... when we speak of Islam as a complete way of life, it includes our life in a non-Muslim state and environment. Our status as British citizens does not and cannot in any

way compromise our global responsibilities as part of the Ummah of Islam. The British government must realise that the Muslim citizens of this country will defend Islam, and the honour of Islam here and in all parts of the world with everything we have. (Qureshi & Khan 1989: 12)

Or, like Shabbir Akhtar, on the ironic centrality of *The satanic verses* in creating another new highly disciplinary and exclusionary Muslim identity which, however, is already incomplete in its inception because of its recognition of the existence of Muslims who have "foundered" at the point of its enactment:

Any Muslim who fails to be offended by Rushdie's book ceases, on account of that fact, to be a Muslim ... These contentions are completely conclusive; there is no room here for private sophistication rooted in hypocrisy and schooled in dishonesty. And God is well aware of the things we do. (Akhtar 1989: 35)

These two assessments are global and metaphoric and aim essentially towards creating a new disciplinary Muslim identity, and thus recognize that such an holistic identity (such as the *umma*) does not exist but can only become manifest, if at all, in its articulation. A third factor becomes relevant here and is present in the British Government's disciplinary notice to Muslims. It reproduces the "mythic discourse" of the West, but is important here for condition-ally inserting Muslims into a local discourse of nation. This is an immanently translocal and mythic identification in which Muslims have local positionality only as a subjected *race*:

[If Muslims] are to make the most of their lives and opportunities as British citizens, then they must also have a clear understanding of the British democratic processes, of its laws, the system of government and the history that lies behind them ... (John Patten, Minister of State at the Home Office, in a letter to British Muslims 4 July 1989)

This nationalism is inherently problematized because of the recognition by Muslims of (some of) the history that actually does lie behind the West and that they are now expected to submit to. This

factor will repeatedly interrupt any future discussion of r identity and "racial" belonging in Europe. There is consi convergence between this conservative position and socialist s of Muslim demands. Socialists could only drag Muslims into l ness by envisioning them as a localized race. But there is a ambiguity in relation to these positions. National sovereignty being compressed and expanded through unsettled global infl and dynamics that Muslims have already participated in demands made by some Muslims of the British state and affiliation to identities outside the national boundary are a red tion of an instability in national sovereignty.

The Rushdie affair transcended sociology and its object of s a single civil society and nation-state, but was also not w describable in the political science of international rela between nation-states. The affair also problematized the abili contemporary social and political theory to explain ideo structure, action and collective agency either within a single s system or within unbounded global economic, political ideological systems. In each of its events, the affair compounded and contingent and refuted the idea of caus exclusive social and political explanation. In this sense, it could be cognitively mapped as a reductive totality. The affair repeatedly and reflexively crossed ontic layers within and betw nation-states and civil societies. Consequently, the affair could "mapped" and "understood" through the deployment of a v range of incommensurable epistemologies, each of which ma sense of the affair within their own discursive logics. It is becau of this that the Rushdie affair lacked a central metanarrative. T affair was endogenous to a global "system" of electror communications and could not have existed or had meanin outside this. The global mass media was a necessary ar acknowledged condition by participants in the affair. However, tl global "system" of electronic communications did not simp represent political events outside itself (this is not its "function' but created and articulated novel political formations (such a *imam*, *umma* and *fatwa*) which only acquired accumulation an meaning in this medium. The affair was importantly cultural bu the meaning of this becomes increasingly obscure. What *doe* "cultural" mean when new hybrid frontier formations ar reproduced across global spaces and resonate in some deepl

identity. All the participants in the riots were Muslims.

That this event shattered the edifice of a unitary "Muslim community" which, in their different ways, "fundamentalists", liberals and socialists had hoped for, is not a cause for celebration. The Blackburn riot contained in its violence a miniature example of national and ethnic communalism. This tendency has become increasingly systematic over the last decade and is following a depressing trajectory. Secular multiculturalism is extraordinarily necessary in opposing communalism, but it increasingly looks defeated and vacant. It is not entirely clear that we possess a political language with which to replace it. The future shape of Islamic fundamentalism, the lives of millions of Muslims and Hindus, the reconfiguration of Western imperialism and the relations between Pakistanis, Bangladeshis, Indians and South East Asians across the world rest on one highly compounded event – the possible coming to power, in India, of the main opposition, the Hindu nationalist anti-Muslim Bharatiya Janata Party. This party articulates a new "nationalism" and a more "authentic" tradition of what it means to be a true Indian and a real Hindu. It owes its historical lineage not to the liberation movement, not to Gandhi, and most certainly not to Nehru but to an obsession with mythic purity, "racial" superiority and the anthropology of blood and land that had earlier taken Western modernity to a murderous conclusion.

CHAPTER 5

Neotraditional Hinduism and the fabrication of purity

[Dandamis the Brahmin speaks to Alexander of Macedon:] You were created of small stature and naked, and came into the world alone: what is it that makes you great enough to slaughter all these people? To seize all their possessions? When you have conquered everybody, and taken possession of all the world, you will possess no more land than I have as I lie down. We control just as much land as we were made from, and we, whom you so despise, possess as much without wars and battles as you do: earth, water and air. Everything I have, I hold justly, and I desire nothing; but you, however, make much war and shed blood and slaughter people, and even if you conquer all the rivers in the world, will drink no more water than I do. I do not fight, or bear wounds, or raze cities, and I have as much earth and water as you. (*The legends of Alexander the Great* 1994: 45)

This is the highest country .... No doubt it was inhabited before any other and could have even been the site of all creation and all science. The culture of the Indians, as is known, almost certainly came from Tibet, just as all our arts like agriculture, numbers, the game of chess, etc., seem to have come from India. (Immanuel Kant, quoted in Leon Poliakov, *The Aryan myth*, 1971: 186)

NEOTRADITIONAL HINDUISM

Introduction

This and the following chapter turn towards an examination of modern right-wing Hindu revival, and in particular the far right-wing organizations that have come to dominate Hinduism in the last decade. All these organizations can be described appropriately as authoritarian religious movements. However, it is becoming conventional to refer to their collective assemblage or ideologies as "Hindu nationalism" and this is broadly the convention I have used, though its descriptive limitations will become apparent. It needs emphasizing that this and the following chapter are focused on far right-wing Hindu formations and are not about Hinduism in general nor the forms of Hinduism practised in South Asian communities.

In much Hindu nationalism, the themes of both "racial" and religious purity, and the pernicious ideologies of caste purity that already exist in Hinduism, are brought together in a new repressive conception of "liberation", "emancipation", nation-state formation (Hindu *Rashtra*) and even "revolution" (*kranti*). These aspects are combined in a modernist narrative that has attempted to create a new Hindu identity, a new mythic world-space and, importantly, a politically effective conception of linear temporality and mythic history both in India and globally. The dominant political formation in right-wing revivalist Hinduism, the anti-Muslim Bharatiya Janata Party (BJP, formed in 1980 and the main opposition party in India in the mid-1990s) has an historical background that, whatever prefixes are used and whatever qualifiers are added, has been far too closely associated with ideologies that were definitive of both fascism and Nazism. This would be valid even if we were to ignore completely the explicit appeal of German National Socialism for some of its principal intellectual founders. Even more instructive are the discursive shifts undertaken by some non-Muslim leftist and also feminist groups in India who have become, to differing extents, apologists for the BJP and its exclusive brand of Hindu nationalism or (as it calls it) "cultural nationalism".[1] In Britain, many secular Hindu leftists often take the position of opposition to the fascistic Rashtriya Swayamsevak Sangh (RSS, formed in 1925) and, sometimes, the Vishwa Hindu Parishad (VHP, formed by the RSS in 1964) but offer qualified support to the "secular" BJP. The BJP is deemed to have only "serious questions to answer".

152

These main Hindu nationalist organizations have "touched the Hitler nerve in India" (Akbar 1988: 165–8). They constantly invoke the themes of "racial" purity, of blood and of soil, nature, essential belonging, purity and cleansing, ideas that manifested themselves in the 1930s and 1940s and do so today in Greater Serbian ambitions. Their popular slogans are just too adjacent to genocidal "reasoning" and their political mobilizations are too bloody, violent and organized and this has caused considerable apprehension about their existence. It is also important for oppositional and secular politics that the BJP-RSS-VHP combine have consistently and vigorously opposed the common secularist accusation that they are "fascist", "Nazi", authoritarian and anti-democratic. This area is examined in more detail below.

Hindu nationalism has the potential to exhibit the same spatial disturbance around "nation" that we have already encountered and some of these tendencies are already apparent in its activism inside and outside India, especially in its conceptions of *Akhand Bharat* ("Greater India"). Like neofoundational Islam it declares itself as a "way of life", a complete commitment to political issues and a critique of traditional religious practice. The same claims that are made by Islamists – that Islam is a legal system, as well as a political ideology, a blueprint for a polity, a sociology for the social formation, as well as being a religion and a code for personal conduct for a global Muslim *umma* – is rehearsed in virtually the same form in Hindu nationalism. Hindu nationalists desire total religious integration with politics. The separation of religion and politics is claimed to be a *Western* "pseudosecular" mystification. The advocates of Hindu nationalism claim to be anti-Western, anti-imperialist, modern, scientific, rational and simply patriotic. However, Hindu nationalism is deeply preoccupied with questions of power, the capture and potential "theocratic-racial" reorganization of the local and federal state and the forging of new politicized, non-privatized and pure Hindu bodies in a "cleansed" civil society. Hinduism, in this vision, is all-embracing and provides a totalizing way of life that encompasses not just the whole Indian social formation but also "the world Hindu community". One important tendency in Hindu nationalism that is also apparent in contemporary Islamism is the claim to power and influence in nation-state formation and civil society by clerical and ecclesiastical groups and organizations that were earlier dismissed by secular modernity.

However, if those older formations of caste hierarchy and religious authority have returned, they have also been reconstituted into political forms that are novel to Hinduism. Hindu nationalism has also been unable to explicate the good life, a new polity or a new economy. Many of the themes encountered in the previous chapter are also important for this new Hinduism: "third routeism", a critique of both capitalism and socialism as materialistic and Western, a conspiratorial tendency, organicism, human agency authorized by God or his texts and fierce visceral religious and "racial" symbolism.

Importantly, a founding methodological claim is made, similar to that often seen in Islamic revivalism, about an essential, transcendental *Hindu civilization* (Jain 1994: 1–13 is the best recent example). This civilizational methodology is perpetually mutable and shape-shifting and provides a mesmerizing universal explanatory paradigm from which any strands in the actual or fabricated histories of Hinduisms can be selected. This civilizational gaze is extraordinarily and increasingly able to aggregate any and all Hinduisms and their institutional structures into its own unitary discourse. "Hindu civilization" is rehearsed by Hindu nationalists as historically tolerant of and providing refuge for all and any faiths or sects, or even that all faiths and sects in India are captured within an all-embracing conception of "Hinduism". At the same time, those that articulate these sentiments can institute bloody pogroms against religious minorities. The combination of universalist and particularist strands within a generic transcendental civilizational methodology constitutes both a dominant ideology and a guide to political organization and activism for Hindu nationalists. It is virtually a Gramscian method: the articulation of numerous, diverse, conflicting and contradictory "philosophies of life" into one potentially hegemonic reconstruction of Hinduism. This attention to a transcendental "Hindu civilization", rather than simply the nation-state or even nationalism, also has important consequences for some of the debates initiated in Chapter 1 and are followed through below.

Both identity and personal politics are extraordinarily important for Hindu nationalism. Despite an embedded and popular view that Hinduism cannot allow conversions into its identity, Hindu nationalists have demonstrated a violent evangelical zeal which matches that of Christian and Islamic neofoundational movements. The "reconversion" of poor Muslims, Christians and Buddhists to what is called their "original" faith has become very important for the Vishwa Hindu Parishad (VHP). The revivalist *Hinduism Today*, by no means extremist, reported with some pride how VHP activists brought "48,000 into [the] Hindu fold". An accompanying photograph shows a woman and child looking out to the sea – "Muslim yesterday, Hindu today, a converted mother quietly reflects on the new life ahead" (*Hinduism Today* 15 (1) January 1993). Virtually all the familiar techniques of social movement identity politics are present in Hindu nationalism: declaration, announcement, prophecy, self-affirmation, pride, the manufacture of identity tokens, body fetishism and body stigmata, a theory of organicist social totality, a theory of "its oppression" by the state and within civil society, a linear "Hegelian" temporality that unfolds to provide an important "history of the present", the formation of core identity through the necessary creation and disciplinary evacuation of dissenters and others on the margins (identity as a process of both constitutedness and constraint), a contemporary permanent dystopia and a promised utopia. "Say it with pride – I am a Hindu!", "Hindi, Hindu, Hindusthan!" It can declare that "anyone who says they are a Hindu is a Hindu" (Dubashi 1992: 4) and this accompanies its extremely narrow view of what constitutes a Hindu, from which dissenters are vigorously excluded (the same kind of universalist claim to hegemony combined with particularist dogmatism that has accompanied Islamism).

Just as the unfolding of the Rushdie affair depended incisively on "diasporic" Muslims, revivalist Hinduism has relied extensively on its followers in the US, Britain, Canada and Europe to generate global support and funds for its political ventures in India. (The agents of Western Hindu revival, especially in the US, display a distinctive combination of vocational success in science and technology and a regressive mystical superstition.) The new Hindu revivalism is quite consciously international in its aims and scope and sees itself as part of "the new global Hindu Renaissance" that will instil pride and glory among the world's "1 Billion Hindus" (the same kind of enumeration that accompanies Islamism's *umma*). Modern Hindu nationalism has created a disciplinarian and intolerant identity based on two separate components: the superiority of what one *believes* (like Islam and Christianity) and who one essentially *is* (like Zionism, racism and fascism). It ties together the themes of "racial" purity with religious purity. It is an extremely dangerous ideology that combines "liberation" with archaeological and anthropological narratives of the authentic inner-self and the authentic body.

There is a vast literature on Hinduism and its multitudinous sects. Most of what is available in the West is preoccupied with Hindu cosmologies, beliefs, customs and rituals. This strictly ethnicizing tendency has become even more ingrained now that aspects of Hindu philosophies have been appropriated in, or dovetailed neatly into the explosive rise of, New Age philosophies and practices.[2] The (relatively few) social theory writings on Hindu communities in Britain also tend to follow ethnicized paradigms. With some important exceptions, sociological theoretical writings on Hinduism outside India have traditionally focused on its metaphysics, mythology, ritual and custom and on patterns of social adjustment and change. Assessments of Hindu supremacist organizations (such as the extremely influential Arya Samaj, or "Aryan Society", of the last century) often simply restate their "religious" themes and ignore their political aims or history.[3] (A fairly typical method is to identify a charismatic male founder, outline his rudimentary beliefs and the nominal contents of his *magnum opus* and provide the name of his sect followers.) Post Second World War Hinduism, partly because of the impact of Gandhianism, did manage to create a contemporary global view of itself as harmless, other-worldly, mythical, renouncing and in some profound way pleasant, tolerant, patient and having an elective affinity with diversity, democracy, multiculturalism, secularism and liberalism. It is now apparent that the latter do not constitute the finished edifice of Hinduism but are contested values in a distinctive battle between secular Hindus and the new Hindu nationalists.

This chapter looks at the background to the history, ideologies and activities of the family of Hindu nationalist organizations (*sangh parivar*). The next chapter examines their ideologies in greater detail. Because of the relative unfamiliarity with the history and content of Hinduisms in Western political sociology and social theory, this chapter presents an initial elementary discussion about aspects of the history of different Hinduisms from which key themes have been appropriated in right-wing Hindu revival. Much of the detail in this and the next chapter relies heavily, if not necessarily accurately or faithfully, on the work of more competent scholars of Hinduism and Hindu nationalism in India, and especially the published work of historians and literary theorists at Jawaharlal University and Delhi University, in particular the historical work of Romila Thapar, K.N. Panikkar and Sarvepalli Gopal (Gopal 1991) and the social and historical research and analysis of Tapan Basu, Pradip Datta, Sumit Sarkar, Tanika Sarkar and Sambuddha Sen (Basu et al. 1993). For detailed reasons that will become clearer as the chapter progresses, even presenting an historical summary of aspects of (northern Indian) Hinduism is a politically charged task, since the histories of Hinduisms and revisionist claims about these histories are both at the core of Hindu nationalism. Indeed, "what is Hinduism" is now a deeply political, contested claim for Hinduism in the West too. The absolutely universal appropriation of the texts and histories of Hinduisms, and their reduction to palimpsests is a dominant methodology in Hindu nationalism, just as the "revenge against" History is one of its dominant metaphors. Just as important are mythic discourses and mythic temporalities. The political appeal to mythic discourse is a core mobilizing factor for revivalist Hinduism, as is its highly selective reliance on (and contravention of) the rules of archaeological and anthropological method.

A highly relevant aspect of this concerns the historiography of myths, legends and fables. The hermeneutic regressions that this can engender, and which indeed are part of the histories of Hinduisms, are vastly exploited by Hindu nationalists. Innumerable legends and myths, as well as the complex refabulations of histories of fables or the tellings and retellings of stories about legends have distinctively contributed to the identity of Hinduisms. However, these complex, iterative hermeneutics that can preoccupy careful realist historians of Hinduism can become singularly reduced in Hindu nationalism to one prophetic announcement, one declaration, one myth and one "history" (Thapar 1991). Similarly, whereas Islam's epistemology is (generally) based on historical time and its historical personalities are (in the main) established and verifiable, this is not the case with much of Hinduism and its personalities. Hence this chapter will need to turn to the themes of history and time, real, imagined and mythic, as well as the substantive content of many mythologies that make up Hinduisms.

(North Indian) Hinduisms: a preliminary narrative

The *Vedas* ("knowledge") are the founding written texts of what, much later, came to be known as Hinduism. They comprise four main books, the *Rig Veda*, the *Yajur Veda*, the *Samar Veda* and the *Atharva Veda*. There is disagreement about the time of their oral composition and transmission and the period when they were set down as texts. The *Rig Veda*, a collection of 1,028 hymns, originated in the hymns to the mythic nature Gods and the religion of the Aryan-speakers who entered as tribes over a considerably long period starting c1500 BC into what is now northern India. The more advanced and "literate" pre-Aryan culture of the Indus valley civilizations of Mohenjodaro and Harappa, which dated from before c3000 BC until c1500 BC, had apparently completely declined by the time the Aryan-speaking tribes began to enter northwestern India from what is now Iran. The Aryans, despite the elevated importance given to them by the founders of the current Hindu revivalism, were not the literate, technologically advanced conquering force they are popularly imagined but were nomadic and primitive tribes with little agricultural technology in comparison with what already existed in the developed urban civilizations of the Indus valley and plains (Thapar [1966]1990: 29–30).

The Aryans originally had no conception of caste as it is now understood, but had a form of social and economic organization divided into the *kshatriyas* (warriors and aristocracy), *brahmins* (priests) and *vaishyas* (cultivators). However, the populations they encountered, the Dasas, were darker in colour and they were marked as the *shudras*. The Aryans subsequently reified their social system along "racial" lines (caste=*varma*=colour) for fear of intermixing with the darker Dasas and this became the basis for a highly rigid but expansive caste system in much later centuries. The *kshatriyas* were the highest caste, followed by the *brahmins*, but much later the *brahmins* usurped the dominant position, primarily through their knowledge of the sacred Sanskrit texts and religious rituals. These two groups were the "twice-born" castes of Aryan mythology – "first" born physically and "then" born into the caste system. The *shudras* were subsequently included in the caste system as cultivators, and the idea of the outcastes or "untouchables" – populations who were outside the caste system and "unclean" – was developed. Over the centuries this idea of four castes became more important as a theoretical frame to a much more rigid and very wide subcaste (*jati*) formation. New populations and groups had to be constantly negotiated into the caste system and there was some small degree of collective mobility when one caste *en masse* changed its occupation in changing circumstances. The system of subcastes and the idea of untouchability became increasingly important, especially from the start of the second millennium right up to the present. The system of subcastes varied enormously across region and depended on local economic and political conditions (such as regional trade and the political power of *brahmins*). The caste system was powerfully threatened by religious, regional, anti-*brahmin* and non-Aryan movements such as Buddhism, Jainism, Sikhism, the Tamil *bhakti* movement and Islam. In contemporary Hindu revivalism, caste constitutes a major presence. Revivalist organizations both denounce the idea of a caste system but are also highly Brahminic in leadership and orientation. For example, at its inception in the 1920s, the RSS explicitly opposed caste and untouchability. However, most of the leadership of the RSS came from Maharashtrian *brahmin* groups. Moreover, virtually any critique of Brahminism, and often the caste system and the ideology of untouchability is vigorously attacked by Hindu nationalists. The racial mythology of the Aryans, in particular the idea that "true" Indians or Hindus are Aryan descendants, that Aryans brought "superior Hindu civilization" to Dravidian "India", and that subsequent, especially Muslim invasions of India are "pollutions" is an important subtext in contemporary northern Hinduism in which an explicit link between "race" and religion is maintained. The fascination with the themes of origin and typology in some strands of contemporary Hindu nationalism has led to eccentric contributions on theories of Aryan origins, including the various selective archaeologies and fanciful speculations of the Belgian Koenraad Elst, who contributes extensively to Hindu nationalist publications and is hailed as an "independent" Western intellectual voice on "Hinduism".[4]

The Vedic hymns, especially of the *Rig Veda*, define the first nature Gods of Aryan mythology, including Indra ("Thunder", probably the most important Vedic God, "lost" in later Hinduism), Agni ("Fire"), Aditi ("Earth-Mother"), Savitri (a solar deity, later another source for the Mother Goddess), Rudra ("Storm", later to "refer" to the Hindu God Shiva) and numerous other members of a vast pantheon. However, the fertility cults of the pre-Aryan civilizations, in particular the worship of a Mother Goddess and the worship of the phallus (*lingam*) were continued into Aryan post-Vedic culture and re-appeared in Hindu form as the Goddess Mataji-Santoshi Ma-Parvati-Durga-Kali,[5] the God Shiva-Shankar and the God Ganesh-Ganpati. In addition to the *Vedas*, a number of other collections, legends, codes of conduct and "legal" texts are important in Hinduism.

The *Upanishads* consist of about 150 collections of extensive metaphysical and philosophical speculations composed probably from 700 BC onwards. They stress the idea of a Universal, an Absolute, an Infinite, an indescribable, called *Brahman*, that is co-extensive with, or pervades everything in the Universe of which other Gods and Goddesses are *maya* (illusion, aspect) to assist the "non-ego self" human soul (*Atman*) to comprehend the Universal and Infinite with which it is (to be) united. The *Upanishads* and the *Rig Veda* were important in defining subsequent "monotheistic" and ascetic Brahminic religion, and, indeed, atheistic Hinduism. The famous Hymn to Creation in the *Rig Veda*, one of the versions of "Genesis" in Hinduism, questions the idea of first cause, a prime mover and the relation between a Supreme Being and Creation:

> Who verily knows and who can here declare it, whence it was born and whence comes this Creation? The Gods are later than this world's production. Who knows then whence it first came into being? He, the first origin of this creation, whether he formed it all or did not form it. Whose eyes control this world in highest heaven, he verily knows it – or perhaps he knows it not. (*The Rig Veda* [trans. Griffith 1896]: 633–4).

The *Brihadaranyaka, Isa, Mundaka* (in which *Brahman* is everything and "no-thing") and especially *Chandogya Upanishads* have also been interpreted as atheistic because of their stress on the subjective self ("Aum", one of the meanings of which is "I am"). However, and importantly, these texts produce a common metaphysical structure that can create or disavow an identity between the Infinite substance, "not that that is not, nor that that is", "not void nor non-void", that exists outside reason, and the (in)finite, terrifying and blissful internal dissolution experienced in mystical apprehension. Both epistemic avowal and disavowal of this identity were important for the subsequent development of Hinduisms. The famous identity, *tat tvam asi* ("thou art that") explained in the *Chandogya Upanishad* (and in a different way in the *Katha Upanishad*) between *Atman* and *Brahman* captures in essence many of the epistemic complexities that arose in the subsequent development of Hinduism, including monotheism and polytheism, speculative-metaphysical and devotional Hinduisms. Numerous Vedantist (post-Vedic) schools provided various interpretations of *Upanishad* metaphysics. The most influential, the diverse *advaita Vedanta* (non-dualist post-Vedic) schools, variously grappled with the problems of what is *Brahman*? What is *Atman*? What is the concrete world? What is God? What is one's relation to God? What is real and what is illusory? How are souls different from each other or from Brahman, if at all? And so forth. They attempted to relate these questions to various systems of good conduct and action.

The metaphysical resources of the *Vedas* and *Upanishads* and their subsequent interpretations could lead to the same religious "decentreing of the subject" encountered earlier, either decentred because it assumed an identity with God, or decentred because it assumed a particular but separated relation between itself and the God it could act for. However, the *Vedas* and the *Upanishads* could also lead to a speculative critique of exactly these kinds of formulations. Perhaps most importantly they institute a tension between essentialism and annihilation of essence. Hindu nationalism discursively appropriates all the texts of Hinduism as its own, with the claim that its ideology is the logical culmination of all Hindu philosophy and tradition. The *Vedas, Upanishads* and *Bhagavad Gita* are extremely important semiotic markers for the new Hindu nationalism which claims them for its historical emergence. This semiotic, rather than hermeneutic, relation to the sacred texts in neofoundational movements was discussed earlier. Hindu nationalism virtually entirely ignores the speculative, transcendental and metaphysical epistemologies that are definitive of the texts it has symbolically appropriated and that can indeed radically disappoint its own ideologies of purity, certainty and Hindu identity. To be sure, *this* critique of Hindu nationalism is itself a difficult one since (ownership or interpretations of) the *Vedas* and *Upanishads* are so closely associated with official Brahminism and its own abhorrent ideologies of caste and gender purity. Moreover, it is a critique of neofoundationalism using the texts it claims as founding, a factor that is addressed in the last chapter. Conversely, Hindu nationalism uses exactly this tension between universalism and particularism, or between essentialism and anti-essentialism to legitimize its incorporation and appropriation of all Hinduisms into its discursive regime. However, it seems important to disrupt the monologically embracing claims of Hindu nationalism.

The *Brahmanas* (speculations and commentaries on the *Vedas*, the *Upanishads* and mythic history) and especially the various *Puranas* (mythic stories and legends based on the exploits of the Gods and Goddess), probably composed from the same period until AD 500, introduce or comment on a new set of Gods who were to become definitive of post-Vedic Hinduism. The epic poem, the *Mahabharata* (literally the "great land" of the descendants of a mythical King Bharata, but now appropriated in Hindu revivalism as identical with "Greater India"), is a drawn-out account of a war over land and sovereignty between two related family-clans, the Kauravas and their cousins the Pandavas. The *Mahabharata*, sometimes called the fifth *Veda*, though it is not traditionally a sacred text, was set down over a considerably long period of time but the surviving versions date from around the first half of the first millennium AD.

The *Mahabharata* contains numerous other narratives and interpolations that are incidental to the main story and are extremely important in themselves. The most significant of these is the *Bhagavad Gita* ("Song of the Lord"). It is important for its focus on ethical, moral and contingent issues that affect the individual conscience, highlighted through a rational dialogue between the God Krishna and Arjuna on the Kuru battlefield (*Kurukshetra*) over Arjuna's reluctance to fight and kill his own friends and relations, itself reflecting a powerful metaphysical and existential crisis about Being, faith, cause and necessity. Several important themes about faith and belief in Hindu cosmology emerge in these dialogues, and engage with the relation between self and the Infinite, including the infinity of cyclical time. One of these themes, constantly rehearsed in Hindu nationalist political discourse, concerns the manifest recognition of religious doubt within oneself and Krishna's response: "he who has no faith and no wisdom, and whose soul is in doubt, is lost. For neither this world, nor the world to come, nor joy is ever for the man who doubts." (The *Bhagavad Gita* 1962 [trans. Mascaro]: 64, 72)

This doubt results from ignorance and must be killed by "the sword of wisdom", one of the few verses where the metaphor of violence is used by Krishna, despite the battlefield setting. In other parts of the *Gita*, Krishna is pretty ruthless about unbelievers. These disciplinary themes have become central to the identity claims within Hindu nationalism, and in particular to their derivative conceptions of good and evil:

> There are two natures in this world: the one of heaven, and other of hell. The heavenly nature has been explained: hear now of the evil of hell. Evil men know not what should be done or what should not be done. Purity is not in their hearts, nor good conduct, nor truth. They say: "This world has no truth, no moral foundation, no God. There is no law of creation: what is the cause of birth but lust?" Firm in this belief, these men of dead souls, of truly little intelligence, undertake their work of evil: they are the enemies of this fair world, working for its destruction . . . . In the vast cycles of life and death I inexorably hurl them down to destruction: these the lowest of men, cruel and evil, whose soul is hate. (*The Bhagavad Gita* 1962 [trans. Mascaro]: 109–10; the "heaven" and "hell" translations are inaccurate and misleading)

Another major theme, again important to Hindu nationalism, concerns necessity and action when faced with a *karmic* cosmology of predestination and a God that is omnipresent and causal (though, of course, *karma* must also necessarily imply freedom of will). Why should one do anything since it is already done? Against this form of doubt, the *Gita* stresses individual responsibility, choice and, especially, the *will to action* even as one is faced with an already inscribed destiny. This particular idea of necessity and action, interpreted as the necessity of political action instead of fatalistic quietism, has become an extraordinarily important trope in contemporary Hindu nationalism, just as the need to suppress religious doubt through violence has been employed metaphorically against Hindu dissenters. Perhaps most importantly, these dialogues in the *Gita* rehearse an important tension between cyclical and linear epistemologies of temporality. Cyclical time, expressed as fatality, is written over by a linear conception of time that has a victorious ending, another emergent theme in Hindu nationalism.

The *Ramayana*, the second major Hindu epic, was set down probably in the same period by "the poet Valmiki" but was considerably revised over the centuries. It had existed as a story in numerous and diverse forms for much longer as the *Ramakatha* (the story of Rama). Rama is another highly important God in contemporary devotional Hinduism. All the above texts were written in (archaic) Sanskrit. Only the Vedic texts were sacred in tradition, whereas the two epics were not. The *Mahabharata* and the *Ramayana* were originally written as "secular" stories and poems and only much later came to have a sacred tone, primarily because of the interpretations and interpolations of subsequent writers, though both are now virtually universally referred to as holy books.

The "*Ramayana* of Valmiki" itself is a text that has been considerably altered over time so that it is not clear what the "original" text or indeed "original" story was; it is one of literally thousands of written texts that tell the story of Rama in India and South-East Asia. However, it, and Goswami Tulsidas' explicitly religious seventeenth-century devotional Hindi retelling, the *Rama-charitamanas*, now constitute the most privileged Rama texts in northern and central Indian Hinduism. These Rama texts are central to the analytical political claims, political symbols, utopias and even the policies and election manifestos of contemporary Hindu nationalism. Valmiki tells the story of Rama, a noble known for his wisdom, humility and compassion. He is a perfect being. In no uncertain terms, Rama is the source of emulation for Hindu manhood. Rama is the devoted son of King Dhasaratha of Oudh (interpreted as "Ayodhya"). The latter has decided that Rama will be his successor. However, the King's youngest queen, Kaikeyi, wants her son Bharata (cf. Bharatmata or "Mother India") to be ruler. Reclaiming a favour owed by the King to her for saving his life during battle, she demands that Rama be exiled for 14 years and that Bharata be crowned in his place. Rama accepts his father's obligations and goes off into the forest with Sita, his devoted wife, and Lakshman, his half-brother. Bharata, on hearing of his mother's various manoeuvres, tries to persuade Rama to return but he refuses. Bharata pledges to serve only in function until Rama's return. In exile, the three have several adventures. In one, a demoness tries to win over Rama's love, but is rejected. She tries to eat Sita in return but Lakshman injures her. She tells her brother, Ravana, the ruler of Lanka (interpreted as "Sri Lanka"), who is enthralled by the descriptions of Sita's beauty. He manages to lure Rama and Lakshman away and flees with Sita to Lanka. While searching for Sita, Rama becomes embroiled in various other political affairs during which he meets Hanuman, the leader of the monkey kingdom. Hearing that Sita is in Lanka, Hanuman goes there and assesses Ravana's kingdom. He sets alight the walled city of Lanka and returns to Rama. The monkey tribe build a bridge across the ocean to Lanka and a huge, bloody and violent war ensues. Finally, Rama kills Ravana. The latter's brother, who aided Rama during the war, is installed as king of Lanka. Rama returns victorious to Oudh where he rules over a land of peace and harmony. This is the utopian period of *Ramrajya* or "Rama's Rule". *Ramrajya* also constitutes the unelaborated utopia of contemporary Hindu nationalism. (Gandhi also used the term Ramrajya to describe the state of utopia that India could achieve after the successful movement of national liberation from British colonialism.) Sita undergoes an ordeal by fire – she becomes a *sati* – to prove her chastity while in captivity, but Rama still refuses to accept her and she is banished. She, now pregnant, sets off to live with the sage Valmiki, the "author" of the *Ramayana*. She gives birth to twin sons and is finally consumed by the earth. Rama, in grief, ascends to heaven.

This is the nominal plot of the "Valmiki *Ramayana*" and its themes for the current shape of Hindu nationalism are highly important: perfect God-figure and Goddess-figure models that are to be emulated, "natural justice", duty, service and patriotism, a warrior (*kshatriya*) world-view, a powerful demon-other, the necessity of unexpected alliances within the "nation" to defeat the demon, the representation of the demon's assault on the nation as an assault on Hindu womanhood, Hindu women as chaste, pure and devoted figures, a massive war of national liberation (the theme of war is central to both the major Hindu epics), national victory and the installation of a utopia. This utopia is explicitly rehearsed in Hindu nationalism. For example, the Bharatiya Janata Party's manifesto for the mid-term elections to the Lok Sabha in 1991 is entitled *Towards Ram Rajya*, which in this context has the meaning Rama's *government* (Bharatiya Janata Party 1991).

However, as Romila Thapar and A. K. Ramanujan have shown, there are numerous popular, but very different versions of the Rama story, some of which often use "Valmiki's text" as a symbolic marker for their tellings (Thapar 1991, Ramanujan 1991). In other texts, it is Ravana who is the noble, the good and the holy and Rama who is vengeful. In other tellings or refabulations, it is Sita who goes to war after Rama has failed, and only she has the courage and strength to defeat Ravana's numerous demonic forms. In others again, Rama is portrayed as of poor character, obsessive and jealous. In yet others, Sita falls in love with, or is seduced by Ravana (or Lakshman) and dislikes Rama. Indeed, several tellings of the story focus on Sita's major role and Rama is relegated to the background. In one telling, the story explores male "womb envy": Ravana becomes pregnant and gives birth to Sita, his daughter. In another wonderful example of intertextuality highlighted by A. K. Ramanujan, Rama refuses to allow Sita to join him in exile. Her retort, which convinces him, is "Countless *Ramayanas* have been composed before this. Do you know of one where Sita doesn't go with Rama to the forest?" (Ramanujan 1993: 33). Similarly, numerous South East Asian traditions have their own local Rama stories and there are many Buddhist and Jaina "versions". These different contents and changing functions of "the story" represent the huge diversity of the Rama story-telling tradition in South and South East Asia. Romila Thapar has argued that many of these stories are political retellings, often Jaina or Buddhist critiques of Hinduism, or regional or caste critiques through which the Rama stories fulfilled social and political as well as cultural functions (Thapar 1991: 150–3). The pre-eminent place of the Valmiki and Tulsi tellings in contemporary Hindu nationalism, including their massive televised rendering, thus apparently reflect another political process. The other Rama tellings, and the diverse polyphonic, multitextual and *cultural*, rather than religious, Rama tradition is quashed.

Hinduism, in particular the caste system, the power of *brahmins*, the authority of the *Vedas* and even the belief in a Supreme Being, was powerfully threatened by Buddhism and Jainism. Buddhism became hegemonic and widespread in "India" and is typically interpreted as a "secular" state "religion" under the emperor Asoka (third century BC). However, it gradually declined in its power within India and was symbolically "reincorporated" into Hinduism, despite its oppositional doctrines. Indeed, "Hinduism" as a more "unified doctrine" probably owed its formation to the threat of atheistic, casteless Buddhism and its sects. At this stage in post-Vedic Hinduism, the principal Gods and Goddesses and its popular cosmology were defined. The main Gods were: Brahma, the "Creator" (not the same as *Brahman*); Vishnu, the "Preserver", a frequent visitor to Earth and best known for his incarnations (*avataras*) as Rama and Krishna; and Shiva, the "Destroyer", but also a creative force, friendly and terrifying, the basis for *lingam* (phallus) worship. These principal Gods, none of whom were exactly the original nature Gods of the *Vedas*, formed Hinduism's trinity (*trimurti*). Their respective consorts, Saraswati and especially Lakshmi and Durga-Kali were the main Goddesses, though Shiva was also worshipped as an androgynous figure. Vishnu and Shiva were the basis of two of the three main Hindu metacults, the Vaishnavites and the Shaivites, each of which believes in the primacy of its main deity. There is apparently no major devotional cult around Brahma, through worship of Brahma is incorporated in numerous other cults. The third major cult is the *Shakta* (literally "power", "energy") movement, which is based entirely on the worship and veneration of female deities, especially Uma-Durga-Kali.

Importantly, these female deities have very different personalities to the passive, devoted, chaste Sita figure of Valmiki's *Ramayana* and, especially, of the Tulsi seventeenth-century *Ramacharitamanas*. They are always powerful, energetic figures who may be benevolent or vengeful, creative or destructive, but still have to be respected and worshipped. The Uma-Durga-Kali mythologies are, in no uncertain terms, explicit about female supremacy over men, and women's superior powers, energies and abilities. Kali is usually depicted as a terrifying figure with a long black tongue, wearing a trophy necklace of men's heads, her trident stabbing a prone male demon while her other weapons fly about her. In one typical depiction, she is also shown stomping violently on her husband Shiva's dead body. Shiva, "the Destroyer", does not just happen to be one of the three most powerful Gods in Hindu mythology, but also represents the phallus (*lingam*). Kali mistakenly killed him during a violent rage while fighting a huge army of demons, which only she could defeat, after all the male Gods had given up in despair. The Durga-Kali deity has acquired an extremely important and unexpected resonance in Hindu nationalism. Sita is often erased or absent in Hindu nationalist political discourse, even though she is Rama's wife, and Durga (literally "impenetrable", "powerful") is deployed instead as the model for women's participation in "national revival" and political mobilization. One dominant representation of Hindu womanhood in BJP discourse is that of *Nari Shakti* ("Womanpower"). These powerful constructions are an embedded and fundamental aspect of *sangh parivar* activism. For example, the proto-fascistic young women's wing of the VHP is called the Durga Vahini (devotee-army, or "the seat of Durga".) In some important respects Hindu-leaning Indian feminism has not simply been undercut by these appropriations but has sided unambiguously with them. We shall return to this theme in the next chapter.

In the northern Indian Vaishnava traditions, the God Vishnu took ten forms (*avataras*), including Ramachandra (of the *Ramayana* tales), Krishna and the Buddha. He will finally appear as the millennial Kalkin, Vishnu on a white horse, who will come to destroy the demons and evil humans when the history of the world ends. Hindu cosmologies defined History as mythical, cyclical time based on four *yugas* (epochs): the *krita*, *treta*, *dvapara* and *kali yugas*, lasting 4,800, 3,600, 2,400 and 1,200 god-years respectively, with each god-year being 360 human years. The four *yugas* constitute one Great Interval. Seventy-one of these constitute one-fourteenth of the period of the *kalpa*, the largest unit of cyclical time. We are in the seventh period of this *kalpa*, each of which lasts some 4,320 million years (Thapar [1966] 1990). Each *yuga* represents a descent from a perfect state of human and Godly existence, peace and love to one of increasing evil, degeneration and chaos. The *kaliyuga* is, in most non-*Shakta* cults, the most evil, chaotic and morally retrograde period and (naturally) we are now in it and will continue to degenerate for several millennia until Vishnu arrives as Kalkin.

It is important to note here that in the "Valmiki" story, the God Rama was born in Oudh and lived in mythic time during the *treta yuga*. This period cannot be historically dated but can be "referring" to a "time" many thousand years before 3102 BC (one traditional dating for the start of the *kaliyuga*, or the *Mahabharata* war, though it is also thought that the latter occurred c800–900 BC. Kosambi ([1964] 1992: 91) suggests c850 BC). Indeed, in some mythologies it could refer to the mythic time of about two and a half million years ago. Panikkar also argues that Oudh was a fictional name that cannot have any bearing on contemporary Ayodhya, which had no significant settlement over the period when the *Ramayana* was composed (Panikkar 1991: 25). If Valmiki was referring to any place, it was probably Saketa, a Buddhist pilgrim town (Panikkar, 1991: 25; see also Kosambi [1964] 1992: 122; Chakrabarti 1995: 193–4).

Gyanendra Pandey has highlighted how, in Hindu nationalism, a fairly typical "dating" for Rama's birth "at Ayodhya" in the latter part of the *treta yuga* is around 900,000 years ago (Pandey 1995: 373). Rama's historical personality is not only unestablished but it is unclear whether it can ever be established. It is exactly this mythical absurdity that was the basis of the apparently "historical" dispute over the Babri masjid in contemporary Ayodhya which unleashed a ferocious wave of communal violence across India, Pakistan and Bangladesh and impacted considerably on British South Asian communities. An extremely important set of themes around temporality emerge here and have been central to Hindu nationalist political epistemologies (cf. Pandey 1995). Perhaps most important is the legitimacy of mythic temporality and the validity and necessity of nebulous or obscure temporalities for contemporary political discourse. Instructively, "time" can be vague (Rama's birth in the *treta yuga*) but "space" is certain (Rama's birthplace, the Babri masjid in contemporary Ayodhya, a town in the state of Uttar Pradesh in northern India). It is also unsurprising that the political appeal to mythic history and mythic time should quite rapidly drift into a highly selective obsession with archaeology and to some extent anthropology (see, for example, Goel 1991). Just as important is the fixation on monument, that supreme signifier of civilizational methodology. Importantly, Hindu nationalist contributions disavow methodologies for the study of "deep time". (As Hindu nationalism claims to be scientific, one would have thought that articulating 900,000 years of the Earth's history would imply an engagement with, at the very least, geology, palaeontology and natural selection, rather than the temporally limited and selective methodological fixation on the archaeology and history of human monuments and the anthropology of human rituals and beliefs.) However, there is a novel temporality in this reconstructive Hindu nationalism that often does not appear in Hindu cosmology. This is the idea of *linear* and monologic temporality (rather than cyclical time) with a clear mythology of origin, a subsequent degradation, the present dystopian moment of renewal and identity-formation and a future state of completed utopia. This also reflects a distinctive feature of social movements in which a legislative history of their present has to be manufactured.

Aside from Vedic texts, the *Upanishads* and the epics, it is important to acknowledge the immense and continuing impact of (broadly speaking) "legal" texts that include moral and ethical codes, jurisprudence, guidance on and prescriptions for caste ritual, worship, relations between castes, purity and pollution, legislative anthropologies for kinship, exogamous group relations, marriage, family, gender and sexuality, astrologies, "economics", relations with rulers, kings, emperors, warriors, *brahmins* or *sadhus* ("priests"), the polity and so forth. Orthodox Hindu sects would have founding moral and ethical codes either as text or as orally transmitted injunctions about some or all of these areas and new ones have been created throughout the history of Hinduisms. One founding legal, moral and ethical code, which also provides another traditional version of Hinduism's "Genesis", is the *Manusmriti* or the *Manu Dharmashastra* ("The Laws of Manu"). The laws are sacred and in the lineage of *smriti* ("tradition"), but are compatible with the laws prescribed in the *Vedas* (*sruti*, "revelation", or "that which was heard"). These are the two most important sources for sacred law, but The Laws of Manu also allow custom ("the customs of virtuous men") as well as "one's own pleasure" as other means of defining the sacred law. In the *Manusmriti*, the story is told of the first Manu, the primeval "self-existent" (*svayambhuva*) born from Brahma, that creates time, the universe, the world, its creatures and plants. Svayambhuva Manu (who is not gendered but is universally referred to as "man") is one of seven Manus or patriarchs, each ruling a different epoch and is the prime law-giver and the founder of the moral and social order of humankind (the *Puranas* define 14 Manus, with their various seers or *rishis*).

The Laws of Manu outline in detail rites, rituals and laws for caste, food, impurity, the duties of women, the duties of husband and wife, the obligations of the King, and extensive rules for "civil and criminal" procedures, including judicial procedure, disputes over money, land or "defamation", theft, violence, adultery, laws of inheritance, and even gambling and betting. It defines the laws for caste boundary or the four *varnas*, the status of "intermediate castes" and rules around caste mixing. The Laws of Manu are important for providing the foundation or inspiration for numerous sect and caste *dharmashastras* (law books) which today govern the lives of Hindus and those deemed to be outside the caste system. Importantly, the Laws of Manu also highlight the legal inflection of *dharma*. The concept of *dharma* has a number of composite meanings that include "religion", "way of life", "the right path", but, and just as importantly, law and jurisprudence.

The latter aspects are extremely important for the more ecclesiastical tendencies in Hindu nationalism, and especially the activities of the Vishwa Hindu Parishad, and they dovetail neatly into the ideas of *dharma* that exist in Hindu communities. Of similar importance to Hindu nationalism are the religious-legal texts that deal specifically with the polity. Hinduism's "The Prince", the *Arthashastra*, was "written" by Chanakya, the mythical *sadhu*-hero of epic Hindu battles, whose story was recounted in a Doordarshan TV serialization of the same name which was shown weekly in the UK on BBC television. Tapan Basu et al. have highlighted the importance of the *Arthashastra* for the VHP and for the idea of Hindu *Rashtra*. They argue that the *Arthashastra* "recommends a police state under a single despotic head" (Basu et al. 1993: 66) and "describes a highly organised surveillance system [with] complete monarchical and bureaucratic controls and monopolies", while the Laws of Manu advise "how best to rule over the subordinate spheres of shudras and women" (ibid: 78). Chanakya's or Kautilya's *Arthashastra* (Kautilya is, in tradition, identified as the same personality as Chanakya) provides or can be interpreted to provide, extensive regulatory "legislature" or rules (*niti*) on physical torture and punishment (*danda*), justice, the regulation of private and civil affairs and the treatment and duties of women. It can also provide organicist theoretical blueprints for public and economic administration, the relation between state and civil society, legal principles and indeed a *dharmic* theocracy. Kautilya has also, rather curiously, given his injunctions about women, been interpreted as a "feminist" (see Kumar 1989: 57–62; *The Rajanitisastra of Chanakya* 1983). The Laws of Manu can also be interpreted as providing a "blueprint" for the polity. It is a moot point, and an area for further oppositional research and discussion, whether Hindu nationalism has the capacity to develop a comprehensive theory of theocratic state and civil society based on invented traditions of political government and moral and ethical frameworks for civil society derived from the antiquated legal-*dharmic* texts of Hinduism.

Bhakti Hinduisms

A much later development, from about the tenth century AD, was the rise of a new set of movements – the *bhakti* ("devotional") movements – that commenced outside formal Brahminic Hinduism, initially in south India, and reached their intellectual and political height in the north around the seventeenth century. *Bhakti* now utterly dominates modern and popular Hinduism, the form in which Hinduism is manifest in the lives of most Indians and the form in which Hinduism is most widely known outside India. This form of Hinduism is also central to the way contemporary revivalist organizations have mobilized political support through the use of both mass print and electronic communications. The *bhakti* or devotional movement is manifested as the popular joyful, loving and ecstatic worship of particular Gods and Goddesses, usually as *murtis* (idols) and images, and manifested in chanting of regional vernacular (not Sanskrit) hymns, as well as dancing, songs, praise and prayer. It was a heterodox movement which, while subsequently incorporated into "mainstream" Hinduism, seriously challenged the power of the *brahmins*, in particular their role as guardians and interpreters of knowledge, but also: a rejection of the authority of the *Vedas*; a refusal to accept the superiority of the Sanskrit language; a rejection of the caste system; of child marriage and women's inferior position; a rejection of the belief in transmigration and the Brahminic sanctions against the remarriage of widows. It powerfully displaced the philosophical and ascetic concerns of earlier Brahminic Hinduism and rejected the morality in much Brahminic Hinduism against "idol worshipping". Brahminic Hinduism existed alongside these forms of popular Hinduism and *bhakti* considerably influenced Brahminism itself, which also became devotional. However, the *bhakti* movement involved a deliberate stress on devotion and direct, unmediated individual access to God without having to undertake the "life-long" endeavour of yoga that was a central aspect of many forms of Brahminism. One could have direct access to one's personal God or Goddess without having to go through the long process of Vedic learning, renunciation and philosophical speculation that was reserved for, and only appropriate to, the men of the "twice-born castes" of Aryan legend. The *bhakti* movement was (and is) especially important for its appeal to women (see Mullatti 1989 for a contemporary account).

The *bhakti* movement started powerfully in Tamil south India in the twelfth century, where it often took the form of Shiva cult worship and reached its peak in the north during the seventeenth century. This popular renewal of Hinduism in the south arose during the same period that a different movement was manifesting in the north: Islam. Extensive Arab trading contact with India goes back to antiquity (as does the presence of Arab communities in India), and this continued into the Islamic period. However, from the tenth century AD, organized, initially ferocious invasions of Turks and Afghans began in northern India. It is necessary to note that the idea of an "India" did not exist, as it does today, at that time. By the middle of the fourteenth century, the (Turkish) Muslim "sultanate" of Delhi controlled parts of north India but was also threatened by Hindu kingdoms, in particular by the Rajput states. Another different movement started when the Afghan Mughal emperor of Kabul, Babar, invaded India in 1525–6, challenged the power of existing Muslim and Hindu rule in parts of northern India and established the Mughal dynasty. The Babri masjid at Ayodhya was built in 1528 in his honour. Mughal rule continued in various authoritarian, tolerant, liberal, syncretic and disintegrating forms until the British colonized and ruled India.

In this period, from the thirteenth to the eighteenth century, *bhakti* flourished in north and central India. Paradoxically, Hinduism became strengthened, widespread, devotional and popular during the period of Mughal rule. This is interpreted in Hindu nationalism as simply a resistance to Mughal rule. However, while there were *bhakti*-influenced movements against the Mughals, *bhakti* was primarily a movement against Vedic Hinduism and, initially, the caste power of *brahmins*. Indeed, and despite the revulsion this suggestion causes for Hindu nationalists, *bhakti* bears comparison with the Islamic *sufi* tradition with which it often intermingled. The two considerably influenced each other and gave rise to various hybrid formations, especially within the medieval mystical tradition in Hinduism. However, *bhakti* has now been associated by Hindu nationalists solely with resistance to the Mughals. In the second part of the seventeenth century, Shivaji, a religious *bhakti* Maratha, fought against Mughal rule and has now become a contemporary Hindu hero, and a considerable source of ideological inspiration for the RSS and the Shiv Sena (Army of Shivaji). Kabir (a Muslim by birth and follower of Ramanand, a Vaishnavite *bhakti* leader) and Nanak (another follower of Kabir and Ramanand) were highly influential *"bhakti"* leaders in the fifteenth and sixteenth centuries and rejected both Islam and Hinduism. Nanak was the founder and first guru of the Sikh faith. His and Kabir's, as well as the teachings of other Muslim and Hindu "saints" were collected by Arjun (1563-1606) into what became the sacred book of the Sikh faith (the *Adi Granth*). However, Arjun's execution by Muslim authorities transformed Sikhism into a martial religion, hostile to Islam and indifferent to Hinduism. Subsequent Sikhism, and its consolidation by Guru Gobind Singh, maintained varying hostilities to Islam but, since it was opposed to caste, it was not incorporated into Hinduism as other *bhakti* cults were. That process is apparently happening now. Some strands of revivalist Hinduism have chosen to re-interpret the history of the Sikh religion as monologically one of war and resistance to Muslim rule, even though some of its founders were Muslims.[6]

In north and central India, the *bhakti* cults in this period manifested themselves almost exclusively as Vaishnavite (worshippers of Vishnu *avataras*). The Vishnu incarnations as Krishna or Rama were the most important. There are a huge number of vernacular Krishna legends and stories and Krishna is an extremely popular God throughout India. However, it was the translation and conservative recomposition from Sanskrit into Hindi of the *"Ramayana* of Valmiki" by Tulsidas in the seventeenth century that propelled the stolid Rama and the ever pure and virtuous Sita into a major focus of popular devotional activity and worship. The older Rama cults became widespread in northern India from the mid-eighteenth century (as the Ramanandi cults) and reached their height in the mid-nineteenth century. The importance, again, of the 1850s should be noted, as should the transformation of Rama from his status as cultural story-figure to his becoming a God for a major religious devotional cult. While many of the *Ramakatha* and *Ramabhakti* traditions are extremely old, the *Ramabhakti* cults that today are being propagated as the ancient essential core of Hindu identity became politically important in the last century during the period of British colonial rule.

The relation between Islam and Hinduism in India over the period of Mughal rule was extremely complex. In contemporary Hindu nationalism, Mughal rule is seen exclusively as a period of *religious* domination, oppression and genocide of Hindus in which their faith was ridiculed and their religious institutions looted and destroyed. Consequently, these "Hindu" religious sites have to be "reclaimed" and the Muslim ones destroyed. There are variously 2,000–3,000 Mughal buildings, including the Taj Mahal, that Hindu nationalists want to destroy. Hindu nationalism, in advancing these claims, combines the most selective archaeological and historical facts with Hindu mythology.[7] Consequently, Hindu revivalism's greatest intellectual adversaries in India are realist history, archaeology and anthropology. The evidence of the latter is that Mughal rule was primarily determined by political and economic factors and not simply religious conquest and conversion (Gopal 1991: 179–82). The destruction of many temples by Mughal rulers was linked to economic factors (the temples had wealth) and political contingencies (the assertion of political power over kingdoms and princely states) rather than simply religious injunctions (*jihad* against infidel polytheism, idol worship, deification and human representation). Muslim rulers were as benevolent towards and tolerant of other religions as they were destructive and authoritarian. The Mughal emperor, Akbar, was considered one of the most benevolent and "secular" of any major rulers India ever had prior to Independence and was opposed to Islamic and Hindu orthodoxy. He courted all religious traditions in an attempt to unite them and synthesize a new religion, but failed because of Muslim orthodox intransigence. Instead, he invented his own syncretic religious philosophy (*din-i-ilahi*), which earned him hatred from Muslim orthodoxy.

Babar, the first Mughal emperor, was also considered a tolerant Mughal ruler. It is unlikely that he ever visited Ayodhya, let alone destroyed a Hindu temple. The only event of religious destruction associated with him was the demolishing of Jaina statues depicting nudity (Panikkar 1991: 28). Babar encouraged Hindu worship and afforded land and grants to enable the building of Hindu temples. It was also economically untenable for Mughal rulers to convert many Hindus to Islam since the gross tax collected for the

175

administration, which Muslims were exempt from paying, would vanish, as would the economic rationale for rule. Mir Baqi, Babar's general, did build the Ayodhya mosque in honour of Babar, but, had this been done at a specially sacred Hindu site, in particular the alleged birthplace of a major Hindu God, this would have been recorded by Mir Baqi as an important religious victory (since *he* was very religious). Babar kept extensive records of his exploits (the *Baburnama*). These do not mention Ayodhya as particularly important, nor do they mention that a masjid was built on Rama's birthplace. The pages of the *Baburnama* that cover the exact period when the masjid was built are missing. However, no Mughal, Persian, Turkish, Chinese, Buddhist or Jaina document mentions any of these factors. Similarly, Hindus, especially *Ramabhaktis*, would have recorded that a temple at the birthplace of their God was destroyed and a mosque built there. But no known Hindu document mentions this.

However, K. N. Panikkar has highlighted a profoundly important event that did occur in 1855 in Ayodhya and has been interpreted as the mythical foundation for the current dispute (see Panikkar 1991: 31–3; the following relies heavily on his discussion). This event emphasizes the complicated way that British colonial discourse around Hindu–Muslim communalism and British colonial texts have acquired a phenomenal authority in contemporary Hindu nationalism. In that year, Muslims protested that the Hanumangarhi, a Hindu temple to Rama's ally, the monkey-God Hanuman, *was built on the site of an earlier mosque*. There was considerable Hindu–Muslim armed conflict over this and Muslims tried to oust Hindus from the Hanumangarhi temple. Hindus violently retaliated, drove the Muslims back to the Babri masjid, defeated them and occupied the mosque. According to Panikkar, they could have easily taken over the Babri masjid if it was believed at that time that it was the site of Rama's birthplace, but instead retreated immediately to the Hanumangarhi. This conflict took place under the political conditions of highly liberal Shi'a rule in Avadh. The Nawab, having broken from the Mughal empire, consolidated his rule by close alliance with Hindu landlords and soldiers and provided for the development of Hindu places of worship. Partly because of liberal Muslim rule, Ayodhya emerged as an important centre for Rama worship by the middle of the nineteenth century. Rama devotion was not centred on the Babri masjid, over which no Hindu claims were made, but on Hanu-mangarhi. It was this that earned the enmity of orthodox and Sunni Muslims who had tried to "retake" the Hanumangarhi.

This episode has been misinterpreted in British historical documents as a dispute over the Babri masjid and Ramjanmabhoomi ("Rama's birthplace"), which, it appears, "were not linked at all in local Hindu consciousness in 1855". There is a complex subsequent relationship between British documentation, local rumours that started to build up around the British view and the memory of the conflict over Hanumangarhi. After the 1857 War of Liberation or "Mutiny", the *mahant* (priest) of Hanumangarhi took over part of the Babri masjid compound and constructed a platform (*chabutra*) for Rama worship. This was a political "checkmate" by Hindus for the Muslim claims over Hanumangarhi. The British reacted by constructing a fence to separate the mosque and the compound, one area for Hindu and the other for Muslim worship. The site was subject to an extended period of legal and political dispute, government intervention and closure, and was finally destroyed in 1992. But it was apparently from 1857 onwards that Babri masjid was associated with Ramjanmabhoomi, and it was from this point onwards that actual history, rumour, myth and irrevocable difference condense, and eventually become symbols for far-right Hindu revivalism.

CHAPTER 6

The land, the blood and the passion: the Hindu far-right

... collective auto-destruction in a very concrete form is one of the ways in which the native's muscular tension is set free. All these patterns of conduct are those of the death-reflex when faced with danger, a suicidal behaviour that proves to the settler that these men are not reasonable human beings. In the same way the native manages to bypass the settler. A belief in fatality removes all blame from the oppressor; the cause of misfortune or poverty is attributed to God; He is fate .... Meanwhile, however, life goes on, and the native will strengthen the inhibitions that contain his aggressiveness by drawing on the terrifying myths that are so frequently found in underdeveloped communities. These are maleficent spirits that intervene every time a step is taken in the wrong direction, leapord-men, serpent-men, six-legged dogs, zombies – a whole series of tiny animals or giants that create around the native a world of prohibitions, of barriers and of inhibitions far more terrifying than the world of the settler. This magical superstructure that permeates native society fulfils certain well-defined functions in the dynamism of the libido.
(Frantz Fanon, *The wretched of the earth*, [1967] 1982: 42–3.)

Every man has to make peace with his country, not the country of his passport, not the country where he has his home, but the country where he has his soul .... This is the real definition of nation, a place where you have your soul.

179

Why did a nation of eight hundred million people sit glued to its TV sets every Sunday morning for four years? Because the Ramayana and the Mahabharata are *our* stories, the Pandavas and the Kauravas are *our* elders, mythical men and women from whom we are descended and from whom we derive our precious nationhood . . . . This is the stuff we Hindus are made of, men who fight for their principles and for their Dharma. And we feel proud that such men and women were born in our land, the same land which gave birth to us five millennia later. (Jay Dubashi, *The road to Ayodhya*, 1992: 35–6)

Introduction

The discussions of the previous chapter are explicitly linked below to the rise of contemporary far right-wing Hindu revival. Exploring this also requires a brief look at intellectual currents that accompanied the first surge of Hindu revivalism in the second half of the nineteenth century and the second wave of Hindu revival during the period prior to decolonization. Hinduism, Islam and Indian nationalism in the mid-nineteenth century laid some foundations for resistance to British colonialism and the *swadeshi* (self-rule) movement, which grew in power from the turn of this century and eventually resulted in Indian Independence and the creation of (East and West) Pakistan. There is considerable debate on precisely the role and impact of religion (either Hinduism or Islam) in the Indian liberation movement. This complex historical debate is appropriated and transformed by Hindu nationalist claims that Hinduism was not only the guiding force for the liberation movement but was subsequently betrayed by the Westernized "pseudosecular" nation-state of Nehru and Gandhi. Indeed, this can be compared with the attitude of the Muslim Brotherhood in Egypt, formed in the 1920s, which opposed Nasserite Arab nationalism for similar reasons. Consequently, Hindu nationalism views itself as "completing" what the secular liberation movement under Gandhi and Nehru "failed" to fulfil: a *Hindu Rashtra* (Hindu nationalism and nation-state formation).

The "Hindu Renaissance"

The rise of Hindu-based, as well as secular Indian nationalism in the
second part of the last century is more closely associated with
movements, riots, "mutinies", insurrections and war against the
British than the post-Gandhi post-Nehru secular and multicultural
reading of that history might indicate. This is a highly sensitive area,
and is precisely at the core of the historical revisionism being
undertaken in contemporary Hindu nationalism which claims that
the insurrections against the British were part of a linear narrative
of Hindu rebellion against all foreign invaders, starting with the
Turkish-Afghan Muslims, the Mughals and then the British. However, while the two are not at all congruent and it is very important
to keep this distance, the rise of nineteenth-century Indian nationalism was integrally also the rise of the first wave of Hindu
revivalism, an intellectual and political project that aimed to
recreate Hinduism in relation to nationhood, social formation and
modernity. In this movement, it is difficult to separate out the
mainly "religious" strands from the mainly "nationalist" ones and
the ostensibly secular ones. This intellectual movement was itself
composed of diverse and often politically opposed reformative
strands within Hinduism, all of which negotiated with conceptions
of reason, rationality and individual rights that were definitive of
the Enlightenment but were also to be found in the Vedic or post-
Vedic texts of Hinduism itself.

Liberal modernists like Ram Mohan Roy (1772–1833) and his
Brahmo Samaj organization (founded in 1828) aimed to modernize
Hinduism thoroughly to enable it to articulate a modern social and
political environment in which obscurantism and backward traditional practices (such as *sati* murders, caste, untouchability, idolatry, child brides and sanctions against widow remarriage) had to be
abandoned. Importantly for the Samaj, the modernization of
Hinduism could rely on what was already in Hinduism, in particular the forms of reason, rationality and "enlightenment" that were
already there in the *Upanishads* and could be syncretically combined with a "Christian" ethical basis.[1] The Arya Samaj ("Aryan
Society"), founded in 1875 by Swami Dayananda, a Gujerati
brahmin, rejected this approach and insisted on a return to the
Vedas themselves. It was a fundamentalist movement which stressed
the self-evident sacred truth of the *Vedas*. The Aryas, like the

Brahmo Samaj, rejected caste, idol worship, child marriage and the isolation of widows. They claimed that these were later distortions of the real Hindu faith enshrined in the Vedic writings and fire rituals of the original Aryans. Dayananda himself claimed a revelatory mantle in which only he had the power to interpret the *Vedas*. The Arya Samaj was extremely popular among Hindus in the Punjab and was highly dogmatic, communalist and violent in its political agitations against Muslims and Christians in northern India (Pandey 1992: 164). Other Hindu revivalists of this period included Ramakrishna Paramhansa, whose devotee Swami Vivekananda founded the international Ramakrishna Mission, and Aurobindo Ghose, a fiercely Hindu nationalist activist who later became a spiritual teacher. (Vivekananda, who would have been highly unlikely to support contemporary Hindu nationalism, is still a considerably important symbolic figure for it.) This strong urge to a revived Hinduism ("the Hindu awakening") was explicitly connected with the removal of British rule and the establishment of a nationalism informed by Hindu thought and precepts. Some of the revivalist writings from this period also sought to demonstrate the theological primacy of Hinduism, the "first" or "oldest" religion, which contained the essential truths of all other religions and philosophies. For them, Hinduism *in some form* had the capacity to create a foundation for Indian nationalism.

We should parenthetically note that revivalist Hinduism in this period also showed a need to demonstrate an essential unity between the discoveries of modern science and the "truths" and knowledge (*jnana*) in Hindu philosophy and cosmology, resulting in highly obscurantist tracts on natural science. Various *advaita Vedantist* (non-dualist post-Vedic) schools of the last century displayed a fascination with the discoveries of modern physics, especially electromagnetism and, sometimes, Newtonian conceptions of gravitation, and identified these with the indescribable cosmic energy (*Brahman*) developed in the *Upanishads* and its essential non-dualistic identity with the human soul. *The holy science*, written by Swami Yukteswar Giri in 1894, is a typical, rather fascinating encounter between a Hindu *swami* and modern human and natural scientific philosophy. Its ostensible purpose is to demonstrate an essential unity between Hinduism, natural science, political science and all religions. Giri describes how electricity and magnetism are misunderstood by modern science and outlines a theory of five electricities, based on the five human senses. (Modern science, he says dismissively, has only managed to discover one form of electricity, whereas the Hindu texts have discovered five.) He also links advances in human and natural sciences, including politics, with a new numerical revision of cyclical Hindu time. Hindu texts had already predicted the advances of modernity (Giri [1894] 1977). Many such syncretic texts used the metaphors of electromagnetism and gravitation as developed in Faraday's and Newton's discoveries (though Maxwell was, unsurprisingly, ignored). The classical formulations of Newton and Faraday had certain "commonsense" qualities of rationalism, empirical realism, determinism and functionalism. Eventually, these were to be either destroyed following the realization of the philosophical implications of quantum mechanics, or significantly remade into vastly different classical formulations in special and general relativity. However, their importance for "Hindu science" was their metaphoric or allusive amenability to "rational" and instrumentalist incorporation into religious frameworks. This factor was important for subsequent negotiations between religious Hinduism and natural science and many of these tendencies have strengthened in recent years. This aspect is looked at in the last chapter.

The revivalist organizations, with the exception of the Arya Samaj, were elite groups with little mass appeal. Their efforts were primarily intellectual attempts at reconstructing Hinduism in the face of modernity, colonialism and the West, and aimed to show that "originary" Hinduism and modernity were inherently compatible or could easily be made to be so. The liberal reformism of the Bramho Samaj, the reactionary fundamentalism of the Arya Samaj and the "Hindu Renaissance" of spiritual teachers were different *reconstructive* strands of an elite Brahminism that influenced modern Hinduism prior to Independence. (The equivalent Islamic responses in India are probably best represented by Sir Sayyid Amhad Khan and Mohammed Iqbal, "liberal modernizers", and the followers of Maududi, a "fundamentalist modernizer"). Some of these strands in modern Hinduism were carried through into the liberation movement and are best represented by the liberal-socialist secularism of Nehru on the one hand and the militant Hinduism of Tilak on the other, with perhaps Gokhale and Gandhi representing a middle ground of liberal Hinduism, the point being that the suppressed conflicts within *the modernity of Hinduism* were an unresolved part of the liberation movement itself. In important ways, some of the theoretical and philosophical foundations for what constituted secularism and multiculturalism were obscured.

During the 1920s a different movement in Hinduism started and bears close comparison with the histories of both the Jamaat-i-Islami in India and the Muslim Brotherhood in Egypt. Particularly relevant to the birth of this movement was the attempt by Gandhi in 1920-21 to win Muslims over to the non-violent non-co-operation movement against the British and to the Indian National Congress by opportunistically supporting the massive *khilafat* movement. In response to the break-up of the Turkish Ottoman empire, the *khilafat* mass movement, which was sweeping many Muslim countries, especially those of South Asia, demanded the restoration of the rule of the Caliphate. (The latter was subsequently abolished by Kemal Ataturk, and provides another interesting reading of contemporary Islamic revival in Turkey.) Gandhi's support for an essentially Muslim-religious movement was seen by various militant Hindu groups as favouring Muslim religious and separatist demands. (Jinnah and other Muslim leaders were, for various reasons, opposed to Gandhi's mobilization around the *khilafat* movement and opposed Muslim agitation around its demands. The Muslim League wanted Pakistan to be a "secular Muslim" state, not a religious one. Indeed, the idea of Pakistan was vigorously opposed by Islamic fundamentalists such as Maududi.) Gandhi's strategy of non-co-operation and his philosophy of non-violence were vigorously opposed by Hindu militant organizations as they were seen to be incapable of fighting British domination. Instead, a stress on the *kshatriya* (warrior) tradition and Hindu unity against Muslims was required both to fight the British and to defend Hindu communities against Muslim rioters, the latter now seen as an uncontrollable, violent, separatist and evangelical force. Innumerable Hindu, Muslim and Sikh paramilitary, sport-based and cultural-religious organizations were formed prior to, during, and after the period of Independence.

Savarkar: anthropogeography and the mystery of blood

The Hindu Mahasabha (Great Assembly) which was initially formed in 1916 to agitate around cow protection among other things, was reformed in the 1920s and argued for the martial Hindu tradition, violent onslaught against the British, martial offence against Muslim communities, and the forced "reconversion" of Hindus who had been converted to Islam. The Mahasabha's intellectual founder, Vinayak Damodar Savarkar is by far the most important figure in the development of contemporary Hindu nationalism. Virtually all the philosophical strands that make up current Hindu nationalism, ranging from the crudely Nazi and genocidal to the ostensibly "secular" were prefigured in Savarkar's writings.

Savarkar is regarded as one of the heroes of the Indian liberation movement ("Swatantra Veer", the "Indian Mazzini"). As a young student, he was involved in various revolutionary activities against the British in India. From the beginning of his political career he opposed the various philosophies of *ahimsa* (non-violence) that influenced the non-violent, non-co-operative direct action strategies of Gandhi. In the early 1900s, he was an important member of the Poona-based Mithra Mela, whose paper was called the *Aryan Weekly*, and was one of the founders and leaders of the secret revolutionary Abhinava Bharat Society. During his period of study in London from 1906–10 at India House, he was heavily involved in Indian intellectual and student groups, such as the Free India Society, that were preoccupied with home rule and liberation activities. This intensely formative period in London from 1906–10 is part of a distinctive political and intellectual journey made by numerous individuals from the colonies to the metropolis; it hugely influenced the leadership and intelligentsia of various anticolonial and liberation movements in Africa, Asia and the Caribbean. In England, Savarkar was arrested and imprisoned for several charges relating to seditious and anti-British activities while in Poona. He spent time in Brixton prison, during which Indian revolutionaries and members of (the then) Sinn Fein attempted to rescue him but failed. He was subsequently sentenced for two life terms and extradited to India (a further rescue attempt was made when the ship that carried him reached Marseilles, and this time he escaped for a short period but was re-arrested). He was imprisoned in the Cellular Jail on the Andaman Islands for twelve years and subsequently interned for lengthy terms in various other prisons within India until he was released in 1924 and allowed to remain in Ratnagiri (Keer 1988).

Savarkar was already well known for his history of the 1857 "Mutiny". But while in London, he was deeply preoccupied with the problem of what constitutes Hindu identity. Consequently, while imprisoned in the Andamans, he wrote the founding text for Hindu neotradition, *Hindutva – Who is a Hindu?* (hereafter *HWH*) which was first published in 1923. In *HWH*, Savarkar develops the entirely novel and modern idea of Hindutva, "Hinduness" or "the essence of being a Hindu". Against the "baseless notion" that the words "Hindu" and "Hindustan" came from "the Mohammed-hans" who used them to mean "the black man", and the "black man's land", Savarkar attempted to demonstrate the mysterious antiquity of the name "Hindu". For him, it denoted strength and vigour, "the valour of our arms, the purity of our aims, the sublimity of our souls". Importantly, Savarkar distances the idea of Hindu, and of Hindutva from "Hinduism". The identity of a Hindu is only partly captured by religion (Hinduism). Hinduism, for Savarkar, is a Western "ism", and "is only a derivative, a fraction, a part of Hindutva" (Savarkar [1923] 1989: 3). What then is Hindutva? For Savarkar, it is "one of the most comprehensive and bewilderingly synthetic concepts known to the human tongue" (Savarkar 1989: 81). Hindutva

> defies all attempts at analysis .... Hindutva is not a word but a history. Not only the spiritual or religious history of our people as at times it is mistaken to be by being confounded with the other cognate term Hinduism, but a history in full. (Ibid.: 3)

This history begins (in true Romantic fashion) with the "intrepid" Aryans, who had arrived in India, spread out to the farthest of the seven rivers (*sapta sindhus*), and had developed not only a sense of nationality and identity but had named themselves in the *Rig Veda* – the Sindu or (its equivalent for Savarkar) the Hindu – to designate "the race, the nation and the people". Indeed, he even argues that the name "Hindu" existed in India from time immemorial, prior to the Aryan arrival. However, the day that the Aryans crossed the river Sindhu (the Indus River), they ceased to belong to the people they left behind and were reborn into a new people. In the new land, the Aryans commingled with the original inhabitants and it was this mixing of the blood that gave a distinctive identity to the Hindu. However, despite this hybrid origin, Savarkar barely discusses the original inhabitants and clearly implies that it was the infusion of Aryan blood that was determining in Hindu identity. The Aryans then came to mean "all those who had been incorporated as parts integral in the nation, people who flourished on this our side of the Indus". Those outside and in opposition to "Sindhustan" were the Mlecchas "who were foreigners *nationally and racially*, but not necessarily religiously" (ibid: 33, emphasis added).

Sindhu for Savarkar also meant both river (the Indus River) and the seas (the oceans that surround India), and hence the geographical limit of nation was "from the Indus river to the oceans". This geographical conception was, according to Savarkar, declared in the sacred *Vedas*, though it is uncertain what physical geographical knowledge of the Subcontinent was actually possessed by the Aryans. The "mission" that the Hindus had undertaken of founding a nation and a country reached a geographical and political conclusion:

> when the valorous Prince of Ayodhya [Rama] made a triumphant entry in Ceylon and brought the whole land from the Himalayas to the seas under one sovereign sway. The day when the Horse of Victory returned to Ayodhya unchallenged ... that day was the real birth-day of our Hindu people. It was truly our national day: for Aryans and Anaryans [non-Aryans] knitting themselves into a people were born as a nation. (Ibid: 11–12)

According to Savarkar, the "ancient cradle name" of "*Sindhu Rashtra*" (*Hindu Rashtra* or Hindu Nation) is preferable to the mythological name *Akhand Bharat* ("Greater Bharat"), founded and ruled in an unknown period by an unknown personality, the emperor Bharat and the "House of Bharat". Savarkar argued that Sindhu (i.e. Hindu) should be used since the *Vedas* themselves use the name Sindhu to refer to "the best nation of the Aryans". Importantly, this ancient foundation of Hindu Nation was a powerful and military one. Consequently, Savarkar views the impact of Buddhist expansion as "disastrous to the national virility and even the nation existence of our race". This, he says, led to the "mealy-mouthed formulas of Ahimsa" (ibid: 18–19) that were unable to defeat the invading Huns and Shakas, the "invasions" of "Chinese Buddhists" and later the Muslims and British.

From the period when Buddhist rule declined up to the invasion of Mohammed of Ghazni, Hindus were united, one race, one people, one nation living in a land where "peace and plenty reigned". All the members of the four *varna* (caste) system and all those who rejected it (such as Sikhs) were embraced in this Hindu unity: "They are ours by blood, by race, by country, by God .... *We, Hindus, are all one and a nation because chiefly of our common blood* – 'Bharati Santati'". (ibid: 39, emphasis added)

It was this blood spirit, the spirit of the Hindu race, that fought with all its vigour against the early Muslim invasions. Those first invasions heralded the day

> ... when the conflict of life and death began. *Nothing makes Self conscious of itself so much as a conflict with non-Self.* Nothing can weld peoples into a nation and nations into a state as the pressure of a common foe. Hatred separates as well as unites. (Ibid: 42–3, emphasis added)

This extremely important and virtually archetypal formulation of Hindu identity politics obsessed Savarkar and all subsequent Hindu nationalist thinkers. Hindu identity is to be based primarily on a fundamentally antagonistic conception of alterity. In important respects virtually all the problems in identity formulations that were discussed in earlier chapters are applicable to this conception of identity. Most importantly, if identity is primarily realized through a difference from an excluded exterior, then that supplementary exterior is already in some way foundationally embedded in, and continues to haunt the centre. Similarly, if identity is formed through a difference that is foundationally antagonistic and conflictual, then the fate of that supplementary otherness from the self is already prefigured as bounded by violence and erasure.

The conflict that Hindus had to endure was, according to Savarkar, an unequal conflict when "nearly all of Asia", including Arabia, "quickly followed" by "nearly all of Europe" were in pitched battle against an isolated India: "day after day, decade after decade, century after century, the ghastly conflict continued". It was this "period" in which Hindutva grew in strength, evolved and advanced, as

... our people became intensely conscious of ourselves as Hindus and were welded into a nation to an extent unknown in our history. The whole family of peoples and races, sects and creeds that flourished from Attock to Cuttack was suddenly individualised into a single Being .... This one word, Hindutva, ran like a vital spinal chord through our whole body politic. (Ibid: 44–6)

Hindutva reached its peak in the wars of the seventeenth and eighteenth centuries against Muslim "invaders" or states, and in particular the war of Shivaji against the Mughals. This was the spirit of *Hindavi Swarajya* (Hindu Empire) and *Hindupadpadshahi* (Hindu Sovereignty).

This "historiography" of origin provides for Savarkar all the concepts essential to defining Hindutva, the "essentialness" and "beingness" of a Hindu, as well as a constitutive definition of a Hindu. Hindutva requires, first of all, a natural geography, a cherished fatherland (*pitrubhumi*) and a motherland (*matribhumi*), "a well demarcated land", that provides for internal cohesion and which, in its geographical and physical features, "vivifies into a living Being". This land, from "sea to sea" also requires an historically authentic "name" (Hindu, or Hindustan) that could by its very mention "rouse the cherished memories of the motherland as well as the loved memories of the past" (ibid: 82).

These two essentials of Hindutva are hardly adequate, however, because they imply citizenship to all residents of the land, including Muslims. Savarkar therefore introduces several further exclusionary essentials for Hindutva, of which the most striking is the anthropology of blood:

The Hindus are not merely the citizens of the Indian state because they are united [by] the bonds of the love they bear to a common motherland, but also by the bonds of a common blood. They are not only a Nation but also a race-jati. The word jati derived from the root Jan [means] a brotherhood, a race determined by a common origin, possessing a common blood. All Hindus claim to have in their veins the blood of the mighty race incorporated with and descended from the Vedic fathers, the Sindhus. [This] ancient Ganges of our blood has come down from the altitudes of the sublime Vedic heights to the plains of our modern history. (Ibid: 84–6)

The "ties of a common blood" are definitive of Savarkar's Hinduness, and the core of his idea of racial unity. Blood is co-extensive with both "race" and "Hindu". According to him, one may lose one's sect or beliefs but not one's Hindutva because its most important determinant is the inheritance of the Hindu blood. Importantly, "blood", in this discourse, has a temporal structure and the capacity to be an agent. Sooner or later, somewhere along the generational lineage, the blood will out and the characteristics of Hindutva will write themselves into the Hindu body and its consciousness. How does a Hindu actually apprehend these bonds of blood? According to Savarkar, it is a structure of feeling, "a question of heart".

> We *feel* that the same ancient blood that coursed through the veins of Ram and Krishna, Buddha and Mahavir, Nanak and Chaitanya, Basava and Madhava, of Rohidas and Tiruvelluvar courses throughout Hindudom from vein to vein, pulsates from heart to heart. We feel we are a JATI, a race bound together by the dearest ties of blood and therefore it must be so. (Ibid: 89–90, emphasis in original)

This mystical and spiritual *volkische* association between the blood of the race and the passion of the race is an extremely important trope in contemporary Hindu nationalist activism and in its political languages. It signals a factor that is often absent in discussions of race: an ontology of emotion as central to "race" formation. Additionally, *jati*, rather than strictly *varna*, more directly emphasizes "type", a typology of origins. If Savarkar's rather modernist view of race is a combination of "typology" (classification) and blood "lineage" (originary descent), it also foundationally embeds a sensuousness and pathos about belonging that emphasizes its Romanticism. This tension between the rational and the passionate becomes important in the subsequent development of Hindu nationalism, especially in the suppression of emotion that is central to the rational-cybernetic "man-moulding" activities of the RSS, which is combined with the libidinal fervour that is at the core of its nationalism and communalism.

Savarkar, however, is also aware that "so far as man is concerned" there is only a single race, the human race, and only one blood, human blood. Sexual attraction is too powerful to prevent the commingling of blood. Nature is constantly trying to overthrow the artificial barriers one raises between race and race. Hence, Savarkar argues, the idea of race is only *relatively* true. But "speaking relatively alone, no people in the world can more justly claim to get recognized as a racial unit than the Hindus, and perhaps the Jews" (ibid: 90).

However, even in this definition, Muslims are included, since, for Savarkar, their "original Hindu blood" is almost unaffected by "alien adulteration". Savarkar thus introduces the concept of common culture and civilization which he defines as *Sanskriti*. This civilization is comprised of the totality of a common Hindu history ("the story of the action of our race"), literature ("the story of the thought of our race"), language (Sanskrit, all other languages being merely derivatives), art and architecture, all Hindu rites and rituals (which, according to Savarkar, reduce to an originary Hindu law and jurisprudence) and finally, feasts and festivals. Hindutva is thus comprised of a common nation (*Rashtra*), a common race (*Jati*) and a common civilization (*Sanskriti*). Importantly, Savarkar's conception of civilization also provides a definition of Hinduism, or *Hindudharma* as

> Each and every one of those systems and sects which are the direct descendants and developments of the religious beliefs Vaidik and non-Vaidik that obtained in the land of the Saptasindhus or in the other unrecorded communities in other parts of India in the Vedic period ... (Ibid: 109)

The motherland and fatherland are now also holyland (*punyabhumi*). For Savarkar, Muslims are now finally excluded from this cultural definition of Hindu Nation because "their holyland is far off in Arabia or Palestine", their names and cultural outlook are of "a foreign origin" and, whatever their feeling towards the land of their birth, their love is divided since they can never look to India as their holyland. Conversely, a Hindu is one "who looks upon the land that extends from Sindu to Sindu – from the Indus to the Seas – as his Fatherland (*Pitribhu*), his Motherland (*Matribhu*) and his

Holyland (*Punyabhu*)" *and* "who inherits the blood of that race whose first discernible source could be traced to the Vedic Sapta-sindhus". Versions of this twofold definition of "Hindu" are at the core of contemporary Hindu nationalism. They rely on a conception of lineage and originary descent, but also on a curious and ambiguous apprehension of place and identity signalled in the phrase "who looks upon" or who "considers". The phrases conceal actually quite contingent beliefs or convictions that can exist beyond and are not amenable to reason (for example, Parsis (Zoroastrians), who are generally treated agreeably in most Hindu nationalism may consider their holyland outside India, whereas many Muslims may well consider India to be all three of mother-land, fatherland and holyland.)

The Hindu identity that Savarkar defines is an eternal, organic, combatant and disciplinary unity that has to overcome the divisions between Hindus:

> ... can any one of you, Oh Hindus! whether Jain or Samaji or Sanatani or Sikh or any subsection afford to cut yourself off or fall out and destroy the ancient, the natural, and the organic combination that already exists? – a combination that is bound not by any scraps of paper nor by the ties of exigencies alone, but by the ties of blood, birth and culture? ... Strengthen every tie that binds you to the main organism, whether of blood or language or common Motherland. Let this ancient and noble stream of Hindu blood flow from vein to vein, from Attock to Cuttack till at last the Hindu people get fused and welded into an indivisible whole, till our race gets consolidated and strong and as sharp as steel. (Ibid: 139)

While this in itself is an admission of Hindu disaggregation, Savarkar's geographical and organicist definition also quickly collapses. For Hindus have also lived in Sind which is on the other side of the Indus river. Savarkar suggests that by "river", ownership of both banks of the river are implied and some people on the northern side of the Indus river who look upon India as their *pitrubhumi* and *punyabhumi* are therefore also Hindus. What of Hindus who leave India? They must recognize, indeed cannot but help recognizing India as their *pitrubhumi*. The blood and the race is eternal. Hence, Savarkar goes further and introduces an important spatial indeterminacy and a global conceptual method:

> ... Hindutva is compatible with any conceivable expansion of our Hindu people. Let our colonists continue unabated their labours of founding a Greater India, a Mahabharat to the best of their capacities .... The only limits of Hindutva are the limits of our earth! (Ibid: 119)

This global method has become particularly important for contemporary Hindu nationalism, even though it seemed to go into abeyance under the parochial xenophobia of the early RSS. The integrity of Savarkar's global Hindutva also depends on the patrilineal transmission of Hindu blood (ibid: 130).

Savarkar's conceptions of Hindutva and "the Hindu" are exhaustive definitions that are unthinkable outside of the classificatory impulse within modernity, despite the uses he makes of "tradition". Importantly, they rely on exclusionary categorization, an obsession with terminology, an obtuse anthropology and systematic methods of rationalist-discursive organization. They form the foundations of Hindu nationalism. The ideologies of the Hindu far-right are transmutations of original themes outlined by Savarkar. In the RSS' Nazism under its second leader, Madhav Golwalkar, Savarkar's Aryan race-blood theory is extended while the "integral humanism" philosophy of Deendayal Upadhyaya and the Bharatiya Janata Party are applications of Savarkar's organicism and historical, cultural and civilizational "method". Hindutva is, like Khomeinism, a very simple conception that articulates what can be termed a Gramscian "commonsense" about land, people and culture. It brings to the fore in a theoretical framework those sedimented "commonsense knowledges" and "memories" that constitute identity, belonging and communion. In this way, a new Hindu identity is discovered at the moment of its enunciation, just as any identity is secured through its authoritative articulation rather than because of any essence it contains.

Savarkar's central concepts of race, war and civilization are articulated within an epistemic framework whose boundaries are a version of anthropogeography, a linear (Hegelian) historiography and an organicist sociology. Savarkar's geography is composed of two elements – an elementary spatial geography of India that is singularly obsessed with physical features that enclose and exclude (the "natural frontier lines" of Himalayas, the Bay of Bengal, the Indian Ocean and the Arabian Sea, the Indus and the Ganges). This identification of physical geography with the imagined or social space, a symbolic landscape of Hinduism under constant threat is deeply resonant today. This physical space is imagined to be socially closed to entry but not exit (though, of course, Aryans entered it and were also usurpers, and so the start of Savarkar's hermetic history of Indian civilization with the arrival of the Aryans is also disrupted and is arbitrary.) Savarkar also demonstrates another geography. This is the geography of "cultural hearth", the merging of physical features into the cultural landscape of the origins and civilization of his Aryan Hindu race. This is a version of Lamarckian environmentalism – the original Aryan race changed and adapted to the environment by changing its *hereditary* qualities, which were then passed down from antiquity to the present and which indeed were formative of the Hindus as a "race".

This biological geography is central to Savarkar's "race concept". Despite the one human race, Aryan-Hindus were still fundamentally different and that difference was in some important way biological. However, while Savarkar most definitely integrates several biological expressions in his concept of race – notably, blood, breeding and heredity – this is not simply a reflection of the scientific-determinist concept of race that was dominant at the turn of the century and in which races were purely biological and definitively hierarchically organized. Indeed, it would have seemed odd for those under British colonial rule to appropriate uncritically *that* concept of race. Instead, Savarkar's race concept relies on several other themes that combine biology and culture with geography in various ways. Importantly, there is a morphogenetic theme in his metaphoric combination of physical landscape with the genesis of the Aryan-Hindu race and culture. In this cultural ecology, not dissimilar in its epistemology to the pre-Nazi *Lebensraum*, the blood of the Aryans, which became the blood of the Hindus, is somehow dialectically influenced by (and influences) the physical environment. This gives rise to a civilization and a culture that is transmitted not simply culturally but biologically (through the blood). This "biogeography" is combined with an iconographic reverence for the physical land – a "geopiety". That this is pure essentialism – biological, geographical, cultural – is less important than the content of these various "essences" and the race concept that is derived from them.

While Savarkar was widely read in Western philosophy and social and political theory, it is difficult to ascertain the impact on Savarkar of Western concepts, such as those derived from Lamarck, Spencer, Gobineau and later scientific racism, though it would be a mistake to think there was no influence of Western intellectual or commonsense race ideas. For example, Savarkar rehearses a pre-Romantic Western race concept in which race and culture are virtually congruent and inextricably linked to the idea of the land, of culture as "cultivation" as well as breeding, and of the importance of a racial aristocracy. In this sense, Savarkar's derivation of race is both original and utilizes Hindu sources that appear to be refracted or influenced by Western ideas. This repeats again the theme of the first chapter – is Savarkar's work originary and "nativist", simply Western, or is it syncretic or a catachresis? It seems possible to derive Savarkar's race concept from (selective) uses of originary Hinduism – the concepts of *varna* (four-caste, and its colour inflections), *arya* ("the noble", the Aryan people), the *dasas* (the darker population), the *mlecchas* (foreigners), as well as the various ideas of homeland and war can easily lend themselves to modernist interpolations of race, colour, minorities, nation and militarism. Indeed, Savarkar's concepts of race, nation, nationalism, the people, the "problem" of minorities, some global conceptual method and the relation of India to the system of nation-states and the (former) League of Nations are unthinkable outside modernity. Even his conception of culture as equivalent to difference has modernist conditions of "thinkability". At the same time, some of the resources it uses are "traditional". Consequently, it is not easily conceivable as an originary "alternative intellectual universe" that can be isolated from modernist or Western concepts, but nor is it entirely detached from ideas in "originary" Hinduisms.

One final theme concerns Savarkar's formulation of culture. While it may be hugely important in situations of colonial and neocolonial domination for nationalism to assert and inculcate pride in its culture and its people, a different strategy is apparent in Savarkar's work and continues in the work of those he influenced. This is the strategy of civilizational aggrandizement, also centrally important for contemporary Islamism. It has several important epistemic themes, some of which have barely moved beyond cultural xenophobia and cultural chauvinism:

- Civilizational genesis – the assertion of an original and founding glorified non-conflictual utopian totality that disappears in the mists of time and is often barely legible temporally (the latter can indeed be central to its discursive power).
- Culture as civilization – the assertion that contemporary or antecedent cultures are equivalent to an originary civilization and that the civilization constitutes an all-embracing totality that is different in its essence from all other cultures.
- Civilization as ontology – the assertion that Being itself and the content of identity arise from the originary civilization.
- Civilization as totality – in this methodology, civilization becomes the totality of all cultural products within all space–times that are deemed to be in congruence with the originary or founding moment of that civilization. Every agreeable aspect, personality, contribution, system of philosophy, historical period, social organization or form of political thought is reduced to a product of this civilization, so that absolute contradictions and conflicts between philosophies and political thought are erased. Individuals with sharply opposing social and political philosophies are presented as a unity, typically as an inventory or catalogue of names. (In the Hindu version of this imaginary, the mythic king Vikramaditya, Rama, the Mother Goddess, Buddha, Shivaji, the king Rana Pratap, Rabindranath Tagore, Gandhi, Subash Chandra Bose, Tilak, Savarkar, Dr Ambedkar, the student-workers' leader Jayaprakash Narayan and past RSS leaders Hedgewar and Golwalkar can all be articulated within a single register of "Hindu civilization". Virtually identical devices exist in contemporary Islamism.)
- Civilizational truth – the assertion that the originary culture discovered truths that are both universal (can incorporate every subsequent cultural epistemology) and transcendental (they are valid, often in their entirety, in all times and at all spaces).
- Civilizational finality – the assertion that the originary civilization or its products provide, in essence, a completed epistemology.
- A comparative civilizational methodology – the assertion that

either the originary culture or its later products have discovered all other cultures to be inherently deficient or limited either in their truths or in their applicability or relevance (other cultures have, in this scheme, nothing to add).

- Civilizational generosity, liberalism and humanism – the assertion that the originary culture, despite its critique of other cultures, was inherently protective of and respectful towards all of them – any conflict was started by the latter.
- Civilizational conflict – a temporality and historiography determined by a transcendental and monumental conflict that drives the civilization forward.
- Civilizational chauvinism – the assertion that civilization can be comparatively evaluated and that the evaluation demonstrates the civilization to be the superlative one (in its intellect, philosophy, mysticism, science, humanity, knowledge, arts, architecture, literature, culture, ethics, morality and so on).

Many of these themes are present, implicitly or explicitly, in Savarkar's view of cultural aggrandizement. However, they are linked very powerfully to the idea of cultural strength, inevitably invoking a "war temporality", a linear time driven forward by war. It is this theme that becomes so important for the subsequent contributions to Hindu nationalism that are examined below.

The Rashtriya Swayamsevak Sangh: organic totality, ordered society and race war

Savarkar's Hindutva philosophy was to influence directly a Congress activist, Dr Keshav Baliram Hedgewar ("Doctorji"). He founded a new organization in 1925 for Hindu men, the Rashtriya Swayamsevak Sangh (RSS, "The National Volunteers' Corps", or more accurately "The National Volunteer Servers' Organisation"). Despite Savarkar's glorious history of Hindu war against alien invaders, Hedgewar was preoccupied with the issue of why Hindus repeatedly and historically failed to repel invaders.

Central to the RSS' activity was a focus (virtually exclusive in its early years) on the highly disciplined psychospiritual change – "character building", "man-making" or "man-moulding" – that was required of the Hindu to make him aware of his inner content

197

and to rebuild him mentally and physically (Andersen & Damle 1987: 34). Literally a new person was required who would identify with *Hindutva* and would be able to resist and fight the foreign influences – these started, according to the RSS, from the first Turkish-Afghan Muslim invasion of "India" that Hindus had failed to repel. The necessity of building new united Hindu people implied an attention on civil society and the need to create disciplined organizations within it. Prior to 1948-9, the RSS rarely concerned itself with the state or strictly "politics" and chose, in its words, to be the independent "conscience of the nation". Involvement in "politics" and the state was seen to be polluting and diverting of its main aim to transform civil society and to create new Hindu-Indians.

The early form of RSS organization developed by Hedgewar was highly authoritarian, centralist, antidemocratic and paramilitary. It exists in virtually the same form today. It was also very modernist in conception and stressed a peculiar Westernized military and boy-scout discipline. All RSS members were required to attend gymnasia and highly regimented *shakas* (military drills, educational classes and branch meetings). Members were required to wear Western (not Indian), indeed almost colonial, military uniform (khaki shorts and white shirt), undergo Indian martial arts training (this mainly involved *lathi* (a bamboo or wooden staff) instruction as well as sword and other weapons training for officers), swear allegiance to the saffron flag and to *Hindutva*, worship *kshatriya* Gods (Rama) or warrior Gods (the monkey God Hanuman), revere Marathi or anti-Muslim heroes and saints (such as Shivaji), perform intimidating public military drills, and attend political education classes and rural training camps (Malkani 1980, Andersen & Damle 1987: 83-92). The RSS membership was recruited primarily from young boys, usually under 15 years of age, but also men. Members were ostensibly from all castes and Hindu backgrounds but included a high representation of upper- and middle-caste teachers, government bureaucrats, soldiers and merchants. The leadership and officers of the RSS were, however, from Maharashtrian *brahmin* castes.

The daily *shakas* that members (*swayamsevaks*) were obliged to attend were the main basis for religious and nationalist inculcation and physical and martial exercise. The *shaka* is the bottom-level structure of the RSS and is divided by age groups with their own leaders (*gatanayak*) and exercise teachers (*shikshak*). These functionaries are below the higher tier of full-time organizers (*pracharaks*), the local secretary (*karyavah*) and higher teachers (*mukya shikshaks*). Above this hierarchy are local and city committees and the state and central assembly. The *pracharaks* are the main organizational, activist and networking layer and are frequently loaned to work on other "non-RSS" projects or in other organizations (Anderson & Damle 1987). The Vishwa Hindu Parishad and the Bharatiya Janata Party were each formed by and still rely heavily on the labour of RSS *pracharaks*. The "Guide and Philosopher of the RSS" is the Supreme Leader or *sarsangchalak*. This mantle was first held by Hedgewar, followed by Madhav Golwalkar and then Balasaheb Deoras.[2]

The RSS gained considerable support for its activities during Partition, in particular through its assistance to Hindu refugees coming into India from (now Pakistan) Punjab and its paramilitary rescue squads of Hindus living in Muslim areas. Partition was seen by Hindu nationalist organizations as an unjustified concession to Muslim separatism and continues today to act as a powerful signifier for Hindu mobilization. The anger at Partition was part of a rejection by Hindu nationalist organizations of all Gandhian methods of liberation, in particular the idea of *satyagraha* (literally "truth force", defeating your enemy by forcefully showing their moral weakness without morally compromising your own position) and *ahimsa* (non-harm, translated by Gandhi as non-violent non-co-operative direct action). These were seen to portray Hindus as weak, effeminate, "unmanly" and, especially, emasculated. The reconstruction of Hindu masculinities was especially important to the RSS and depended on selecting violent *kshatriya* histories and violent masculine Gods for their devotional, symbolic and pedagogical appeal.

The Rashtra Sevika Samiti (the "National Women Volunteers Corps") was formed in 1936 by Lakshmi Kelkar. It also stressed the martial and violent aspects of Hindu mythology (Andersen & Damle 1987: 38–9). It focused, as it and similar organizations still do today, on disciplined training of young Hindu women in martial arts. It glorified powerful Goddess and female historical figures. Women were to emulate the Goddess Durga, and not necessarily the devoted, subservient, suffering and passive Sita figure. Women were expected to be active and prepared for war in defence of their *Hindu*

Rashtra. The Sevika Samiti was the RSS' first affiliated organization, and had a similar authoritarian and centralized organizational structure.

Following Gandhi's assassination by Nathuram Godse, who was previously a prominent member of both the Hindu Mahasabha and the RSS, the new Hindu nationalist organizations were banned during the period 1948–9 by the new Congress Government of India. (Godse had been Savarkar's "lieutenant". Consequently, Savarkar also stood trial for Gandhi's murder and was found innocent.) However, during the ban there were extensive and often secret negotiations between the anti-Nehru pro-Vallabhai Patel leadership factions in Congress to get the RSS to become, *en masse*, part of the ruling Congress Party (Golwalkar 1962, Andersen & Damle 1987: 52–4). This potential depended on negotiation with the RSS to make its constitution suitably acceptable to Congress leaders. Patel negotiated extensively with Golwalkar, the RSS' *sarsangchalak* after Hedgewar's death, to democratize the RSS, accept the secular Constitution of India, renounce political activity and even become part of Congress itself (Golwalkar 1962). These negotiations failed, but did result in the unbanning of the RSS, which then adopted an increasingly political, rather than strictly "cultural" orientation. In many ways, this process highlighted the unresolved secularism in the liberation and independence movements, and in particular the unsettled nature of what role modern Hinduism was to play in a democratic, multicultural and secular state. That factions of the Congress leadership of the national liberation movement were prepared to negotiate with a Hindu-Aryan supremacist body that preached hatred of Muslims demonstrated a considerable underdevelopment in secular thinking.

The RSS' organizational philosophy was classically totalitarian under Hedgewar. However, if Hedgewar had supreme organizational skills – "Organization! Organization! Organization!" sums up the RSS' day-to-day philosophy – then the most important theoretical and philosophical input came from Madhav Golwalkar ("Guruji") who became the RSS' second *sarsangchalak* after an extremely close association with Hedgewar and after the latter's death. Golwalkar is a profoundly important figure in the political development of the RSS. Some of his earlier writings, and in particular his Nazi-like treatise on nationalism, *We, or our nationhood defined* (first published in 1939, hereafter *WND*), have been suppressed by the RSS because of some embarrassment about their contents. Later works, such as *Bunch of thoughts* (published in 1966) are promoted instead, though, in essence they reproduce the philosophy of *WND*. BJP president, L. K. Advani, was questioned about the Nazi-like contents of *WND* during a BBC TV investigation of Hindu nationalism and replied:

> Just one single book and that too he [Golwalkar] virtually dissociated himself from, from the views that were expressed there. And it was more of a translation. He wrote it very early, in '37 or '36. [*Interviewer: But it was reprinted in 1946*] Yes I know that! But that one single paragraph keeps being repeated over and over again. I don't agree with that at all and [Golwalkar] himself did not agree. (Assignment BBC2 15 June 1993)

This indeed has been a fairly typical Hindu nationalist response to accusations that *WND* is a Nazi-like tract.

We, or our nationhood defined was written and published at a time (1938–9, republished in 1944) when National Socialist doctrines of race purity, national purity and antisemitism were flourishing in Germany and having significant impact across both western and eastern Europe, and in parts of Latin America, South East Asia and the Middle East. However, they were also vigorously opposed and challenged. It cannot be claimed, as it often is, that Golwalkar's philosophy was simply and naturally a consequence of that time, or that support for National Socialist Germany was a valid choice in opposition to British colonialism. The vast majority of colonized people, including Hindus and Muslims in India, opposed National Socialist doctrines and were to fight against Germany and the Axis forces in the Second World War.

Golwalkar's main concern in *WND* (the second edition of *WND*, published in 1944, is used in the following section), as in Savarkar's earlier contribution, is identity politics. He sought to provide a meaning and a definition of "nation", which he identifies in opposition to "state" – that "haphazard bundle of political rights" (Golwalkar 1934: 3). "Nation", for Golwalkar, is a cultural unit and "state" a political one and while they may overlap, they are distinguishable. The form of state is secondary to the national concept (ibid: 51). The political context for his analysis was the movement, discussions and negotiations for Indian self-rule (*swaraj*) and independence. These, for Golwalkar, were "strange times" when "we do not live but merely exist", and in which "traitors should sit enthroned as national heroes and patriots heaped with ignominy":

> The idea was spread that for the first time the people were going to live a National Life, the nation in the land naturally composed of all those who happened to reside therein and that all these people were to unite on a common "National" platform and win back "freedom" by "constitutional means". Wrong notions of democracy strengthened the view and we began to class ourselves with our old invaders and foes [the Muslims] under the outlandish name "Indian" .... We have allowed ourselves to be duped into believing our foes to be our friends, and with our own hands are undermining true Nationality .... In our self-deception, we go on seceding more and more, in hopes of "Nationalising" the foreigners and succeed merely in increasing their all-devouring appetite. (Ibid: 14)

Against this "betrayal", "the wild goose chase after the phantasm of founding a 'really' democratic state", and what he considered to be the "amazing doctrine" that the nation is composed of all those who live in it, Hindus should instead be "at war at once with the British on the one hand and the Moslems on the other".

Hindus must start afresh, they must ask "who are we?" Golwalkar, like Savarkar, starts with the *Vedas*. While all other civilizations can trace the history of their civilized life back only "a couple of thousand years", it cannot be determined how far back Hindus discarded their "state of nature". Perhaps, he argues, "it seems as if we were never uncivilised". That originary point of Hindu-Vedic civilization is in the time of the dim past, "the mysteries of which History dare not venture" (ibid: 5). However, Golwalkar does venture: "Undoubtedly ... we Hindus have been in undisputed and undisturbed possession of this land for over 8 or even 10 thousand years before the land was invaded by any foreign race" (ibid: 6).

Golwalkar, unlike Savarkar in *HWH*, is unwilling to accept the "White Man's" view that Aryans came from outside India, settled and merged with the existing "aborigines", and then slowly degenerated. As for these Western hypotheses,

> ... we reject all and positively maintain that we Hindus came into this land from nowhere, but are indigenous children of the soil always, from time immemorial and are natural masters of the country .... And we were one nation – "Over all the land from sea to sea one Nation!" is the trumpet cry of the ancient Vedas! (Ibid: 8)

This is his originary genesis of nation. However, this glorious civilization started to degenerate (the fall from originary utopia), much as in Savarkar's *Hindutva*, but this time because Hindus became too secure in their glory and therefore careless. The "one nation" fell into small principalities, consciousness of the one Hindu nationhood and the one race waned, and Buddhism was misinterpreted and caused "over-individualization". Thus "when the first real invasions of murdering hordes of Mussalman free-booters occurred, they indeed found the nation divided against itself and incapable of stemming the tide of devastation they brought in their wake" (ibid: 10).

And "yet the race spirit did not wholly die out. The Race Spirit is too tenacious to be dead so easily." Indeed, Hindus are "an immortal race with perennial youth". Golwalkar, like Savarkar, establishes the now-familiar Hindu nationalist historical narrative of endless war, "this 800 years' war" and of immeasurable Hindu heroism virtually identical to Savarkar's story of war, Hindu strength and martyrdom. Indeed,

> History is the story of our flourishing Hindu National life for thousands of years and of a long unflinching war continuing for the last ten centuries, which has not yet come to a decisive close .... And Race Spirit calls, national consciousness blazes forth and we Hindus rally to the Hindu standard, the Bhagawa Dhwaja [saffron flag], set our teeth in grim determination to wipe out the opposing forces. (Ibid: 13)

After the long "war", the Hindu nation was exhausted and unable easily to fight the new invaders, the British, who had entered the land "with the help of the Mussalmans". However, even then, and especially in 1857 and in the independence movement,

> The Race spirit has been awakening. The lion was not dead, only sleeping. He is rousing himself up again and the world has to see the might of the regenerated Hindu Nation strike down the enemy's [the British] hosts with its mighty arm. (Ibid: 12)

This Hindu nation, for Golwalkar, is composed of the "unassailable" and "scientific" understanding of the "famous five unities": Country, Race, Religion, Culture and Language. "Race", for Golwalkar, is the fundamental concept of nation:

> It is superfluous to emphasise the importance of Racial Unity in the Nation state. A Race is a hereditary Society having common customs, common language, common memories of glory and disaster; in short it is a population with a common origin under one culture. Such a race is by far the most important ingredient of a Nation. Even if there be people of a foreign origin, they must become assimilated into the body of the mother race and inextricably fused into it. They should become one with the original national race not only in its economic and political life, but also in its religion, culture and language, for otherwise such foreign races may be considered, under certain circumstances [as] at best members of a common state for political purposes, but they can never form part and parcel of the National body .... We will not seek to prove this axiomatic truth, that the Race is the body of the Nation, and that with its fall, the Nation ceases to exist. (Ibid: 21)

Despite Golwalkar's claim of the generosity and the tolerant spirit of "broad Catholicism" that is the essence of Hinduism (ibid.: 42), his organic Hindu-racial totality is emphatically intolerant:

> ... in Hindusthan exists and must needs exist [sic] the ancient Hindu nation and nought else but the Hindu Nation. All those not belonging to the national i.e. Hindu Race, Religion, Culture and Language, naturally fall out of

the pale of real "National" life .... All others posing to be patriots and wilfully indulging in a course of action detrimental to the Hindu Nation are traitors and enemies to the National Cause ... all those who fall outside the five-fold limits of that idea can have no place in the national life, unless they abandon their differences, and completely merge themselves in the National Race. So long, however, as they maintain their racial, religious and cultural differences, they cannot but be only foreigners, who may either be friendly or inimical to the Nation. (Ibid: 45–6)

Alongside his national-racial totality, Golwalkar also proposed monolithic conceptions of culture and religion. Culture, for Golwalkar, is virtually reducible to and difficult to distinguish from religion. Both these create "the peculiar" race spirit and race consciousness. Religion has become "eternally interwoven" into every aspect of the life of the race. Indeed, "every action in life, individual, social, or political is a command of Religion". Religion cannot be the practice of private faith or individual beliefs, but instead regulates society in all its functions. Indeed, religion

... cannot be ignored in individual or public life. It must have a place in proportion to its vast importance in politics as well. To give it a go-bye or even to assign it an insignificant place would mean degeneration on all hands. Indeed, politics itself becomes, in the case of such [true] Religion, a small factor, to be considered and followed solely as one of the command of Religion and in accord with such commands. (Ibid: 24)

This avowedly theocratic concept of politics and civil society is combined in Golwalkar's philosophy with a racial concept of the nation. Importantly, both institute an organic functionalist and totalizing conception of the social formation, an integrated and unitary state and civil society. One of Golwalkar's pet hatreds was anything that could upset his imagined organic racial-religious totality. Hence, his philosophy towards minorities, a barely disguised metaphor in his writings for the Muslims of India, becomes especially important. Golwalkar was scathing about the rights and protection treaties for national minorities that were negotiated under the former League of Nations. He was opposed to both minority rights and minority protection. These, for him, amounted to "preferential treatment". In discussing minority rights,

> We will only state one small sentence that for such a foreign race [he is referring to Muslims] to claim preferential treatment at the hands of the Nation, it should not be an upstart, a new, voluntary settlement, and it should not be below 20% of the total population of the state. (Ibid: 31)

No one should "tax the generosity" of the Nation by "demanding privileges" as minority communities. Moreover, every national race has conferred upon it

> the indisputable right of excommunicating from its Nationality all those who, having been of the Nation, for ends of their own, turned traitors and entertained aspirations contravening or differing from those of the National Race as a whole. (Ibid: 34)

Consequently, no minority that chooses to remain so is deserving of any "right what-so-ever" or "any obligations from the National race". Such minorities

> ... live only as outsiders, bound by all the codes and conventions of the Nation, at the sufferance of the Nation and deserving of no special protection, far less any privilege or rights. There are only two courses open to the foreign elements, either to merge themselves in the national race and adopt its culture, or to live at the sweet will of the national race. That is the only logical and correct solution. That alone keeps the national life healthy and undisturbed. That alone keeps the Nation safe from the danger of a cancer developing into its body politic of the creation of a state within a state. From this standpoint, sanctioned [by] the experiences of shrewd old nations, the non-Hindu peoples of Hindusthan must either adopt the Hindu culture and language, must learn to respect and hold in reverence Hindu religion, must entertain no ideas but those of the glorification of the Hindu race and culture i.e. they must

not only give up their attitude of intolerance and ungrate-
fulness towards this land and its age-long traditions but
must also cultivate a positive attitude of love and devotion
instead – in a word they must cease to be foreigners, or may
stay in the country wholly subordinated to the Hindu
nation, claiming nothing, deserving no privileges, far less
any preferential treatment – not even citizen's rights. We
are an old nation; and let us deal as old nations ought to
and do deal with the foreign races who have chosen to live
in our country. (Ibid: 48–9)

This is barely different from the National Socialism that Golwalkar was contemporaneous with. Golwalkar's philosophy contains virtually all the themes that constituted official Nazi ideology:
a superior race, a superior, ancient and mystical culture, an organic
nationhood, a national landscape, and destructive and polluting
minorities and traitors to the race and nation that should be
stripped of all their rights, though Golwalkar also used more
visceral metaphors.

Golwalkar and National Socialism

It was Golwalkar's laudatory discussion of Nazi Germany, the small
poorly translated "single paragraph" that Advani dismisses, that
accumulated a great deal of notoriety for the RSS, and which the RSS
has been keen to suppress. Golwalkar's thoughts on Nazi Germany
are worth examining. For Golwalkar, the eternal race consciousness
is awakened by its desires and aspirations. These aspirations of the
race are historic and are embedded in its distant past and in the call of
ancient tradition. A nation cannot but "tread the road" that the
traditional past has "opened out for it". If a nation abandons this
"fixed groove" of tradition and race spirit, it seriously endangers "the
whole fabric of its existence" and its life soul. The individual and the
race as a whole is conditioned, or has its "mental frame" shaped, by
this historic awakening of tradition in the race spirit of today
(Golwalkar 1994: 31). This, for Golwalkar, was the situation in
Europe in the 1930s: "Look at Italy, the old Roman Race consciousness of conquering the whole territory round the Mediterranean Sea,
so long dormant, has roused itself, and shaped the Racial-National
aspirations accordingly" (ibid: 33).

Similarly with modern Germany, where "The ancient Race spirit which prompted the Germanic tribes to over-run the whole of Europe has re-risen" (ibid: 31). Golwalkar claims that each of his five constituents of the "nation idea" have been "boldly vindicated" in National Socialist Germany. The national spirit in Germany, he claims, is logical, and merely seeks to bring into its ownership what is "originally" German land:

> Modern Germany strives, and has to a great extent ach-
> ieved what she strove for, to once again bring under one
> sway the whole of the territory, hereditarily possessed by
> the Germans but which, as a result of political disputes, has
> been portioned as different countries under different states
> .... German pride in their Fatherland for a definite home
> country, for which the race has certain traditional attach-
> ments as a necessary concomitant of the true Nation
> concept, awoke and ran the risk of starting a fresh world-
> conflagration, in order to establish one, unparalleled,
> undisputed, German Empire over all this "hereditary terri-
> tory". This *natural and logical aspiration* has almost been
> fulfilled and the great importance of the "country factor"
> has been once again *vindicated* in the living present. (Ibid:
> 36, emphases added)

Germany has also fulfilled Golwalkar's other prescription for nation – a nation that contains only a pure race with no "pollu-tants". Golwalkar's race concept, which includes culture, language and religion, is similarly framed, and when combined with his aversion to minorities, provides an instructive example for what Hindu race formation should become:

> German race pride has now become the topic of the day. To
> keep up the purity of the Race and its culture, Germany
> shocked the world by her purging the country of the semitic
> Races – the Jews. Race pride at its highest has been
> manifested here. Germany has shown how well nigh impos-
> sible it is for Races and cultures, having differences going to
> the root, to be assimilated into one united whole, a good
> lesson for us in Hindusthan to learn and profit by. (Ibid: 37)

Organic corporatism and the cybernetic personality

If these explicitly Nazi-like doctrines were later disavowed by Golwalkar, there is no doubt that his entirely totalitarian and fascist vision of a perfect, pure, organized, disciplined, organic, integrated, non-democratic single-minded social order continued to thrive, as it still does in the RSS. The fetishism of order, discipline and organization is at the core of RSS ideals, vision and social and political philosophy. In its vision, the ideal social formation was to be a rigorously organized and ordered one. It was to be a world comprised of men having the same visions and beliefs.

In both Hedgewar's and Golwalkar's philosophy, the RSS was to be literally *a society in microcosm*, with the aim of remaking Hindu society in its image of perfect organization and discipline. Importantly, for the RSS, it *was* the society and the Indian social formation had to be moulded into its shape: "Right from its inception the Sangh has clearly marked out as its goal the moulding of the whole of society, and not merely any one part of it, into an organised entity" (Golwalkar 1966: 341)

The RSS, in this sense, disowned the actually existing social formation. Its emphasis was on slow patient work in civil society, from the bottom, literally the creation or moulding of a new man whose influence would cascade into the existing civil society that would in turn become increasingly organized.

> The ultimate vision of our work, which has been the living inspiration for all our organisational efforts, is a perfectly organised state of our society wherein each individual has been moulded into a model of ideal Hindu manhood and made into a living limb of the corporate personality of society. (Golwalkar 1966: 61)

The "right path" for undertaking the moulding of men cannot be a mass movement or revolutionary activity but the technique of organization, discipline and *shaka* developed by Hedgewar "by taking individual after individual and moulding him for an organised national life" (ibid: 332). This "technique" is seen to be inherently Hindu – it is claimed that the RSS "has eschewed [all] self-defeating alien types of organisation" (ibid: 342). Golwalkar describes a *shaka*:

There is an open playground. Under a saffron flag groups of youths and boys are absorbed in a variety of Bharatiya games. Resounding shouts of joyous enthusiasm often fill the air .... The leader's whistle or order has a magical effect on them; there is instant perfect order and silence. Then exercises follow – wielding the lathi, Suryanamaskar, marching etc. The spirit of collective effort and spontaneous discipline pervades every programme. Then they sit down and sing in chorus songs charged with patriotism. Discussions follow. They delve deep into the problems affecting the national life. And finally, they stand in rows before the flag and recite the prayer: Many salutations to Thee, O loving Motherland! whose echoes fill the air and stir the soul. "Bharat Mata ki jai" [Long Live the Motherland!] uttered in utmost earnest [*sic*] furnishes the finishing and inspiring touch to the entire programme. (Ibid: 333–4)

The RSS, in facing the problem of having to inculcate its philosophy across different Hindu sects,

... have evolved a technique, an emblem, a "mantra" and a code of discipline in keeping with our ideal of a unified and disciplined national life. The great and inspiring emblem that we have chosen is the immortal Bhagwa Dhwaj [saffron flag] which brings before our eyes the living image of our ancient, sacred and integrated national life in all its pristine purity ... (Ibid: 335)

The purpose of regular discipline is essential for ideological teaching and hence character-building. In an enlightening passage, Golwalkar states: "It is a common experience that if a particular idea is repeated at a fixed hour regularly it goes deep into our being and becomes an inseparable part of our character. Hence the untiring stress on regularity and punctuality in the Sangh" (ibid: 347–8)

Instructively, despite the ancient, eternal and powerful call of the Hindu race, *swayamsevaks* still have to be ideologically indoctrinated into Hindu identity. The core aspect of this "man-moulding" and "character-building" is to "imprint" the correct *samskars* ("impressions", "values", "world-views"). Psychologists, Golwalkar informed us, tell us that three factors are necessary to permanently "imprint" ideas into minds, to "fashion" new persons, to "make men out of dust":

> ... firstly, constant meditation of the ideal that is to be formed into a samskar; secondly constant company of persons devoted to the same ideal; and finally engaging the body in activities congenial to that ideal ... (Ibid: 350)

Indeed, in the body activities, "all the various apparently little things like games, wielding of lathi, singing, marching" have "the potency of instilling deep *samskars*". This "daily imprinting of *samskars*" is an urgent necessity since the bad habits and tendencies of centuries "cannot be washed off in a single day". The crux of those bad habits is indiscipline, "our great undoing". However, even a "disorderly crowd of even hundreds of persons stands nowhere in comparison with a handful of disciplined men". Hence, mind, intellect and body have to be trained "to become a living limb of the great corporate society". Golwalkar uses the metaphor of bodily cellular destruction to describe this process. In a human body, every cell not only feels its identity with the entire body, but more importantly is "ever ready to sacrifice itself for the sake of the health and growth of the body". It is this literal "self-immolation" of millions of cells that releases the energy of the human body. Thus so for the *swayamsevaks*. They have to undergo this process of self-annihilation and sacrifice for the Sangh, and eventually, the society. The strict training of the *shaka* gives the individual "the necessary incentive to rub away his angularities". This includes all his emotional urges, which are detrimental to the moulding of character:

> ... all our great authorities on mental discipline have ordained us not to succumb to overflow of emotions and weep in the name of God but to apply ourselves to a strict discipline of day-to-day penance. Effusion of emotions will only shatter the nerves and make the person weaker than before leaving him a moral wreck. It is just like a liquor-addict who is left imbecile after the effects of liquor subside. (Ibid: 349)

We should note the disjunction between the emotional being that Golwalkar sought to suppress and the intense and essential emotional passion that needs to be "roused" in resurgent Hindu nationalist identity. That passion is central to both Savarkar's and Golwalkar's conceptions of race and blood. In repressing their emotional being, the *swayamsevaks* "learn to obey a single command", to behave in the spirit of oneness with their brethren "and fall in line with the organised and disciplined way of life. Discipline enters their blood." Golwalkar was utterly unconcerned about the loss of individuality or opinion or feeling among the *swayamsevaks*, and was scathing towards those who made this criticism:

> There are some others – probably finding it rather troublesome to undergo the regular course of our organisation! – who say that they do not desire to be bound by any restrictions, that these are the days of "individual freedom" and so on. One such gentleman charged the Sangh as being "fascist" because according to him all persons in the Sangh from Kashmir to Kanyakumari whether aged or in their teens gave the same kind of reply to a question, which indicated there was no freedom of thought in the Sangh! ... It is natural that the persons in the Sangh imbued with the correct national perspective react spontaneously to the various national problems that arise from time to time in the same manner. To mistake it for mental regimentation is to call the spirit of nationalism itself an instrument of regimentation! It is the undigested modern ideas like "freedom of thought", "freedom of speech" etc., that are playing havoc in the minds of our young men who look upon freedom as licence and self-restraint as mental regimentation! (Ibid: 355–6)

Golwalkar, of course, only confirms the gentleman's anxieties about the RSS. There are several important themes in Golwalkar's philosophy that, even if his discussions of National Socialism are ignored, make his social thought classically fascist and in parts virtually congruent with official National Socialist philosophy, especially in his conception of the nation as an organic totality with a single, transcendental collective consciousness comprising the national soul as well as the importance of mystical-intuitive knowledge. Anderson and Damle suggest that its main difference from classical fascism is its rejection of the leadership principle since it is ego-oriented (Anderson and Damle 1987: 82). It has also been suggested that its disavowal of claims to state power make it essentially non-fascist. However, its internal structure and the complete authority of the *sarsangchalak* are surely based on an unmediated *Fuhrerprinzip*, just as its disavowal of formal politics and the quest for state power have also to be qualified by its intense political orientation in civil society and its formation of numerous explicitly political mass movements. It is better seen as a variant of the Italian fascist model with strong philosophical strands that are epistemically similar to those within German National Socialist philosophy, and that bear an ideological affinity with the numerous *volkische* "cultural" mass organizations that existed prior to and during the Nazi period. Needless to say, Golwalkar's philosophy is thoroughly modernist in the strictest sense of the term, despite his selective use of traditional texts. It was born, as was Savarkar's *Hindutva*, out of a political engagement with Indian nationalism, nation-state formation and the development of the international system of nation-states during the early part of this century, and especially in the inter-war and post-war periods.

Similarly, the RSS is a classically authoritarian semi-paramilitary urban social movement. There is virtually nothing traditional about its forms of organization and discipline, its "man-moulding" mission or its cybernetic view of the human personality. On the contrary, the systematic forms of rational bureaucratic organization and algorithmic inculcation suggest not religious sensibilities but scientific, technical-rationalist ones. Rational method is central to its aim of ordering the social formation in accordance with its vanguardist imagination. This rationalism commences with the need to "create the proper type of man", who is then to be integrated into the proper type of social order. Golwalkar was explicit that this should be the *Varnashrama* (four-caste) system, "the best order for achieving human happiness". "Even those who loudly trumpeted individual liberty had to accept collectivism and the doctrine of heredity". The "feeling of inequality" attached to caste has, according to the RSS, "crept into the caste system and is not proper". However, "the Geeta tells us that the individual who does his assigned duties in life only worships God through such performance" (Golwalkar 1956: 50).

> If a Brahmana becomes great by imparting knowledge, a Kshatriya is hailed as equally great by destruction of the enemy. No less important is the Vaishya who feeds and sustains the community through agriculture and trade, or the Shudra who services society through his art and craft. [sic] Together, and by their mutual interdependence, they constitute the social order. That, indeed, is the spirit of our land. (Ibid: 50)

This structural-functionalist organicism is not simply an adherence to tradition but a selective appropriation of caste that both wilfully ignores its injustice and evades the deeply traditional historic movements against the caste system, such as Buddhism, Jainism, *bhakti*, Sikhism and Islam. This organic social order is, for the RSS, overdetermining of the state. The role of the state is subsequent to, and important only for, maintaining the created social order. Each aspect of the social order – economy, the state and civil society – is integrated and non-conflictual. Economic differences – such as class conflict – have no place in this social order and have to be suppressed. The form of government is both idealized and undemocratic. The village council or *panchayat* system is idealized, not because it leads to greater decision-making power or airing of grievances but because it leads to organic totality. *Panchayat*, in this vision, will lead not to fragmentation but rather to "a reinforcement of the centre". The form of state is not only unspecified but unspecifiable

> If the basic structure of society is strong and enduring, any form of Government, from monarchy to democracy, will be workable. None of them will be able to shake off the basic structure. This is why there is no insistence on any particular form of Government in our way of thinking. (Ibid: 56)

This is disingenuous since the RSS has always been committed to building a powerful, xenophobic, heavily militarized, warlike Hindu-Bharatiya *Rashtra* (Hindu Nation) that would govern a heavily ordered and disciplined civil society. This is inconceivable as anything other than a despotic, totalitarian, authoritarian or, at best, an antidemocratic state form that is both internally and externally aggressive. Golwalkar's xenophobic nationalism, as well as his inclement attitude towards the not-yet-proper inhabitants of Indian civil society was demonstrated during the war with Pakistan in 1965 and earlier with China,[3] following the latter's invasion of India in 1962. Golwalkar was frustrated with the limited nature of these wars and called instead for "a total war". Such a war "would involve every one of our countrymen in active participation in an all out war-effort and would have been a great chastener of the national mind" (Golwalkar 1966: 312). According to him, the centuries have bred vice and weakness, indolence, selfishness and parochialism in Indian men.

> It is therefore that a bigger and total war is welcome in spite of the temporary hardships it may entail us. In fact, we should heartily pray for such a war, though we are traditionally incurable lovers of peace and not war-mongers; for that is the price we have to pay for peace with freedom and honour and the sooner we pay the price the better. (Ibid: 312)

The *sangh parivar*: visceral mutilation, radical difference and ethnic death

After Golwalkar's death in 1973, Madhukar Dattatreya (Balasaheb) Deoras, previously (joint) general secretary, became the RSS' *sarsangchalak*. Under Deoras, the RSS became more directly involved in formal and mass politics, especially because of the experience of the totalitarian Emergency period under Indira Gandhi during which the RSS – and numerous left-wing organizations – were persecuted or banned. However, it was the adjacent organizations that were initiated and controlled by the RSS under the Golwalkar period that became extraordinarily influential.

During the 1960s the RSS expanded its activities by forming several affiliated organizations, of which the Vishwa Hindu Parishad (VHP – World Hindu Council) and the political party, the Jan Sangh were the most important. This was the formative period of the Hindu nationalist social movement. The vHP was a federation of Hindu religious leaders (*sadhus*, *sanyasis* and *mahants*, and later the main *shankaracharyas*) whose activities were to dominate Hindu revivalism in the 1980s and 1990s. The Jan Sangh, whose leadership was composed of rss members and which was created and supported by the considerable labour of rss *pracharaks*, was to become part of the ruling Janata coalition following the defeat of Indira Gandhi's Congress Party in 1977. The rss membership of Jan Sangh MPs was at the root of the attacks upon it by other Janata partners and led to the dissolving of the coalition and its consequent defeat at the polls. Subsequently, the Jan Sangh reformed itself as the Bharatiya Janata Party (BJP – Indian People's Party) in 1980 under the leadership of Lal Krishnan Advani. From 1985, the BJP committed itself to the late Deendayal Upadhyaya's philosophy of "integral humanism". Integral humanism is a self-consciously modern, holistic and developmental vision of the social totality in which individuals and collectives are seen as interdependent and should be mutually non-conflictual under the greater principle of nation. The basis of conflict is indeed seen as a weakening of nationalism and *dharma* among individuals, and consequently some form of *Dharma Rajya*, which Upadhyaya insists is not a theocratic state, needs to be established. Integral humanism employs Hindu ideals of *dharma* which encapsulate, according to Upadhyaya, *karma*, *artha* (translated as statecraft and social and economic policy development) and *moksha* (liberation). Interestingly, the Darwinian metaphor, together with various organicist and biological tropes, is heavily employed in Integral humanism (Upadhyaya et al. 1979)

The leadership and intelligentsia of the BJP, including Upadhyaya, Atal Behari Vajpayee (the current BJP leader) and Advani, are or were all influential rss members and rose to prominence through their rss activities. Advani is a prime example of an rss activist who entered mainstream politics. He joined the rss at the age of 14 and he, like Vajpayee,[4] still demonstrates complete loyalty to it. The BJP has already had a role in government as part of its minority alliance with the Janata Dal and the Communist Party of India (M), an alliance that collapsed because of agitation around Ayodhya. The BJP has risen spectacularly in Indian national politics since 1980. Its two seats in parliament in 1984 increased to 89 seats in 1989 (and almost 120 seats following political realignments in 1991). It has seen similar successes in state assembly elections, including control of the prize state Uttar Pradesh[5] (though after the destruction of the Babri masjid, the centre government took control of the BJP states). In 1995, it won a two-thirds majority in Gujarat state and took control of Maharashtra state in a coalition with the fascist Shiv Sena.

The broader "family", or *sangh parivar*, of contemporary Hindu nationalist organizations in India are mainly aligned to the RSS–VHP– BJP axis. The RSS has about two million members in India and its role has been to advise, guide and organize the other revivalist formations. These have grown rapidly since the 1970s:

> For example, the Bharatiya Mazdoor Sangh, [the RSS'] labor affiliate, claimed that it had grown from about 1.2 million members in 1977 to about 1.8 million members in 1980, making it the second largest national union after the Indian Trade Union Congress. The Vidyarthi Parishad, its student affiliate, grew from 170,000 to 250,000 members between 1977 and 1982, further strengthening [its] position as the largest student group in India. (Anderson & Damle 1987: 215)

The Vishwa Hindu Parishad, the Bharatiya Janata Party, the Rashtra Sevika Samiti (the RSS' women's affiliate), the violent Bajrang Dal ("Hanuman's army", the youth wing of the VHP), the Durga Vahini (the young women's wing of the VHP), the Mahila Mandal (the VHP's women's section formed in 1980), as well as the organizations formed to destroy the Babri masjid have been the most active during the late 1980s. Other older organizations such as the Arya Samaj are also relevant. In addition, there are thousands of local organizations, including welfare, cultural, student, peasant, farmer, tribal, youth, trade union, women's and religious organizations, some of which are explicitly linked to the formations mentioned, or sympathetic to them and others that use alternative local epithets but are essentially branches or local projects of the RSS and the VHP. Importantly, various older missionary movements, including the Swaminarayan Mission and the Chinmaya Mission, undertake joint projects with the VHP, and in many cases the exact organizational boundaries and personnel affiliation between the RSS and (especially) the VHP and other groups has dissolved. Tapan Basu et al., in their research on VHP activities near Nizamuddin, found that

> At the Arya Samaj Mandir at Jangpura, we were directed towards the Sanatan Dharm Mandir by a Samaj official who said that the *sanatanists* would expound the same basic principles [as the VHP]. The late nineteenth to early twentieth century heritage of bitter Arya–Sanatani conflict seemed utterly forgotten. At the Dharm Mandir pujaris told us that their Lajpat Nagar premises are shared by the VHP. At the Namdev Temple Samiti office on Lodi Road, we came across busy mobilization for a march under VHP auspices which would protest against a recent judgement of the US Supreme Court against ISKCON ['the Hare Krishnas'] properties. On Ram Navami day in April 1990, we saw trucks sporting VHP placards in front and Arya Samaj ones at the back. *Rashtrasevikas* [RSS women members] told us that all VHP, Arya Samaj or Sanatan Dharm premises were freely available for their activities. (Basu et al. 1993: 58)

This is a practical demonstration of a strictly hegemonic political strategy in which diverse, eclectic and unrelated strands are knitted together into an overarching political discourse within which their discursive unity "makes sense". The RSS–VHP core derives this vanguardist political legitimacy from one important trope that the RSS developed. This is the central idea of the political organization encapsulating within itself the society it wants the social formation to become. This is not simply an ideological flourish or a crude vanguardism but a deep belief that within itself a new society is being created that will extend outwards and embrace the whole social formation. It is central to its forms of organization in civil society. There is one important traditional metaphor that the RSS, and especially the VHP, repeatedly use to "legitimize" this diffusive, expansive and rapaciously all-embracing ideology. This is the idea, especially important in high-caste Hinduism, that both the singularity and the infinity is *Brahman* and everything is either co-extensive with, or an aspect of it. Consequently, every Hindu person or belief is but an aspect of this totality, no matter how varied, different, contradictory or opposed the contents of that totality are. In this sense, all non-semitic (i.e.

non-Judaic, Christian and Islamic) formations are Hindu formations (including all Buddhist, Sikh, Jain, Vaishnava, Shakta, Shaiva, animist, tribal or even atheistic belief systems) and all Hindu formations can legitimately be incorporated into, articulated by, spoken for and substituted with the political-religious formations, discourse and symbolism of the RSS and the VHP. Despite the Hindu idiom, this is strikingly similar to the totalizing vanguardism in modern Islamic movements and reflects many of the epistemic structures discussed in the previous chapter. It is additionally interesting that it exhibits a strong dynamism committed to total social change, while the classificatory and denotative ideologies and practices in Savarkarism and RSS philosophy are emblematically static and rigid.

One other Hindu far-right organization that is important to consider is the Shiv Sena (Army of Shivaji). It has a different history to that of the RSS "family" of organizations. The Shiv Sena was formed in 1966 by Bal Thackeray, formerly a cartoonist, as an anticommunist "pro-Maharashtrian" Hindu regionalist organization. The Sena's ideology has ranged since then from initially crude anti-Tamil, anti-southern Indian and anticommunist to anti-Gujarati and finally anti-Muslim political rhetoric. It very quickly became an extremely violent, fascistic anti-Muslim communal force, especially in Bombay. Historically, the Sena has been aided both financially and politically by Congress and by Maharashtrian industrialists, especially in its strike-breaking anti-communist activities and in its role of providing volunteer shock troops for various internecine battles (Hiro 1976: 184). Thackeray is an open and ardent admirer of Hitler and National Socialism and refers to Hitler's "greatness" and "artistry" in his speeches today (*The Guardian* 13 May 1995). The Sena are Maharashtra's *pogromshchiks*. They also control Maharashtra state in a coalition government with the BJP. They were responsible for the brutal attacks on Muslim communities in Bombay during early 1992 following the destruction of the Babri masjid. The Sena acts through extreme terror and brutality. For example, in the first half of the 1990s this has resulted in so many bombings and attacks on journalists and newspaper offices and the breaking up of any meetings that dared to criticize it, that a city-wide strike of journalists took place in Bombay in the summer of 1993 just over the Sena's terrorism and extortion (*The Hindu* 5 September 1993).

While communalist language and violence has been a part of Indian post-Independence politics, the more recent activities of the *sangh parivar* have framed this within a larger metanarrative of Hindu nationalism, Hindu superiority and mass social movement. Since the 1960s, communal violence against Muslim communities and beatings and murders of Muslims have been framed within the discourse of "necessary punishment" for a minority that is "too vociferous" and "unruly" and too demanding of "special privileges" and "rights" that are "denied" to the Hindu majority. A formative point for this new Hindu communalist language was the war between India and Pakistan in 1965. The incidents that perhaps best indicated this transformed discourse were the Muslim demonstrations in Gujarat that resulted from the Israeli storming of the al-Aqsa mosque in Jerusalem. The demonstrations caused resentments among Hindus and resulted in several days of rioting against Muslims. These events were celebrated by many Hindus with "triumphant pride": the Muslims "deserved to be taught a lesson". Further wars with Pakistan, Indian support for Bangladesh's separation, the intensification of the conflict in Kashmir, the growth of Islamic revival in the Subcontinent following the Iranian revolution and the war in Afghanistan resulted in further Hindu nationalist resentments.

Three events in the 1980s, all of which centred on the purity of the body, were extremely important for both Hindu and Muslim revivalists (Chhachhi 1991: 162) – the mass conversion of "untouchables" to Islam in Meenakshipuram, Tamil Nadu in 1981, the Supreme Court ruling on the Shahbano case in 1985 and an incident of self-immolation by a widow in Rajasthan in 1987. The Tamil Nadu incident directly changed the work of the VHP towards massive conversion, fundraising, Ekatmata ("Integration") and "Hindu Enlightenment" campaigns all over India. In Rajasthan, a young Hindu woman (Roop Kanwar) immolated herself on the funeral pyre of her husband and was hailed as a *sati*, leading to huge feminist and secular protests. These protests were interpreted by Hindu nationalists as "Hinduism under threat" and the suicide-murder was militantly defended as Hindu Rajput "tradition". Shahbano, an elderly Muslim woman, was divorced and abandoned by her husband and she subsequently filed a petition for alimony. The case went to the Indian Supreme Court which, in April 1985, ruled in her favour, overturning the legitimacy of Muslim Personal

Law in India. This was seen as both a victory against Muslims by Hindu revivalists and a victory for women by feminist and progressive organizations. However, after considerable lobbying by Islamic organizations, especially the Indian Jamaat-i-Islami and the (Deobandi) Jamaat-i-Ulema-i-Hind, Rajiv Gandhi's government intervened and overturned the court ruling by introducing new legislation.

We should note that it was virtually this same Islamic coalition which formed around the Shabano case that was also directly involved in starting the Rushdie affair in India and in Britain. Almost the same coalition was involved in political agitation in defence of the Babri masjid against Hindu fundamentalists. An extremely important political thread links Shahbano with Salman Rushdie and with the Babri masjid and emphasizes the fundamental importance of Hindu–Muslim communal relations in South Asia in shaping the global form of religious-political activism by Muslims and Hindus. In this register, incidents in the Middle East become less important in comparison with those in South Asia, as the Rushdie affair and the destruction of the Babri masjid demonstrated.

Many Indians viewed the government's intervention in the Shahbano case as an unjust concession to Islamic fundamentalists, an attack on women's rights and an opportunist strategy by the ruling Congress (I) Party to keep the Muslim "vote bank" (Muslims have traditionally voted Congress). Hindu nationalists saw this as a further appeasement towards a backward, intransigent Muslim minority: why should Hindus have to follow a "secular" common civil code but Muslims have their own separate legislation in matters of family law, divorce, polygamy and alimony? (The issue of personal law in India is extremely complicated for both Hindus and Muslims, and, especially, for women from both religious communities.) In Hindu nationalist political language, this is the "pseudosecularism" that "keeps Hindus enslaved in their own country". The similarity between this discourse and new-right and far-right racial discourse in the West should be apparent. Just as central are the personal politics of Roop Kanwar's death, the Shahbano case and the religious conversion cases in framing the national agendas of both Islamic and Hindu fundamentalists. In Hindu nationalism, as in Islamism, the personal is intensely political. Importantly, both the Shahbano ruling and Roop Kanwar's suicide-murder critically expose the recent fabrications of Hindu nationalism around women's rights. The same Hindu nationalist claims justified both these incidents. If Hindu nationalism could claim ownership of women's rights in the Shahbano ruling, it also vigorously defended the grotesque mass public spectacle of the murder of a woman in Rajasthan.

It is the way in which these recent developments have been articulated through a new Hindu tradition based on mythic history, new conceptions of blood superiority and new ideas of Hindu nationalism, that has led to the political language of the body in Hindu nationalism becoming especially violent. In the chants at Ayodhya, Muslims were called "the sons of Babar", who must "pay with their blood". The following quotations from the secular film *Ram ka Naam* (In the Name of God) made by Anand Patwardan (India 1991) are of Hindu *kar sevaks* (volunteers-servers) on their way to Ayodhya to destroy the Babri masjid:

> Those who dream of Babar, we will wipe out their aspirations. We will crush underfoot this poison ivy spreading in our garden. A looter destroyed our temple 462 years ago. It is a stain on our honour. While the mosque stands it reminds us of our slavery. We will not rest until we have destroyed it.

> *Was Godse right to kill Gandhi?* Absolutely right! Whoever betrays our nation will meet the same fate.

> Traitors beware! Lord Ram is awake! Victory to Lord Ram! Victory to Bharatmataji! ['Holy Mother India'] Any Hindu whose blood does not boil has water in his veins!

This language is not accidental, transient or simply contingent on the events taking place at Ayodhya. It is a deeply structured political language that definitively rehearses virtually all the themes of blood, martial tradition, race and race war, mystical and originary belonging, "cultural hearth" and disciplinary identity-formation that were at the core of Savarkar's and Golwalkar's political philosophy. This language is inserted into a religious idiom and a martial "tradition", symbolically reflecting a *brahmin–kshatriya* caste alliance. Its core is the theme of essential belonging by virtue of blood and soil to "Bharat". Indian Muslims do not belong to "Bharat" since "they are Pakistanis" – "If they wanted a separate state why don't they go and live there now? Why do they remain in India", "our" nation?

Alongside this *Hindutva* political language resides a vast repertoire of prejudice that would be instantly familiar to students of racism and ethnic hatred. Muslims are "intolerant" or "dirty", responsible for crime, prostitution, drug trafficking, they take away "our" jobs and homes, they have four wives or child brides, their population will overtake us (the fertility trope), they get favourable treatment and special rights, the state favours Muslims, Muslims have an absolute political veto, multiculturalism favours Muslim culture, equal opportunities policies and job reservations favour Muslims, secularism discriminates in favour of Muslims and against Hindus, Muslims are fundamentalists, Muslims are proselytizing and converting "*our* Hindus, *our* untouchables". Racist languages are themselves highly structured and extraordinarily capable of dismissing realist history or sociology. Hence, factors such as the higher levels of unemployment among Muslims compared with Hindus, or the roughly equal incidence of polygamy among Hindus and Muslims are elided. One route of escape from the brutality and prejudice of the Hindu caste system for many *dalits*, lower-caste Hindus and *adivasi* (tribal) peoples was to convert to Buddhism and Islam within which they have, technically, formal gender-differentiated equality. In Hindu nationalism this simply becomes Islamic fundamentalist proselytizing.

The political rhetoric of murder and death to the body of "the other" has always accompanied communal violence. But its articulation in this new Hindu nationalist metanarrative is often explicitly genocidal. Communal violence is manifestly about the recognition of difference in civil society, and the legitimation of physical attacks on, and murder and rape of those who are different. Aside from a few extremely important interventions (Das 1992b), it has been common on the Indian left to view communalism as "false consciousness" (Vaniak 1990: 153), a strategy of the state or ruling class to divide the masses along communal lines. Communalism is also invariably viewed as a phenomenon that commenced with, and was a strategic practice of British rule in India. It is also common to view communalism as an ideological epiphenomenon rather than a material practice carried out by cognitive agents who are not simply uncritical bearers of discursive formations that reside outside their communities. However, a common thread in most assessments of communalism is that, despite its "external" or institutional causes, a reservoir of violence lies just below a deceptively thin surface of peace and it requires a relatively minor incident ("a Muslim-owned dog bites a cow") or intervention ("a speech by Advani or Shahabuddin") to trigger it. Most assessments of communalism combine this reservoir–tinderbox view with an explanatory paradigm of external institutional cause.

However, communalism highlights important factors about the structuration of many modern, civil societies and the identities that are reproduced within them. Communalism is manifestly a problem of modern urban civil society. It is a highly dynamic cultural-political formation that may (or may not) be related to state ideology or social policy but is strictly autonomous from it. Significantly, communal violence is not generally directed against the state. Identities are thus formed not through eternal ethnic traditions but through new forms of difference constituted as martial territorialization of the urban city and routine acts of semi-organized and disorganized violence against affiliates of another identity. Murder might be terrifying but it becomes essentially mundane. In important ways, some civil societies are organized through the enactment of communal violence against others so that disorganized or semi-organized collective violence can become a permanent constitutive mechanism of identity formation in complex modern civil societies.

Of particular importance in the reproduction of violence are the local "historiographies", folk genealogies and folk memories that are created during periods of communal violence (of which the most important is the memory of past communal violence itself). This is an iterative and compounded memory whose nature is encapsulated in the phrase "the cycle of communal violence". The importance of "explanatory temporalities" in communal violence has been highlighted by Veena Das: "there are certain social practices which are defined by the fact that their temporal structure, direction and rhythm are *constitutive* of their meaning (Das 1992b: 15, emphasis in original).

Das discusses an investigation of Sinhala–Tamil conflict in Columbo which found that participants in both communities had very different versions of the sequence of events that led to a riot.

The tracing of these sequences back to some originary point is extremely difficult "since the precise sequence of events within which it is to be placed remains one of the most contested sites in the interpretation of violence". Similarly, it is exactly the alternative interpretations of the sequence of events – contested temporalities – that "constitute the meaning of the violence for people located in different social positions" (Das 1992b: 15). The "active forgetting" or "active retention" of past moments – "the capacity to contract two instants into a single sequence" – is itself an imaginative synthesis of time that provides both a local "historiography" of past violence and strategies for the anticipation of future action (ibid: 16). In important ways, this is highly suggestive of the general temporalities that are created by social movements and that give metanarrative meaning to local, small or particularized actions by their affiliates. It is here that the metanarratives of Hindu nationalism make routine communal violence possible and meaningful, and consequently even more dangerous. Local "historiographies" compound local myths, rumours, history and interpreted events of past violence. In the related spatial frame, urban areas are symbolically translated as communal territories – public civil space becomes territorialized and segmented without any necessary intervention by the state. In Hindu nationalism these local stories are contained within a broader hegemonic narrative that can articulate these local disorganized "historiographies" into a vast period of "time", itself imagined to be commencing from mythic or archaeological time-frames.

Another important aspect of communal violence is the celebration of visceral mutilation and the annihilation of the body of the other, an obsessive fixation on the body within a modern urban ritual of carnage and bloodshed. Importantly, there is an embedded aspect to disorganized collective violence that is about ecstatic "joy" and "rapture" in the riotous situation (cf. Gilroy's discussion of riots in Britain (1987: 238)). Communal violence is also a highly gendered phenomenon that focuses on the meaning of masculinity in a complex social formation where gendered difference is continually overdetermined by other differences. However, recent acts of communal violence in India have involved women as core mobilizing agents of men, as well as agents themselves of communal violence. The hate-filled political rhetoric of the VHP "*sanyasinis*", Sadhvi Rithambara and the (conveniently named) BJP MP Uma

Bharati, has been absolutely fundamental to this process. The reproduction of Rithambara's inflammatory and genocidal rhetoric by audio-cassette has been seen as fundamentally sufficient to create a permanent wall of communal hatred. As Tapan Basu et al. have argued,

> Rithambara's voice circulates with the ubiquity of a one-rupee coin in north India. Rithambara has in the process become the first mass leader in our country who has been created by a recorded cassette: she has herself become an extension of that cassette, for all her highly successful public speeches draw upon its format. But more than drumming up support for particular movements, this cassette has generalised and intensified communal attitudes to the point that they have become the meaning of existence for many. The Pesh Imam of the Babri Masjid implored us to do something about this cassette, for it, above all, had destroyed completely the affective basis of their relationship with their Hindu neighbours . . . (Basu et al. 1993: 100)

In much Hindu nationalist activity, Hindu women are frequently placed in important leadership, organizing or activist positions and very much *not* in the home. At Hindu rallies women speakers, often the main mobilizing speakers, taunt, abuse and insult the predominantly male audience: "Are you cowards?", "Are you real men?", "Are you effeminate weaklings?", urging them to commit acts of violence against Muslims – "can't you do any better than that, you pathetic idiots?" Similarly, during communal riots, women on the sidelines taunt and encourage men and women participants to go further. This includes the raping and murder of Muslim women and children, rapes of other women being justified because they are major violations of Muslim womanhood and consequently major indignities for their husbands or family. Women are mobilized in huge numbers under a powerful and violent conception of Hindu womanhood and are encouraged to engage in acts of violence against Muslims. In the communalist idiom, it becomes productive to efface Sita and Lakshmi – instead it is the *duty* of women to become Durgas:

Just now you tried weapons but they were only wooden.

Now you need to learn to use real weapons. The time to use
them is coming, the nation is in crisis.[6]

The activities of the Rashtrasevika Samitis (RSS-affiliate wom-
en's organizations) and the Durga Vahini have created a major
problem for secular Indian feminism which has never witnessed
anything like this mass mobilization of Hindu women before.[7]
In this Hindu nationalist idiom, some previously progressive
feminist voices have embraced the need to build a powerful,
exclusive *Hindu Rashtra*. *Manushi*, the renowned Indian feminist
journal, editorializes "in defence of *dharma*", and the necessity
of strengthening Hinduism and the nation, while also criticizing
men's oppression of women (*Hinduism Today* 17 (5) May 1995:
5). This novel Hindu nationalist discourse around womanhood
extends to the BJP, which can talk openly about "women's
liberation" and "womanpower", and about the necessity of
bringing women into the political, educational, economic and
social processes. Both these aspects can be articulated as part of
the same discourse. The extremely visible and militant presence
of Hindu women in Hindu nationalism has led some commentators to view this as an unforeseen but progressive and emancipatory development because Hindu women are being mobilized
in huge numbers under a militant and active conception of
womanhood, political participation and women's rights. However, at the same time, and through the same process, the most
brutal and violent masculinities are being constructed. Similarly,
a "naturalized" understanding of women as "homemakers" is still
dominant, especially in strictly religious Hindu nationalist ideology. Moreover, Hindu nationalist womanpower is a deeply
particularist understanding of women's liberation that is completed and hermetically sealed before the moment that Muslim
women can be articulated within it. This creation of Hindu sex/
gender systems is a novel rehearsal of Hindu "tradition" in
modern civil society.

One extremely important gendered trope for Hindu communalist
agitation has been that of "Bharatmata" – "Holy Mother India".
The Motherland definition that is essential to Savarkar's *Hindutva*
is hugely influential in contemporary discourse. "India" is represented as a frequently chained, bound or gagged woman and the
Muslim presence within it is thus signifies "a pollution", "a rape".

The intended conclusion is elementary – "Hindu womanhood is being raped", or more powerfully, "your mother is being raped" by Muslims and she is powerless to resist because she has been bound and chained like a slave by secularists and Hindu traitors. Similarly, Partition is often represented as the beheading of a sobbing, grieving Hindu woman. One popular VHP hoarding portrays a beautiful woman having her head slowly sliced off by secularists with a massive tooth-saw. An immense amount of blood is gushing from the wounds in her neck and pouring down her clothes. She is looking down at her bloodied body ("India") but her arms and legs are shackled and she can do nothing but cry. Her tears intermingle with her pure, wasted, Hindu blood.

It does not require a major leap to relate the visceral and intensely sexualized nature of these national symbols of Hindu nationalism, especially the continual representation of appalling and horrifying acts of mutilation of the body, to the actual practice of communal violence. Communal violence celebrates the frenzied mutilation of the flesh and destruction of the human body of "others", a tragic form of "personal politics". Of particular relevance to its reproduction is the importance of sexual narrative in constructing both the visceral symbols of communalist agitation and in providing various explanatory methods for local communalist violence. In the communalist idiom, sex, gender, femininity, masculinity, fertility, death and blood are used in both metonymic and metaphoric senses. These intensely libidinal tropes that are used in Hindu communalist agitation are the paradoxical end-products of a founding discourse that actually claims to suppress and "order" sex and sexuality. Golwalkar, for example, was quite explicit about the destructive nature of sexuality and the need to repress it:

> The "modern fashion" of young men is to appear more and more feminine. In dress, in habits, in literature and in every aspect of our day-to-day life "modernism" has come to mean effeminacy. "Sex" has become the one dominating theme of all our "modern" literature. History of countries the world over has time and time again shown that sex-dominated literature has been an unfailing precursor to the ruin of nations and civilisations. (Golwalkar 1966: 230)

The iterative, semiotic nature of communal violence also significantly evades a moral and ethical dimension about the killing of humans and the worth of human lives. This repeats the discussions of previous chapters – religious discourse, in its capacity to decentre the subject, also naturally and powerfully displaces philosophical humanism. While, indeed, the defeat of communalism requires a political strategy within the *personal* institutions of civil society, it is difficult to view such a strategy as simply one that stresses secularism – the ideal of a non-religious ethic – when communalism is so firmly fixed on the highly gendered and sexualized destruction of the body through an autonomous dynamic of local myth, rumour, memory and fabricated histories of purity.

Conclusion: modernity and the violence of purity

In both Hindu and Islamic fundamentalism the obsession with the body is strikingly repressive and violent. There is little celebration in revivalist discourse of the real erotic traditions of Islam or Hinduism, of the sexual pleasures of the human body. The sexual body is instead to be disciplined, contained, silenced, obscured or erased. However, just as important for communalist symbolism and mobilization is the continual manufacture of visceral symbols through which subjects are mobilized against "others". These symbols are explicitly libidinous and constituted through barely disguised sexual narratives. In this symbolism, the woman's body often becomes the privileged site of revivalist agitation. In both the Shahbano case and the Rajput Hindu glorification of the *sati*, the woman's body became the territory on which Islamic and Hindu neotraditions condensed. The identification in revivalist discourse of women as the bearers and reproducers of culture, and of women as equivalent to tradition, has a contrary side because women are also explicitly identified with unrestrained sexuality, and relentless temptation. In neofoundational discourse, women represent both the tradition that is to be preserved but are at the same time constitutive of the transgressive sexuality that is to be repressed. This is a ruptured and unsettled identification. Consequently, neotraditional discourse has to keep reproducing sexual narratives of the gendered body even as it ostensibly claims to repress sexuality. This pivotal place of sexuality in otherwise righteous revivalist discourse forms a core aspect of its obsessions with purity.

Noting the importance of sexuality and purity to neofoundation-alist discourse is far easier to do than explaining it. There are several themes that appear to be important, though they barely constitute an explanation and require further discussion. The regulation of sexuality is a characteristic feature of modernity (Foucault 1981) that, in the West, has had complicated historical links with the establishment of racial and class purity (Weeks 1981: 126–38). The creation of Hindu and Muslim Personal Codes and legislation dealing with sexuality, the family, polygamy, *sati*, and so forth in nineteenth-century India was informed by essentially British colo-nial mappings of sexual discourse that instituted British regulations of sexuality as an ideal. These British colonial codes are still considerably influential today and, arguably, dominate Indian regulations of sexuality. In this sense, the "traditional" purity strand within Hindu revivalist constructions of sexuality is essentially a Puritan strand. In important ways, British colonial codification of sexual morality and sexual practice also dovetailed into some forms of traditional *brahminic* asceticism and sexual renunciation. The colonial frontier also becomes important in another sense. The importance of slavery and colonization in constituting a sexual narrative for the West's sense of its own racial identity has been noted by numerous writers. However, what is at least as important is how these narratives impacted on the populations they colonized and instituted indigenous constructions of sexuality as a marker of communal difference within the social formation. Nineteenth-century colonial discourse imposed – possibly for the first time ever – legislated differences between different Indian communities through the narratives of sexuality, sexual practice, reproduction, fertility and the family. There is a deep link between British constructions of communalism and the sexual narratives of moder-nity. Indeed, it is instructive that contemporary Hindu nationalist constructions of Muslim "difference" reinstall aspects of British colonial discourse about Muslim sexual practice.

"Hindu communalism" has rarely acquired its potency in a *foundational* way, except perhaps during the period of Partition. It has, even during national waves of communal violence, tended to reactively follow localized or singular national or international events. However, today communal rhetoric is deployed within a metanarrative of Hindu revivalism that structures quite neatly the legitimacy of killing within an overall explanatory and generalized modality. The complex social formation acquires elementary intelligibility as a somatic "polluted" totality. This Hindu neotradition is not reducible to previous examples of communalism. Instead, Hindu communalism is legitimized within a systematic, ruthless formation of superiority, prejudice, state power and "Hindu revolution" (*kranti*). This modernist will to totalitarian power has deliberately created a dangerous gaze on an underprivileged minority "Other". The great challenge is in promoting a new counter-hegemonic "culture of social change" that embraces new political visions. This oppositional task is not restricted to secularists and progressive activists within India. The ideologies, organizations, political language and activities of Hindu nationalism have been hugely influential in diasporic communities outside India, just as Islamic revival has impacted on Muslim communities across the globe. Within the UK, the communalist idiom has increasingly structured the ethical relations of community and solidarity among South Asians. This is one area that is considered in the final chapter.

CHAPTER 7

The new materials of ethnogenesis: communalism, the body and science

> Mowgli, his head on Mother Wolf's side, smiled contentedly, and said that, for his own part, he never wished to see, or hear, or smell Man again. (Rudyard Kipling *The second jungle book*, [1895] 1968: 44)

> ... the source of the bloody barbarism of National Socialism lies not in some contingent anomaly within human reasoning, nor in some accidental ideological misunderstanding ... this source stems from the essential possibility of *elemental Evil* into which we can be led by logic and against which Western philosophy had not sufficiently insured itself. This possibility is inscribed within an ontology of a being concerned with being ... Such a possibility still threatens the subject correlative with being as gathering together and as dominating ... (Emmanuel Levinas, *Reflections on the philosophy of Hitlerism*, Critical Inquiry 17, Autumn 1990, p. 63.)

> Into blind darkness enter they who worship non-becoming. Into darkness greater than that, as it were, they who delight in becoming. (*The Isa Upanishad*, stanza 12 [trans. R. Hume 1877])

Introduction

The preceding chapters have argued that the authoritarian religious movements recovered under resurgent Islamism and Hindu nationalism are both novel and in important ways modernist.

233

There are two historical periods that have been important in the formation of neofoundationalist ideologies: the period of nineteenth-century colonial modernity and the period of decolonization. Each of the "traditional" sects that intervened in the Rushdie affair was formed either after the middle of the last century (the Deobandi and Barelwi movements and the Ahl-i-Hadith and Wahhabi sects) or in the period from the 1920s to the 1960s (the Jamaat-i-Islami, the Muslim Brotherhood, Khomeinism). The nineteenth-century sects were formed explicitly in relation to, though not all of them in opposition to, the colonial frontier. They primarily constitute the "orthodoxy of tradition" which Muslim communities in Britain have tried to preserve. These sect "traditions" are no more, and often far less, than about 150 years old. The authoritarian religious movements of this century were formed in explicit relation to the period of the formation of nation and nationalism from the first decades of this century. These Islamic sects became mass movements mainly from the 1960s. They, and the "traditional" sects of the previous century, engaged forcefully with the discourses of modernity, science, rationalism and nationhood.

In Hindu nationalism, virtually the same pattern recurs. While the numerous Ramakatha traditions are ancient, the Rama devotional cults that have dominated contemporary Hindu nationalism became politically important, as did the Babri masjid issue, from the 1850s, again in a complicated, non-reductive relationship to the British colonial frontier and modernity. The "tradition" now celebrated as ancient and eternal owes much to the activities of Hindu revivalist and reformist organizations of the last century. The Hindu authoritarian religious movements were created in the 1920s and became mass movements from the 1960s onwards. They were formed in explicit engagement with the modernist discourses of nationalism and secularism.

Both nineteenth-century and contemporary Islamic and Hindu revival thus have endogenous relationships with Western modernity but cannot be seen as congruent with a Western *telos* of modernity. However, all these formations have relied explicitly on modernist discourse. The Hindu revivalism of the last century cannot have a meaning if we remove its discourse of nationalism, liberation, emancipation and rights to which British colonialism was opposed. The Islamic sects were similarly formed in relation to what "nation" was to mean in the context of colonial domination. The neofounda-tional movements of this century are explicitly modernist. Neither Khomeinism, nor Maududism, Savarkarism and RSS philosophy, nor contemporary Islamic and Hindu mass movements have any meaning without their modernist core of revolution, a conception of total society, nationalism, nation-state formation, identity, the people and the mass movement, ordered civil society, the aim to modernize in some way, and an intensely rational, ordered and algorithmic structure to their political ideologies. Their ideologies are also practically organized within, and obtain their conditions of existence from the modern urban city. They owe their selective use of archaeological and anthropological methods to modernity and their reformation of individual identity is a modernist strand. Similarly, neofoundationalism, unlike "tradition", is not about stasis but radical change.

The ideas of liberation and purity that characterize authoritarian religious movements are products of Enlightenment and Romantic discourse and exhibit the tensions within and between both these traditions. The mystery of land, of blood, or nature or God is combined with the specialness of (some) humans, their civilizations and their beliefs. These factors are articulated within a generally rationalist discursive framework of order, classification, totality, instrumentality and reductionism. These latter themes were at the core of the scientific-technical or procedural rationality that was definitive of Enlightenment human and natural sciences.

Importantly, each of the authoritarian religious movements exam-ined in the book demonstrates several characteristics that were a definitive aspect of European fascism in the 1930s and 1940s: the combination of natural mystery, human mysticism and rational, virtually "scientific" order in a political project that depends on mass mobilization of the people, a will to political power and a political economy that rejected both capitalism and communism. The reli-gious authoritarian movements described in previous chapters incor-porate much of this same quality of "holistic-national radical Third Way" (Eatwell 1996: 11). Pantomimic versions of Darwin and Newton, and the kinds of ready-made evolutionism and determinism that were created by Comte and Spencer, Lamarck and Gobineau, often frame the epistemic boundaries of these social movements.

This mystical-natural, religious-political domain is not entirely reducible to nationalism. Instead it has existed in parallel with the development of modernity along nationalist, capitalist and communist lines. It needs to be seen in the same large conceptual way that we characterize other strands of modernity. However, accepting the latter means that Western conceptions about modernity have to be significantly revised. There is no meaningful way in which any of the religious formations examined can be described as premodern. But neither are they modernist in the accepted Western sense. This either means accepting the claims within Western modernity of the latter as *telos*, or asserting an historical perspective in which the impact of modernity in the "Third World" is "actually existing modernity" and the latter captures the global nature of modernity, its differential manifestations and its existence within a world-system of domination and exploitation.

This final chapter moves away from this discussion to focus on a number of densely interrelated themes that are important for mapping some of the shapes that neofoundational ideologies are taking. A diverse range of areas is engaged with, ranging from social policy and communalism in the context of UK multiculturalist policy development, via globalization and new communications technology, through to the importance of physics and biology for new religious movements. Each of these disparate areas is becoming important for both religious revivalist and authoritarian religions ideologies and in many ways provides the deep content for their ethnogenetic projects. The areas are discussed below as essentially markers for further political research rather than as forming a hermetic conclusion to the book. However, the theme of ethnogenesis runs through all of them and is discussed first. Perhaps most importantly, each area raises important *epistemic* and *ethical* issues, especially around universalist knowledges and particularist ones, and about ethico-political strategies founded on sameness or difference. The chapter concludes with a discussion of ethical themes that seem important to register for a secular black oppositional politics that lies within the socialist and feminist traditions, those enduring remnants of Enlightenment.

Ethnogenesis and being

It has been implicitly argued throughout the book that the transnational political importance of British black communities far outweighs their relation to the economics of labour exploitation or migration. Indeed, the political spaces that Asian, African and Caribbean communities have created in the UK are undetermined by the spaces of nation, civil society and community. Black communities constitute new non-contiguous communities based on affiliations and identities whose actual material of culture and ethnicity cannot be taken for granted. These communities are social as well as imagined spaces, and have acquired a physically translocal presence through the means of mass print and electronic communications and the technologies of time–space compression. Those "cyberspatial" relations have become essential for identity formation and for new rehearsals of ethnicity, tradition and religion. Importantly, they open up the possibility of displacing the historical narrative of community formation and social movement that has been definitive of both British black socialism and the field of race and ethnic relations. Indeed, the sociology of nation-state, civil society and community and the historical narratives of colonialism, migration and diasporic communities were disarranged during the Rushdie affair and in the global activities of Hindu revivalists.

These new authoritarian religions provide, like all identity formations, an epistemology of time, space and Being. The cultivation of ethnicity in new Hindu formations is, as we have seen, hugely dependent on elaborating an integrated temporal and spatial epistemology. Mythic, archaeological and modern times and their associated God-mythic space, the space of empire and the modern space of nation, city and community are the threefold space–times that frame their differential contents of land, blood and compulsive war. The eclectic combination of mythic, civilizational and modern times and spaces gives structure and meaning to the common sense of identity in the present. It enables local affiliates of that identity to construct folk genealogies that explain their Being in the present.

Consequently, new ethnicities can be seen as epistemologies of the present that seek to make sense of time, space and transcendental Being. Transcendental Beingness – immortality and significance – is achieved by manufacturing a grand epistemology that explains the present state of quotidian existence. Importantly, the new authoritarian religious movements examined in the book project a utopian universalism and humanism into both the past and the future but construct a deep and forbidding dystopian particularism that makes up their present. This dystopia makes sense of the temporal and spatial organization of modern nations, cities and communities, in which new religions can remain dormant or can become animated and dynamic.

Racism, religion and the desecularization of social policy

One consequent problem is how these new religious-ethnic projects in UK Asian communities co-exist with the *race* formation of these communities, especially in this troublesome period of European identity formation within which race has occupied a central place. To be sure, religious differentiation has become an important component of popular discriminatory discourse in the West against its minorities, especially Muslims and, increasingly, Hindus:

> MERRY KRISHNA – Kids Santa do axed for Hindu feast ... Santa Claus and his sleigh were ditched and the youngsters treated to an Indian Festival of Light Ceremony instead ... MP John Carlisle labelled it an "affront to traditional Christian principles". (*Daily Star* 12 November 1993)

The dogmatic formation of Christian fundamentalism in the US and Europe severely undermines the idea of Western social formations as unproblematically secular. The activities of Christian fundamentalism, itself closely allied in the USA to militaristic Romantic fascism (such as Christian Identity and the militia movements), have increasingly focused on Muslim and Hindu minorities. The extreme right-wing Senator Pat Robertson, for example, declared in 1995 that Hinduism was "demonic" and thus Hindus should be barred from entry into the US. (For the Hindu nationalist response to this, see Ram Swarup, "Mr Pat Robertson on Hinduism", *Hinduism Today* 17 (12) December 1995: 9.) Consequently, the threat that subaltern religious identification poses for the symbols of British and American nationalism and the various Christian traditions suggests very different materials for minority identity formation and it is not obvious that these can be conceptualized as "race formations".

Similarly, the affiliations being created in Asian communities, and the translocal spaces they represent, cannot be viewed as racial or, indeed, even ethnic identifications, if the latter are conceptualized as attributes, rituals, boundary formations and belief systems. The complex effects of global Islamic and Hindu religious resurgence, the national discrimination or racism faced in the West by Muslim or Hindu minorities, and the slower processes of community formation and socioeconomic participation in the West are all important factors.

This also means that the right-wing Islamic and Hindu formations we have examined by no means complete the identities, activities and concerns of members of South Asian communities in (or outside) the West. While authoritarian religious movements do constitute formidable disciplinarian political forces, they are also contingent formations that have barely begun to address the totality of social, economic, political, ideological and cultural issues facing South Asian communities. In important ways, their religious *epistemes* – despite the universality that is monotonously claimed for them – severely limit their capacity to address any of these issues aside from reductively condensing them to a set of religious aphorisms that soon begin to lose their discursive power against the glacial persistence of social and economic problems. However, the activities of these organizations can quite fundamentally divert attention away from the social, economic and political discrimination faced by South Asian communities in the UK. In particular, the articulation by entrepreneurial "ethnics" of a mesmerizing "authentic cultural unity" deftly erases the severe differences in class and gender interests between them and the working-class communities they speak for.

There is a rather cynical and highly particularist political strategy often used by religious organizations to appropriate the suffering or racial oppression faced by (only) their putative constituencies while at the same time failing to provide anything like a coherent or feasible analysis of, or opposition to, racial oppression or discrimination that travels any distance beyond an established set of religious aphorisms. For example, it would be disingenuous to provide an analysis of racist oppression against South Asian Muslims in the UK without looking at the historical processes that have shaped racial discrimination against South Asian, South East Asian, Jewish, Caribbean, Irish and African communities. However, the selective privileging of particular religious constituencies such as Hindus or Muslims in the (quite lucrative business of)

239

creating a hierarchy of racial oppression is becoming a persistent desecularizing strategy in local antiracist and multiculturalist social policy initiatives in the UK.

The discursive structures through which many of these interventions are articulated in social policy and activist politics are applications of some of the themes of civilizational aggrandizement, permanent dystopia, chauvinism, identity politics, the decentreing of the subject, social totality and so forth that were discussed in previous chapters. The argumentative structure seems to be made up of several factors:

- exclusive holism and totality – the form of argumentation that the favoured religion is the only solution to any or all social, economic, cultural and political problems under consideration, and that the favoured religion can provide both a holistic and a completed solution to these problems
- idealized utopia – the identification of the favoured religion as definitive of "the good", or the claim that some abstract universal good has always existed in the religion at all times and in all spaces. Importantly, what is actually "the good" and what is "evil" are tokens that are barely elaborated.
- epistemic overreach – the legitimacy of authoritarian religious discourse in articulating demands that are strictly out of its discursive orbit of comprehension let alone a basis for policy formulation
- reductionism – the reduction of the complexity of social factors, including social structures and class conflict, to bare, and often antagonistic, religious factors that in some way provide final explanations of the social factors under consideration
- religious maxims as explanation – the reduction of complex hermeneutics, description and policy formation to what can be derived from a minimum set of religious maxims, many of which can be widely and differently interpreted
- counterfactual explanation – explanation of the kind that, if the religious injunctions had been followed in their totality, then the social, economic, political or cultural problems under consideration would not have arisen
- substitutionist legitimacy – the argumentative style that institutes an imagined totalized, unfragmented constituency, such as "*umma*", "The Hindus", as the subject of the argument for

which it provides legitimacy: "Muslims [i.e. all Muslims] say
..." or "Hindus [i.e. all Hindus] want ..."
• the reduction of religion to an authoritative token and a
  character-agent that speaks autonomously to the subject that
  articulates its injunctions – this argumentation is of the kind:
  "Islam/Hinduism says ..."
• idealized platonic totality – an obscurantist dogmatism of the
  kind that in the favoured religion, the social, economic,
  political or cultural problems under consideration simply do
  not exist
• idealist sanction – an authoritarianism of the kind that in the
  favoured religion, the social, economic, political or cultural
  problems under consideration are forbidden, and therefore
  should not exist or should not be practised
• substitution of deep empiricism or critical empirical investigation by (atemporal) anecdote, personal experience or naïve
  rationalism

In this schema, the social and political issues under consideration
could be anything from racism, child sexual abuse, alcoholism, drug
abuse to imperialism, economic exploitation, the environment and
so forth. It is often simply the rhetorical force of these dogmatic
argumentative styles and the abstract religious authority they
invoke, rather than any reasoned, analytical and usually complex
understanding of the social issues, and the consequent social
policies that may be necessary.

Shabbir Akhtar's defence of the "virtues" of Islamic fundamentalism is one such example, perhaps a more sophisticated form of
this argumentative style, occasionally supplemented with a good
dose of Nietzschean *Schadenfreude* (Akhtar 1989: 95–106). It is
based on an uncomplicated understanding of social, political and
historical processes which, in his methodology, seem to be mostly
comprehensible from the narrow gaze of analytical logic. Indeed,
his methodology is dominated by an individual argumentative style
in which false (op)positions are constructed and then dismantled,
and from which apparently universally applicable observations are
derived. Akhtar clearly believes reason, or at least one Cartesian
form of it, can thoroughly assist in the defence, or reconstruction,
of fundamentalism. His argument, however, conceals three essential
circularities: fundamentalism (which he does not define) exists for

its own sake, since religion must have "an internal temper of militant wrath"; Islam is a "unified enterprise of faith and power"; and the ultimate end-point of the contemplation of religion by reason has to be faith, since reason cannot go further. However, all Christian, Hindu, Sikh, Jewish and Islamic fundamentalisms have their own internal temper of destructive militant wrath and their affiliates would see them as unified enterprises of faith and power. "Wrath" barely constitutes an analytical, explanatory or even prescriptive device, and seems to have the role of a military token, one of many metaphoric associations between war and religion that Akhtar seems to celebrate. Moreover, "wrath" is essential for all religions according to his schema, the consequences of which are already apparent and that he presumably approves. His closure of reason by (the leap of) faith is also essentially dogmatic, for reason can still continue to question faith after one has submitted to the latter (or, where faith stops in faith, reason can still continue in the doubt of faith). Faith also demands adherence to, or at least the necessity of facing and negotiating with, the scandals of religion that reason has already discovered to be false and unwarranted. But Akhtar is silent about which scandals of religion one should own and which should be abandoned. Similarly, his discussions of oppression, exploitation and liberation, barely venture beyond those terms themselves. They act as motifs and tokens without any real theory of oppression or exploitation beyond the aphorism or the palimpsest.

The kinds of social policy options that religious-political revival has produced are illustrated in the vast and burgeoning literature produced by Islamist and traditionalist Muslim organizations on education, gender, parenting, health, family, religious, political and social welfare issues in Britain. With few exceptions, these are focused on non-empirical, anecdotal information and a selective appeal to the authority of the Qur'an, Sunna and the hadiths. From a religious frame, and from bare impressionistic, anecdotal and personal experiences, policy options are derived that do not even start to address the actual social policy, health care, educational, employment, housing and social care issues that are relevant to Muslim communities in the UK. Shabbir Akhtar's handbook for Muslim parents (Akhtar 1993), for example, is focused virtually entirely on the need to provide Islamically oriented education. Fairly typically, this includes the right of Muslim girls to wear approved dress, the right to withdraw from comparative religious education and religious assembly, fully-clothed single-sex sports activities, halal school meals, a balanced approach to the portrayal of Muslims in history and religious education, the right to practise religious worship in schools as required, "mother-tongue" and Arabic teaching, the right to withdraw from sex education, and an appraisal of the "liberal arts" in order to cultivate non-representational and calligraphic art forms. Additionally, Akhtar also highlights another fairly typical revivalist agenda, whose moral and political conditions of possibility are those framed by official neoconservatism: the need for single-sex, separate, voluntary-aided, or grant-maintained Muslim schools together with some acknowledgement of linguistic needs (including Arabic language teaching). Issues such as truancy or poor educational performance are simply reduced to the lack of a strong Islamic identity. Moreover, multiculturalism and equal opportunities stop for Akhtar before the point where other national minorities have legitimate needs to be addressed in social policy:

> Muslims welcome the stipulation in Section 28 of the Local Government Act (1988) which forbids local authorities to use public funds to promote homosexuality or to teach that homosexual behaviour can be part of an acceptable family relationship. (1993: 32)

Akhtar here uses multiculturalism (formally, a universalist discourse) to articulate a discourse of minority rights for Muslims through which disciplinary substitution ("Muslims welcome ...") and authoritarian exclusion are used to deny the minority rights of another group. This rehearses a key ethical issue in ostensibly universalist, pluralist discourse – its use to claim particularist rights that deny the rights of other minorities. If one accepts the legitimacy of a pluralist framework of rights, and one necessarily demands a deep, committed and learned consideration by others of the needs of one's own constituency, is there not also a necessary responsibility for one to undertake that same deep, committed learning and consideration of other groups outside of (or inside) one's own constituency? (Put differently, when does a particularist demand have to demonstrate itself to be a universal principle, at what stage is a particularist maxim under the obligation to represent itself and

243

demonstrate itself as a valid universal moral law?) Suffice to say, Akhtar's dismissal of the rights of others barely begins to address the complexities of human sexuality and sexual identity, or indeed of the needs of Muslims or non-Muslims who may be gay or lesbian.

It additionally seems remarkable for a handbook on education that there is virtually no discussion of education: vocational training, transferable skill development, reading, writing and comprehension skills, computer-based training, (non-European or European) language learning, school discipline, the responsibilities of parents in education and learning, teaching and learning methods, or of the content of education – the physical sciences, English, literature, geography, mathematics, the social sciences, information technology and so forth. There is an implicit assumption that either these are irrelevant to the future of Muslim children, or that they already accommodate their needs and identities as Muslims, though below we shall see how even the area of natural sciences education and canon formation can become an ideological battleground.

The focus on educational institutions by Islamist organizations is unsurprising, since these are conceived as one of the primary vehicles of cultural reproduction. However, it is the organicist, structural-functionalist approach to these institutions that is most striking. This is essentially a variant of the view that the social formation or any of its constituent structures is comprehensible as an elementary reductive totality into which religious discourse can simply be injected. This has consequences for how subjectivity is imagined in these discourses. One important educational issue in recent years for UK Islamist groups has concerned the teaching of comparative religion, and the consequent demand to withdraw Muslim children from religious education classes. The only argument that has been used for this withdrawal is that Muslim children will be "confused" by (necessarily neutral or secular) study of the world's main religious traditions (more confused than when they first encounter arithmetic long division?), and consequently any teaching of comparative religion has to be undertaken from an Islamic perspective (*The Guardian* 5 February 1996). Both these views of social totality and human personality are distinctive for the elementary relationship that they assume between ideology and social institution, and between ideology and human personality development. The other side to the view of a hermetic social totality is the cybernetic and algorithmic personality that was encountered in the last chapter.

South Asian communalist discourse in Britain

The above examples of the potential desecularization of social policy in the UK illustrate the effectiveness of global religious revival in setting the overall agendas within which the issues facing South Asian communities are increasingly framed. It is through these same hegemonic ventures that the political languages of communalism become disseminated and effectual. The predominance of new communalist language in informing relations between Asian communities makes for a depressing assessment. The swiftness with which an internationally effective communalist language is now structuring intra-Asian relations was illustrated in November 1993 when the Abu Bakr mosque in Southall widely distributed a leaflet that contained a photograph of an Ealing council building and a strong appeal to Muslims.[1] The leaflet stated that Hindus had raised more funds than Muslims to buy the building and feared that Muslims would be unable to outbid the Hindus. The leaflet asked Muslim readers for their help and donations and stated their responsibility: "you make the decision – mosque or mandir". It is some measure of the power of neofoundational ideologies that an appeal for funds to purchase a local authority building should explicitly invoke the bitter experience of Ayodhya and present a disgraceful and cynical choice between mosque or mandir, this time in a west-London suburb. This choice, as we have seen in the last chapter, is a very recent one and perhaps highlights how religious intolerance in Islamic and Hindu fundamentalism is a modern concept that has erased the strong older traditions in both religions that were based on tolerance and protection of other religious groups.

Hindu nationalism has not been dormant in disseminating its antisecular agendas in British, European and American Hindu communities. In the early 1990s, a RSS–VHP video cassette made by J. K. Jain Studios in India was widely disseminated in the UK. This video was reproduced by an Asian video company in Brent and distributed by the Hindu Sahitya Kendra in Birmingham and by local VHP and RSS branches to Hindu temples, cultural organizations, shops and homes in the early 1990s. Indeed, the video was distributed door-to-door to Hindu homes, in many cases for free. It was among one of several "Hindu nationalist texts" that have assisted in creating a view among many Hindus in Britain of "Indian history" and the Muslim presence. The 90-minute video, called *The story of Ramjanmabhoomi – past, present and future* (a version of *Bhaye Prakat Kripala* in India) was expensively produced and deployed computer graphic technology and extensive special effects. The video contains several narrative forms, including dramatized play acts, linear historical narrative, graphic illustrations, devotional songs, footage lifted from fictional war films (some of it patently absurd given the historical context), and film of Hindu demonstrations and mass rallies.

The video commences with a computer-generated *bricolage* of Hindu – and interestingly Sikh – religious symbols circling the screen and condensing into the "tree" logo and slogan of the VHP, "the protector of the faith" urging "Hindu unity". This demonstrates the inclusivist and tributary nature of VHP propaganda (though rhizomic or filamental would probably be a better description). An introduction states its unapologetic and militant nature and confirms the support of the VHP and RSS. It emphasizes the international, as well as the national nature of the "struggle for Ramjanmabhoomi" ("Rama's birthplace") and the importance of recreating India as a *Hindu Rashtra*. The video makes explicit appeals to Hindu women, traditional Hindu *sadhus* (priests) who may not be willing to follow the VHP's line, and poor, lower-caste and "tribal" people. It skilfully inserts the idea of martyrdom using the Hindu concept of *moksha*, the final liberation of the soul from the cycle of birth and rebirth. *Moksha* can have an importance in Hinduism similar to Paradise in Islam and Heaven in Christianity. The message to viewers is clear – defend Hinduism and you will attain *moksha*.

The video presents an epic historical narrative commencing with *Brahman*, the force of cosmic creation. This demonstrates inventive use of NASA astronomical and stellar photography, including a photograph of a supernova onto which a pulsating neutron star has been superimposed. The booming cosmic narration quickly identifies *Brahman* with Rama, "the only true manifestation of *Brahman*", a typical disciplinary substitutionism in Hindu nationalism. The whole of cosmic creation therefore condenses towards

Ayodhya in *Akhand Bharat* ("undivided Bharat") after which a history of India is presented. The political geography of India is transformed in this narrative into a selective religious geography. Ayodhya is now placed at its pre-eminent symbolic core, the heart of the imagined geographical nation. The historical narrative is also virtually identical in structure to Savarkar's "historiography" of originary Aryan civilization, a long period of brutal war with "alien conquerors" and the contemporary need to strengthen Hinduism, but this time because of "the struggle for the liberation of the Ramjanmabhoomi" (*Sri Ram janmabhoomi mukti andolan*). The historical content emphasizes numerous themes of war that are intended to appeal to a wide and diverse constituency of "Hindus", both men and women. The video continues with the militant and caustic speeches of Sadhvi Rithambara. An RSS bugle march portraying the future that India can look forward to completes the video. Each presentation in the video of Indian Muslims is designed skilfully to portray Muslims as a threatening, amorphous, violent and especially dehumanized force – for example, they are never depicted using a full colour palette but are instead portrayed in a few dusky colours accompanied by a menacing soundtrack.

Just as insidiously, the video restructures the Hindu devotional idiom in its portrayal of Rama by a precocious child actor who is playing about "his compound", the Babri masjid. While there are mythical narratives about Rama's childhood, the use of a child-God is a strong appeal to Krishna devotees for whom Krishna's childhood (*lalo*) is especially important. This use of electronic video technology to represent a deity for mass consumption significantly transforms the meaning and impact of the devotional mode of Hindu worship. The deity is no longer static and iconic but a representing agent, a simulacrum more real in its miraculous special effects than any God likely to be encountered through personal devotion to idols. The deity engages directly and forcefully with the devotee viewer who is obliged to abandon him– or herself to this pixel God. It appropriates the method of Bollywood as well as the Doordarshan TV broadcasts of the *Ramayana* and the *Mahabharat* in the period 1987–9 which were watched by up to 80 million people. We should note that this electronic representation is not only novel but transgressive. It creates not just a new medium but constitutes a new meaning for what *bhakti* Hinduism – and Hindu identity – is now to become. While we should not assume an uncritical consumption of electronic idolatry, or that the same medium cannot also be used to oppose it, the RSS–VHP video representation extremely skilfully transforms the Hindu devotional idiom. It layers highly emotional religious chants with a representation of an innocent child-God who just happens to be at the site of the disputed Babri masjid. This is a fusion of an intense emotional appeal with formally devotional themes that no believing (Vaishnava) Hindu could rationally contest or fail to acquiesce to. The articulation of these themes into a doctrinaire narrative of contemporary events is a deep political-hegemonic strategy that has the capacity to create the powerful feelings of hurt, offence, insult and, consequently, action among Hindus who are not actually or formally required to believe everything that the RSS and the VHP say. The importance of this technique is in practically reproducing the structure of feeling that had been described in a different context by Savarkar as constitutive of Hindu identity.

The RSS and VHP have both managed to establish an international structure and large followings in Britain, Europe, Canada, the USA and, reputedly, at least 70 other countries. The RSS is usually called the Hindu Swayamsevak Sangh (HSS) outside India, but has several affiliate organizations or support networks. These include the Vivekananda Kendra, a sport and education organization for youth (this was first formed in India by Eknath Ranade, an important early RSS activist and ideologue), the American Hindu Students' Council and various Hindu "cultural heritage" associations in the US and in the UK for youth and young children. The Arya Samaj groups have also been important in Britain and exhibited the fundamentalist obsession with purist representation by organizing protests against Gurinder Chadha's feminist film *Bhaji on the beach* in 1994 for its "insulting" and "blasphemous" portrayal of a woman who, during a dream sequence, stubs out a cigarette at the idol of Rama. (The film was withdrawn in India.) Violence against Asian women was a dominant theme in the film but this did not incite the Samaj to organize similar protests against male brutality.

The RSS is reputed to have about 40 *shakas* in Britain alone. The Vishwa Hindu Parishad has at least 100,000 members in Britain, Canada, the US and Europe and many more supporters. In Britain it has its own publication and is reputed to have 40 branches and camps to train workers. The VHP outside India has grown phenomenally. Its tenth session in New York in 1984 attracted 5,000 delegates, in comparison with the 35 delegates who attended its first session in Ohio in 1970 (Andersen & Damle 1987: 136–7). The VHP and the American RSS were the sponsors for the Hindu "Global Vision 2000" conference held in Washington DC in early August 1993. This had over 10,000 delegates and, though most were not VHP affiliates, their presence indicated the impact of the VHP's shape-shifting and inclusive political strategy (*Hinduism Today* 15 (10) October 1993). Britain is the base for the VHP's European network, which has organized several Europe-wide conferences. In 1989, the VHP held an explicitly political, *Hindutva*-dominated, *Virat Hindu Sammelan* (Hindu Congress) in Milton Keynes that attracted 50,000 people. The brochure for the *Sammelan* was dedicated to Hedgewar and the RSS and contained messages of support from both Buckingham Palace and 10 Downing Street, as well as numerous other organizations. The VHP's fifth European Hindu conference was held in Frankfurt in August 1992 and had 1,200 delegates. The conference was subject to tight police security because of demonstrations by some Sikh groups (*Hinduism Today* 14 (11) November 1992). Both the RSS (as the HSS) and the VHP are represented on various Hindu councils across Britain. They have received significant funds from (usually left-wing) local authorities, often given under the guise of religious, cultural heritage, educational or language-learning activities. Both the RSS and VHP have focused strongly on mobilizing American, Canadian and British Hindus through educational initiatives (especially for youngsters) and through international fundraising campaigns such as the 1989 Brick Appeal of the VHP during which the VHP urged Hindus in 25 countries to send "blessed bricks" and money for temple construction at Ayodhya. Many British temples sent money and symbolic bricks to Ayodhya.

It has not required the presence of the VHP or the RSS to demonstrate caste prejudice in Britain. Hindu organizations, including most temples, many of which may be opposed to the extremism of the RSS, are universally structured through caste (*jati*) membership, as well as *gotra* (exogamous clan), *sampradaya* (a movement or loose community based around a spiritual leader), religious sect and regional origin. Every Hindu council in Britain is composed mainly of caste-defined organizations. These Hindu councils receive significant local state, Labour and Conservative Party patronage, as well as some local authority funds. The persistence of caste prejudice in Hindu communities has barely received attention or opposition from black socialism. It also demonstrates a considerable underdevelopment in secular thinking within multiculturalist and antiracist efforts in Britain.

Unsurprisingly, some of the activities of the (now abolished) left-wing Greater London Council (GLC) illustrated the state of socialist secularism in the 1980s. The GLC funded several RSS and VHP activities in London (one of which was an RSS–VHP Hindu temple in Newham). This funding process was investigated by Channel 4's *Bandung file* series in the summer of 1986. Similarly, of the 362 South Asian groups that were on the GLC's directory and mailing list,[2] almost half were explicitly based on religious (i.e. religious exclusionary) identification and over half of the Hindu organizations showed some explicit caste or sect affiliation. It is striking that only one explicitly anticaste organization, an Ambedkarite group, was on the list. Of the Hindu, Sikh and Muslim organizations on the list, nine were associated with the RSS–VHP network, two were Arya Samajist or related to other Hindu revivalist formations, five were Sikh fundamentalist and one a Jamaat-i-Islami group. About 16 per cent of Hindu organizations on the GLC's list were far-right groups. While these numbers only give an indication, they do highlight the predominance among Hindu organizations of caste organization and the striking presence of far-right groups. Similarly, the Brent Hindu Council (BHC) in north London, which has an established relationship with the local authority, has, among its 54 affiliated members for 1993, the RSS and the VHP, as well as Brahmin, Kshatriya, Patidar, Dhobi, Darji and Lohana caste-*jati* organizations. Of its member organizations, 24 are explicitly caste-based. Only three of its member organizations use the secular category of "Asian" in their names. Not a single *dalit* ("untouchable") or explicitly anticaste organization is affiliated. The Brent Hindu Council, like many Hindu organizations, has become stridently revivalist in recent years and has vigorously promoted the "Hinduism under siege" line: "throughout the world, the very existence of Hindus is threatened by others' efforts to convert, discredit and persecute" (*Hinduism Today* 14 (11) November 1992). This coded communalist language is well understood by Hindus. It invokes a global conceptual concern as well as the "genocide" of Hindus, and, in its last three words, Islam, Pakistan and the Mughal period. The increasing reliance on the communalist political idiom during the

1980s and 1990s within British Hindu, Muslim and Sikh communities was dramatically illustrated after the Babri masjid was destroyed:

> Members of Britain's Hindu and Muslim communities are taking extraordinary security measures as the wave of arson attacks on places of worship, sparked by the destruction last weekend of the Ayodhya mosque in India, continued yesterday . . . . Two fires were started deliberately in a Hindu temple in Leeds yesterday. In Derby, about 20 worshippers attending morning prayers at the Jamia mosque extinguished a minor blaze . . . . Three days ago, the ground floor of the city's Hindu temple was gutted . . . . In Sheffield arsonists hurled petrol bombs into the Hindu Samaj temple in Burngreave . . . . A Hindu temple in Ealing suffered slight damage . . . . It was the third such attack on a temple in the capital in two days . . . there have also been incidents in West Bromwich, Coventry, Birmingham, Luton, Bolton and Bradford. (*The Independent* 11 December 1992)

Globalization and ethnic identity formation

It is through these complex processes, international and intensely local, involving community formation and state multiculturalist apparatuses, as well as international religious networks and community antagonisms in civil societies, that new forms of ethnic-religious identification are created. The global component of this has become particularly important for the recovery of religious "tradition". One dramatic illustration occurred in 1995, and highlighted the distinctive importance of instantaneous electronic communication technology for religious revival. Idols and depictions of the elephant-God Ganesh in South and South East Asia, Britain, Europe, Australia, the USA, Latin America, Africa, Canada, the Caribbean and the Middle East "suddenly" started to absorb milk. The "Ganesh milk miracle" began on 2 September 1995 and

251

lasted for about one day (variously, 18 or 24 hours) after which the divine thirst was quenched. The extraordinary rapidity with which the event spread and involved millions of Hindu individuals and families, believers and non-believers alike, in mass self-similar social agency should not detract from the uniqueness of the "miracle" of Ganesh drinking milk, which owed practically nothing to ethnic Hindu tradition. The intense debates on all the main national television and cable news channels and newspapers in the UK about the surface tension of milk, absorption and capillary action in varieties of stone, granite, fired clay and marble or other physical and chemical processes, highlighted the confidence of religious revivalists in facing and articulating natural science, a factor we examine below. The miracle had, however, rather more secular beginnings in both India (where, in the midst of a local religious dispute, a *sadhu* dreamt that Ganesh was drinking milk) and the UK (when an RSS member in the UK went to the Vishwa Hindu mandir in Southall and offered milk to a Ganesh idol). The VHP and RSS were quick to mobilize their international networks to generate the miracle globally. (The VHP also intervened in the bovine spongiform encephalopathy (BSE) scandal in the UK by helpfully suggesting that the human Creutzfeldt-Jakob disease was retribution for eating sacred animals (a variant of the counterfactual argument). It was also suggested by VHP representatives that cattle infected with BSE, instead of being slaughtered, could be adopted by Hindus in the UK.)

The importance of mass global communications for religious revival in the Ganesh "milk miracle" and the Rushdie affair highlights the fundamental appropriation of the means of communication by religious revivalists or fundamentalists as a central aspect of their political methodology. (The American Christian fundamentalist, evangelical and revivalist obsession with cable, radio, TV and satellite has a similar but more intense and longer pedigree.) Indeed, a current political dispute in Britain concerns the activities of Mohammed al-Masari and the Committee for the Defence of Legitimate Rights in Saudi Arabia, an Islamist organization that became important through its use of the fax and e-mail to oppose the Saudi dictatorship. The skilful and determined use of mass electronic communications by Hindu nationalist and Islamist groups extends to the Internet, especially the World Wide Web, and includes several Usenet newsgroups, various Listserv services and influence over numerous Internet Relay Chat channels. The BJP

(Kamal Darshan), the RSS, the Hindu Swayamsevak Sangh, the RSS–VHP aligned Hindu Students' Council (GHEN – The Global Hindu Electronic Network) and its American and Canadian network, as well as the Chinmaya Mission and the Swaminarayan Mission,[3] have extensive sites, mostly based on US Web servers. Similarly, the Jamaat-i-Islami, the Muslim Brotherhood (and its numerous branches and affiliated organizations, each portraying the Brotherhood's Qur'an and two swords logo and its oath of struggle), the UK-based Muslim Parliament, the Committee for the Defence of Legitimate Rights in Saudi Arabia, Hizb-ut-Tahrir (and its various branches in the US and the UK), the Khomeinist Islamic Centre of England (probably the most dedicated Khomeini site) and numerous other Islamist organizations are represented on Web sites and offer extensive activist and political resources on the Internet. The secular, agnostic or atheistic Hindu and Muslim oppositional presence on the Internet is paltry in comparison.

However, Hindu nationalists have, like their Christian and Islamic counterparts, focused more critically on the content of mass global electronic communications technology. A recurring theme in both Hindu and Islamic neofoundationalist discourse is the corrupting influence of Western TV, satellite and cable, while at the same time, neofoundationalism privileges this medium for its messages. During the early 1990s, the immoral, impure and degrading content of television and satellite programming became an important topic in Indian public culture (as well as in Iran, Saudi Arabia, Pakistan and numerous other countries). The astonishing growth of satellite and cable TV in India, interpreted as "an onslaught against Hindu tradition", has included Star TV, Star Plus, Asia Today Network (ATN), CNN, MTV and the BBC. Star TV, now owned by Rupert Murdoch, broadcasts Indian-language and English programmes from Asia Sat I. ATN, which is owned by Western Indians, uses the Asia NET satellite. The success of satellite and cable TV in India has generated major moral panics, often orchestrated by Hindu revivalists and far-right organizations, about the effects of Western multimedia on Hindu youth and morals: "White, Western, Monstrously Rich, Morally Broke – TV's new icons of worldliness now guide India's Youth" (*Hinduism Today* 15 (1) January 1993: 17)

While one can see the appeal of this kind of invective, its doubling and reversal should be noted, for this is an exact reversal of the colonial discourse that placed Indians at the core of uncivilized sexual depravity. Now, the West is identified with immorality and Hinduism with sexual, moral and ethical purity. This discourse is about the purity of "cyberspace", often identified with the purity of the woman's body, and compared directly to mythic purity: "Today, when Hindu schoolgirls socialise, they allude not to Sita of Valmiki's *Ramayana* but to Gina of Star Plus' Santa Barbara" (*Hinduism Today* **15** (1) January 1993: 17). It is doubtful that many Indian schoolgirls ever chatted about Valmiki's *Ramayana* and even more doubtful that *Santa Barbara* is going to destroy Indian civilization, at least not for the reasons being given by Hindu nationalists. However, the alternative disciplinarian and exclusionary symbols that Hindu nationalists want to substitute for "Western TV" should be noted. In October 1990, the VHP, the BJP and the RSS organized a *rath yatra* ("chariot pilgrimage") from Somnath to Ayodhya. A motor-jeep was redesigned as the God Rama's chariot and was driven towards its final "victorious" destination where an attempt was made to storm the Babri masjid. Each stop on the "pilgrimage" was an important Hindu religious place and was symbolically "captured" by the masculine warrior advance. The itinerary relied on a selective religious cartography of northern India. This "traditional pilgrimage" would have had no meaning outside its reporting on television, radio and newspapers. It was designed for mass electronic and print consumption. BJP leader, L. K. Advani, who rode the "chariot", was explicit that the importance of the pilgrimage was its semiotic and symbolic quality. It was, for him, irrelevant whether or not Rama was born at Ayodhya. Predictably, it resulted in a wave of communal violence throughout India. Prior to the "pilgrimage", Doordarshan, the government-controlled national TV network, partly in response to competition from other TV stations as well as the threat of cable and satellite TV, broadcast productions of the two Hindu epics, the *Mahabharata* and the *Ramayana*. These productions are being hailed by Hindu nationalists as the privileged model of electronic representation (Mitra 1993). The importance of the televised religious epics was through their direct contestation and replacement of Western corrupting influences. Their value for formal politics was illustrated when the actress who played Sita in the *Ramayana* production stood for election as a BJP candidate and won a seat in India's parliament.

Neofoundational "science" and the control of freedom

The neofoundational political method based on new communications technology highlights an important orientation among religious revivalist and fundamentalist organizations towards natural science. This has sharp ethical consequences that have often not been noted by progressive forces, and highlights the necessity of critical engagement by the left with natural scientific discourse. In extremely important ways, the appropriation of natural sciences, as well as their physical and biological technological products, have formed the contents, and even the metaphoric shape of some of the new ethnicities that are recovered under religious revivalism. This may appear to be anomalous – natural science and religious discourse are typically comprehended as adversaries. To be sure, there are widely varying religious attitudes to natural science, and some of the fundamentalist orientations are one strand. However, there are important epistemic leaps undertaken in much religious revivalist and fundamentalist discourse that, for their affiliates, pose little difficulty in cultivating a parasitic or metaphoric relation with natural science. Much of this is prefigured in the mutilated Cartesian rationalism and naïve and delimited empiricism with which religious fundamentalism approaches the human sciences. But it also shows in the disciplines that formed the intellectual development of many of their founders – especially engineering, as well as chemistry, physics and classical economics.

It was noted in previous chapters that neofoundationalism persistently invokes the textual method, but does so in an eclectic, selective and semiotic manner. Neofoundationalism presents a deconstructive case with regard to its (paradoxically) privileged texts. This semiotic relation to the text is extended to be universally applicable to all texts – an unwarranted breach of epistemic and disciplinary boundaries – and allows various pseudo-isomorphic relationships to be established between a superior religious discourse and an inferior natural science that the former nevertheless still attempts to embrace. Several characteristic themes are present in this relationship. Revivalist discourse often makes the founding, and false, assertion that natural science makes claims to both universal and complete knowledge whereas it is limited by human intellectual capacities that only religion or God can transcend. (In reality, of course, natural science cannot ever claim certainty or completed knowledge for it would lose its *raison d'être*: natural science is foundationally based on the unknowable and the uncertain.) However, religious revivalist discourse, much like New Age philosophy, also has a dependent relationship on the discoveries of natural science.

In many forms of modern Hindu and Islamic revival, there is a striking obsessive and iterative reliance on each new discovery of natural science, which, it is consequently argued, either had already existed in religion, or is limited in its capacity for total explanation anyway. Natural science is also seen as materialistic, mechanistic, determinist and particularist and in some consequent way evil, though this is typically compared with a totalizing, holistic, "infinite" and completed religious discourse. Moreover, the critique of natural science's materialism elides the rather materialist obsessions of fundamentalist discourse – those of land, nature, state, political power, technology, economy and so forth that were discussed previously. Interestingly, "materialism" is seen as evil and particularist, whereas "nature" is virtually universally constructed as good, benevolent, amiable and infinite.

Most importantly, though, much religious revivalist discourse seeks to demonstrate a deep isomorphic, or even chiral relation between itself and the discoveries of natural science, especially physics, without, however, accepting the critical consequences for itself that the methods resulting in such discoveries may have. The rather liberal excavation of religious texts is undertaken to illustrate the relations between modern cosmologies and ancient religion. To be sure, much of this is the result of the necessary need to "cultivate civilization" against the erasures and distortions of Western colonialism, imperialism and racism, to demonstrate the rich classical and medieval traditions of learning in the natural and human sciences that existed in Arabic and Indian traditions, particularly in philosophy, astronomy, arithmetic, literature, the arts, mathematics, optics, cosmology, historiography and natural history. (Significantly, the contributions of non-Western intellectual traditions to modern human and natural sciences may have received more substantial recognition prior to and during the Enlightenment that they perhaps do today.)

However, the insertion of non-Western traditions into the process of world history that imperialism has erased is not always or necessarily what is actually being undertaken by modern religious revivalists. Of particular importance in recent years has been the labour devoted to illustrating the congruence between quantum mechanics and the (to be sure, phenomenal) philosophical speculations about ontology that result from mystical apprehension, as elaborated in the *Vedas, Upanishads* and in the bhakti, sufi or gnostic traditions. That nothing like actual quantum physics, relativity, electromagnetism or Newtonian mechanics has existed in ancient texts is irrelevant to the *ex post facto* project being undertaken here.

Pervez Hoodbhoy, in a lonely critical assessment of "Islamic science", has provided important examples of this semiological approach towards science and technology (Hoodbhoy 1991). Indeed, his study confirms just how important natural science is to neofoundational movements. The International Seminar on Qur'an and Science organized in June 1986 by the Pakistan Association of Scientists and Scientific Professions included a paper by a senior governmental scientist who gave chemical formulas for calculating the level of anti-Islamic hypocrisy (*munafiqat*) or "corruption" based on a model of the polarizing forces that act on molecules in a liquid. Delectably, the West is given a hypocrisy value of 22, but no value is given for Pakistan. Another theory from the chairperson of Pakistan's Space Organisation

> proposed that an explanation for the Holy Prophet's [ascension to Heaven] be sought in Einstein's Theory of Relativity. As every believer knows, the Ascension took almost no time .... This apparently short duration has been interpreted – and most recently in a slick film produced by the International Islamic University – as an example of relativistic time dilation. (Hoodbhoy 1991: 143)

Similarly, a senior director of the Pakistan Atomic Energy Commission, a scholar of nuclear reactor theories, described in a book how the transition to the Final Day of Judgement is similar to the formation of electromagnetic fields around a current-carrying conductor. Another major scientist at the Defence Science and Technology Organisation speculated how God produced *djinns* (genies) from methane gas and other physicists showed how Pakistan's energy crisis can be solved by using the energy of *djinns*.

A delegate to the Islamic Science Conference held in Islamabad in 1983 calculated the angle of God as π/N (N is not defined). A leading figure in the Pakistani nuclear science and physics establishment calculated the coefficient of per capita spiritual activity and worked out how much reward (in Paradise) is earned through prayer as a function of the number of people praying with you. This, presumably, is a scientific argument to encourage more people to pray. Hoodbhoy provides numerous other examples. These individuals are trained scientists and are establishment figures who control the state of scientific education in Pakistan. Hoodbhoy traces this tendency to the growth of Islamic revival in Pakistan under the Zia regime, especially through the activities of the Jamaat-i-Islami. One consequence of this process of Islamicization has been, with a few notable exceptions, a disintegration of rational education throughout the educational infrastructure in Pakistan.

One relatively recent concern within Islamism has been a critical (and ironic) focus on Darwinism along much the same lines as Christian fundamentalism. The mechanism of natural selection and the theory of evolution directly challenge both the creationist mythologies and the central and privileged importance of humans in the three semitic religions, as well as Hinduism, and therefore need to be invalidated. For example, Khurshid Nadvi's *Darwinism on trial* is celebrated as one of the most important Islamic critiques of evolution and natural selection (Nadvi 1993). However, the critique of (neo-)Darwinism in such writings is usually founded on several important strategies: a lack of comprehension of deep geological time; a fundamental misreading of Darwin's theory of natural selection, which additionally also assumes that evolution and natural selection are identical; a misconception of natural selection as entirely random rather than contingently random; a crucial identification of both pre- and post-Darwinian teleological evolutionary frameworks as definitive of and constituting the totality of Darwinism; an anthropomorphic and a static conception of what constitutes selective advantage or what might make ideal or conducive natural environments; a misreading of natural science which assumes that the latter claims total explanatory power for any and all situations and that it has explained all these situations; an inability to provide empirical arguments that help explain the existing evidence or any anomalies in the evidence, except perhaps for an iteration of religious aphorisms; the disingenuous identification of neo-Darwinian critiques of early Darwinism, including those that propose other physical (i.e. non-religious) mechanisms in addition to natural selection, as constitutive of a rejection of Darwinism *in toto*; and a wilful evasion of the overwhelming paleontological and genetic evidence that exists for natural selection.[4]

In Nadvi's book, natural selection itself is virtually ignored, the theory of evolution is identified with a gradualist and teleological conception of evolution (and hence the "missing links" prove it is wrong) and neo-Darwinian critiques of gradualism are seen to be a refutation of all processes of evolution and natural selection (even Stephen Jay Gould is mobilized against Darwin). Moreover, Nadvi relies heavily on a familiar religious critique of discomforting natural science, the presentation of prosaic evidence, anecdotal argumentation, a rehearsal of past issues, problems and critiques that few would accept today and the presentation of evidence that it is claimed disproves Darwin, though nothing about the evidence does. However, after demolishing Darwinism, Nadvi undertakes the important civilizational paradigm shift described earlier: intellectual ideas about evolution were not indigenous to the West but had been originally discovered in Islam and were subsequently appropriated by the West.

Contemporary Hindu revivalism exhibits similar tendencies, and highlights again the privilege that natural science can have in neofoundational discourse. It is striking how many modern Hindu revivalist or devotional texts include the word "science" in its modern sense in their titles and happily use modern cosmology (anything from early relativity and quantum physics to contemporary theories of supersymmetry, superstrings and even $N=8$ supergravity) to prove the essential truths of the *Vedas*, the *Upanishads* or the *Bhagavad gita* while at the same time condemning materialism. Erwin Schrodinger's wave equation (which is solvable for simple quantum systems and results in solutions that demonstrate the fuzzy and probabilistic nature of the position of a particle), Heisenberg's principle of uncertainty,[5] the various philosophical interpretations of the results of versions of Young's double-slit experiment (which demonstrate both holism and the central importance of sentient observation for the results of quantum processes), the refutation of the Einstein–Podolsky–Rosen thought experiment by Alain Aspect's work with polarized light in the early 1980s (which essentially verified holistic "action-at-a-distance" in quantum mechanics, and verified the critique of classical – Newtonian and Einsteinian – ideas of causality), Gödel's incompleteness theorem, as well as chaos theory[6] have provided rich material for religious revivalist mysticism.

The tropes of quantum mystery, indeterminacy and holism are selectively appropriated in religious revivalist discourse as religious-natural metaphors while at the same time the rather complexly determinist and practical uses of quantum indeterminacy or holism are carefully ignored. For example, quantum uncertainty is at the core of why semiconductors (and various combinations of semiconductors) conduct electricity. This indeed has led to the phenomenal revolution in information technology that we see. Similarly, the mathematical models devised by Richard Feynman for the inaccessible mysterious area of quantum-level interaction have resulted in quantum electrodynamics, usually seen as the most successful theory to have ever existed in physics in the veracity and numerical precision of its predictions. Chaos theory, instead of being inclined towards religious mystery, is its virtual opposite, a rather determinist theory. The holistic and beautiful structures that are a consequence of chaos result not from some mysterious or sublime force but from the determinist iteration of some mathematical equations. Chaos has itself led to more overarching explanatory theories (such as complexity theory[7]) that allow and put to use chaotic states. To be sure, there are (at least) two extremely important discussions about the relation between quantum physics and consciousness, one focused on the nature of consciousness itself, and one based on the nature of the "anthropic" relation between sentient observation and reality. However, they do not necessarily lead to either religious or anthropomorphic interpretations (Penrose 1989, Zohar 1991).

Of recent importance in the West is the work of Deepak Chopra who, in his book *Quantum healing*, brings neatly together the New Age obsessions with health, holism, nature, medicine and modern science within an overall metanarrative determined by the Vedic and Upanishadic conception of the Sublime, or *Brahman* (Chopra 1990). Chopra employs many of the orientations to science listed above, including the standard isomorphic fallacy: the uncertainty at the core of quantum mechanics, which he calls the "? field", is essentially identified by him with the infinity or uncertainty that arises through mystical apprehension, as related to us by the Vedic seers. His "? field" is identified with the unknown in the quantum-level processes that are involved in the nervous system, and therefore human consciousness (though quantum processes are involved in all matter, energy and space, sentient or otherwise.) This unknown quantum field is also linked by Chopra to various other religious tropes such as the holistic and cosmic "bliss" and "intelligence" that exist beyond the Western limits to rationality but which have been apprehended by the Vedic seers. This is the form of argument that iteratively appropriates the most recent discoveries of natural science for essentially religious purposes while claiming that natural science or rationality is limited. According to him, it is also valid to attribute a human concept of recent lineage – intelligence – to molecules, peptides and indeed the quantum field and the whole of nature. The further links he develops between quantum uncertainty, human consciousness, healing and then God or infinity are another religious decentreing of the subject of the kind already encountered. This is a characteristic anthropomorphic fallacy in which the real is determined or described through selective human ideological constructs. Why, for example, does quantum uncertainty have the quality of "bliss" (a form of the argument that benevolence and goodness are attributable to and constitutive of nature)? Why should recognizing this quantum bliss in human consciousness heal human diseases (the latter are also natural and equally dependent on quantum processes)? Do not the proteins and peptides in cancerous cells or on the surface of the Human Immunodeficiency Virus have this same blissful intelligence and benevolence? One is led to wonder whether the Vedic *rishis* ever caught a cold. (The general emphasis on holism, goodness and the cosmic centrality of (some of) humanity that is derived from various New Age appropriations of natural science ignores, perhaps deliber- ately, the central relevance of the Second Law of Thermodynamics for all physical processes, and the relentless increase in entropy ("disorder", "disintegration") in the universe as a function of directional time that is a general consequence of the Law. Perhaps it will be appropriated as a dystopian trope for the *kaliyuga*.)

While much of this obscurantist "Hindu science" and its impact on Western New Age thinking may seem ethically inconsequential, some forms of modern Hinduism have also shown just how dangerous the obsession with science can become, especially when the new technologies of the body are combined with what is seen as "ethnic tradition". Ultrasound scanning technology and amnio-centesis in India are now almost routinely used to abort female foetuses and a massive private industry in ultrasound femicide clinics has grown in just the last few years. In the period 1978–83, 78,000 cases of female foeticide took place directly after biological sex selection tests (SSTS). Almost one hundred per cent of 15,914 abortions (all of female foetuses) in urban Bombay in 1984–5 were carried out after high technology SSTS. The sex ratio of women to 1,000 men in India was 972 in 1901. It was 929 in 1991 (Patel 1992, 1989). In Britain, several hospitals, such as Northwick Park Hospital in northwest London, deny families the full results of ultrasound scans because of the increasing incidence of female foeticide among Hindu families. One private clinic in northwest London specializes in providing discrete and expeditious female gender-selective abortion. It should be noted that the same claim to "tradition" that preaches non-violence, vegetarianism and non-killing is content with femicide.

However, Hindu revivalist discourse has also intellectually opposed feminist demands around abortion using ancient texts and slivers of modern science to generate the most appalling obscurant-ism: "At the moment of conception the soul connects to the newly fertilized egg first overshadowing it from the inner planes, then 'moving in' fully as the new physical, pranic and astral bodies become sufficiently mature" (*Hinduism Today* 15 (6) June 1993: 9). The metaphoric identity created here between the soul and the male sperm should be noted. The demand for abortion as part of a demand by women for control over their fertility is reconstructed in many strands of modern Hinduism as a sin[8] (though in Hindu traditions, Gods can be also be evil and demons can also be good). These essentially semitic conceptions of sin have also informed Hindu revivalist discourse on HIV disease. *Hinduism Today*, whose editor informs us that AIDS is part of God's divine plan, ran a four-part series by Dr Devananda Tandavan to educate its global readership about HIV/AIDS. Tandavan is a member of the Amer-ican Medical Association, the International College of Surgeons and the Society of Nuclear Medicine. He informs his readers that "there is *irrefutable* evidence that HIV is man-made". Furthermore,

[HIV] can be transmitted through kissing ... possibly through exchange of tears, possibly airborne by transmission through droplets of sputum and lung secretions. No studies have been done yet to determine whether or not transmission by mosquitoes or other insect bites is possible, but there is no scientific reason why this should not be a pathway. It is also possible for transmission to occur through infected food handlers. (*Hinduism Today* **15** (9) September 1993: 4)

Naturally, infected people should be incarcerated. Each one of Tandavan's speculations on HIV transmission is erroneous (numerous and widely published laboratory, clinical and epidemiological studies have been conducted in each of these areas). However, this is the acceptable stuff of revivalist scientific education for Hindu readers. It is unfortunate that such "science" is propagated by religious revivalists at a time when India and Thailand are considered by the World Health Organization to be the epicentres of the Asian HIV epidemic (another divine choice?).

It is difficult to see how "neofoundational science" will develop in the future but its current trajectories, especially those fixated on the body, are considerably reactionary, when not just plainly mendacious. This should underline why, for tendencies affiliated to the left and feminism, an ethical and critical re-engagement with natural sciences is essential. It is in opposing these repressive syncretic combinations of natural science and neofoundational religious ideologies that the value of ethical, critical realist natural and human science becomes especially important. Opposition to repressive scientific technologies in the West is just as important for a critical orientation towards natural science. In many sections of the left, natural science has typically been reduced to "positivism", and this has been seen as constituting of a sufficient ethical critique of it. However, natural science cannot be conceived as simply positivist. It is a social product comprising a philosophically unsettled but effective combination of empiricist (constant conjunction, experiment), realist (deep structure, linear and holistic causality and modelling), rationalist (induction and deduction, verification and falsification) and idealist (*a priori* conditions, theory and holism) strands. For the most part, its ontologies in relation to its objects of enquiry, and the epistemologies it creates are entirely different from the human sciences in relation to their objects and knowledges. It is this fundamental difference in orientation towards nature and the social that is elided, both in mechanistic fundamentalism and in the reductive and determinist forms of natural science that claim explanatory power in the social and political field.

Conclusion: black socialism and feminism and transgressive challenges to religious authoritarianism

These various and complicated strands of science, the body, new information technologies and new ideologies of communalism form important components of the type of authoritarian identities that religious fundamentalism needs to secure for itself, the new ethnic traditions it wants to create, and wants to claim over younger South Asians. However, all these areas are permanent sites of contestation rather than already constituted edifices. That religious fundamentalists claim substitutive and legislative privilege over South Asian communities in the UK is the strongest evidence that their claims about identity and ethnicity are not secure but are indeed sites of struggle. The secular political tradition in South Asian communities in the UK is a deep one, perhaps symbolically, and arbitrarily, captured by the Grunwick strike (in the 1970s), the Bradford 12 campaign (in the 1980s) and the victory of Kiranjit Ahluwalia (in the early 1990s). However, the existence of fundamentalist and communalist languages announces that secularism, multicultural-ism, democracy, liberalism, humanism, socialism, the best ethical, rationalist and humanist religious traditions that have been erased by fundamentalism, and indeed the scheme of reason itself are necessarily and always unfinished projects that demand constant repetition, movement, transformation and activism.

The one political-activist force in Britain that is in any position to challenge authoritarian religious movements at a community-based level and develop an alternative secular culture of change within British South Asian communities, while at the same time remaining committed to an anti-racist and ostensibly anti-imperialist politics, is made up of the small black socialist and feminist groupings that now constitute "the independent black left". However, with the important exceptions of the Indian Workers' Association branches across the country and the small number of anticaste organizations, only black and multiracial feminism has actively and consistently opposed religious fundamentalism. The Institute of Race Relation's various class-reductionist systems of antiracism and socialism, often combined with an intense disavowal of the power of ethnicity, has barely looked at the consequences of the changes that have affected the constituencies it speaks for (Sivanandan 1982, 1985, 1990). The IRR has attempted to construct "black struggle" within the parametric boundaries of racism and antiracism while concurrently displacing ethnicity. This results in an unusual kind of black nationalism, the content of which is basically antiracism, that jostles for position with a strong socialist commitment (reproducing the older debate between Marxism and nationalism). This paradigm seems incapable of challenging other black or cultural nationalist formations that are derived from more comprehensive and substantive materials of "ethnicity" and "tradition", however imagined or manufactured their realms might be. For these "nationalisms", the elementary critique of white racism usually does not present a problem. Even though white racism may not ostensibly be within their purview, or occupy a position of discursive significance, they can mount substantial and effective local challenges to it by virtue of their own, albeit particularist, ethical or moral systems.

Early black socialist feminism in Britain faced similar issues: what forms the ethical basis for, and what is the content of positive "racial" difference, solidarity and autonomy beyond just antiracism? Early black feminism also often harmonically oscillated between an IRR type of antiracist black identity politics and anthropological mystical black nationalism:

> Many white feminists have argued that as feminists they find it very difficult to accept arranged marriages which they see as reactionary. Our argument is that it is not up to *them* to accept or reject arranged marriages but up to *us* to challenge, accept, or reform, depending on our various perspectives, on our own terms and in our own culturally specific ways. (Amos & Parmar 1984: 15, emphases added)

This rehearses another version of the problem of particularist representation and universalism. A discursive field is created in which two processes take place: racial reduction (racial discourse is reduced to racist discourse, whites are thence excluded) and the creation of an unproblematic Habermasian inner space where undistorted black communication can take place. At the same time, the universality of women's oppression is stated, particularly through assertive statements like "women's oppression in black communities cannot be deemed more severe than in white communities". This is a diverting type of universalism. It asserts a general equivalence in the condition and extent of women's oppression across boundaries that are also constructed as anthropologically incommensurable because black feminism defends the particularism and specificity of its experience. Identity censorship in the new social movements has been defended as a necessary "autonomy", and the latter has sometimes been analytically distanced from anthropological "separatism". While one can be in pragmatic sympathy with this position, one can doubt its ability to create a *strong* ethical argument for antiracist autonomy that is different from black nationalist separatism, especially at the point of the practical politics of autonomy where "races" have to be separated.

Generally, since the later 1980s, black socialist feminism has been far more pragmatic in political practice than the above assessment of nationalist racial closure suggests. Indeed, it had to be because it began axiomatically with an analysis of "the intersection of race, gender, class, sexuality and imperialism in shaping our lives, experience and struggles". The perception of complexity and contradiction rather than the elemental monologism that infects the black socialism of the IRR was certainly an advance, and indeed, black feminism had to minimize the degree to which it upheld a self-defeating link with anthropological black nationalism. However, is it possible to create let alone sustain an ethical political project that can manage to negotiate these different polyvocal and contradictory issues all at once? Moreover, is there not an axiomatic impossibility about such a project if it requires simultaneous assessment of personal experience, ideology, agency and structure along all the different "axes of oppression" that it identifies at that time?

Well before the Rushdie affair, the campaigns against violence against women had permanently shattered the idea of a unitary black community and had raised irreducibly ethical issues that black ascetic socialism (and its various aphorisms) had repeatedly failed to address. There is, indeed, an *intense* disjunction between the Institute of Race Relation's ascetic utopian socialism and its avoidance of a discussion of gang culture, weapon culture, violence against women and issues of the family in general, ethnic communal and political violence, misogyny, homophobia, drug use, drug economics – and actually even class – and the formidable impact of these factors on the quality of life for members of African, Asian and Caribbean communities in the UK. Racially based reasoning, in particular antiracism and black nationalism, prohibits elaboration on these issues unless they are accounted for as a consequence solely of racism. However, black absolutist, religious and ethnically based political formations have not been tardy in fashioning reactionary postures on many of these issues, often within the crucibles of local and state multiculturalism. It is mainly black feminism that has been there to confront them, and to develop a critique of reactionary and antisecular multiculturalism (Southall Black Sisters 1990, Sahgal & Yuval-Davis 1992, Women Against Fundamentalism *Newsletters* 1990–94).

Monological constructions of "community" and "family" have also been critically subjected to other transgressive secular Asian formations that have been unable unproblematically to create visible spaces in public culture in the manner that African-Caribbean and African-American youth cultures have. These include the articulation of pleasure through progressive syncretic cultural styles in Asian nationalist Indi-pop, hip-hop, rap, ragga[9] and some reformative bhangra, Asian women's ascension in community and cultural politics, the growth of Asian lesbian and gay groups and cultural spaces, the development of Asian youth spaces in daytime and night-time disco, (utilized unconventionally by Asian young women as much as men), the production of irreverent Asian youth media and the staunch celebration of "sexual emancipation":

ASIAN STRIP SHOW ANGER. Ban this filth say Muslim protesters .... Showing two scantily-clad Asian girls in provocative poses, the posters promise punters a feast of "mujara bhangra followed by a topless striptease with a two-girl duo" .... The girls encouraged the leering audience to fondle and dance with them, and later they performed their striptease as well as simulated lesbian acts. (*Eastern Eye*, 15 October 1991)

These cultural spaces do not have an elementary concern with anything approaching antiracism but are informed by the organization of pleasure times and spaces against the obdurate, but constantly re-organized conventions of community probity. Qumar Ashraf and Zarina Ramzan, the young Muslim women who organized the show in Southall elicited the wrath of young Muslim men not simply for daring to unclothe, but because of their sceptical re-appropriation of the symbols of their oppression. Their performance not only invoked Pakistani Muslim courtesan traditions, constituted through the pastiche of *Pakeezah*, but involved the brazen display of religious adornments during the show. Most significantly, however, the women were uncompromising in their autonomy and for this they received numerous enraged calls, death threats and organized pickets of their shows. The women responded unequivocally through the language of universal rights: "We have a right to act as we choose. In our culture, the men are allowed to drink, smoke and have mistresses, but a woman can have her legs broken if she is seen talking to a man."

The sexual and cultural politics of this incident are highly complex and transgress feminism and antiracism just as they transgress Islam. The appeal to freedom from patriarchal religious fundamentalism to engage in activities – the sexual display and objectification of women for the benefit of men – which feminism has traditionally protested against creates a space which, even if carefully constructed as an autonomous right of women, still refuses to conform easily with feminism, though the two women powerfully valorize their rights over their bodies through its language. But, in illustrating the need for active, indeed activist, policing of the female body and, by extension, policing of women's control over their sexuality, the incident signifies the incompleteness of "family" and "community".

It is at this juncture that a strange alliance between black and antiracist administrative socialism, antiracist youth formations and the institutions of religious revival has become apparent. A striking development in the mid-1980s was the formation of Asian youth gangs along primarily ethnic (Muslim, Sikh and Hindu) parameters in east, west, northwest and southeast London, in the Midlands and in the north. The notation "gang" implies a more organized basis and structure to Asian youth formations that only very rarely existed, and was easily dealt with by the police. It is more accurate

CONCLUSION

to speak of local, mainly disorganized, collective youth affiliations, some of which became semi-organized for different events. This included Sikh-identified and Khalistan-identified gangs in Southall and Birmingham, Hindu gangs in Brent, Muslim and Sikh gangs in Newham, Muslim (but primarily Bangladeshi-nationalist) gangs in Tower Hamlets, predominantly Muslim, but regionally and linguistically identified gangs in Bradford and the northern towns, and various other groups in Hounslow, Crayford, Hayes and Camden. However, the manifestation of gang activities is far more complex than ethnic or religious identification allows and refers us to syncretic associations between criminal activities, male subcultural ritual, surveillance and sexual harassment of women, "antiracist" formations, renunciation of patriarchal pedagogy and recreation of patriarchal tradition, as well as explicitly religious-political identification. The struggle for Khalistan might have preoccupied a couple of Sikh gangs in Birmingham, but, for example, in Bangladeshi-nationalist youth activity in Tower Hamlets, there was a more complex hybrid negotiation with African-American expressive culture and the traditions of the "East End". Similarly, the (now defunct) Hindu Billy Boys of Brent and the Tooti Nungs in Ealing acquired peripheral associates from the local Caribbean communities. The minor moral panic and extraordinary police attention[10] over Asian gangs in the mid-1980s resulted in antiracist defence of their activities by black constituencies (*New Life* 28 March 1986). However, it was left to Asian feminists to point out that these gang activities, while disruptive of the "traditional normativity" of Asian communities, still enforced the control of patriarchal institutions over the activities of young women (Southall Black Sisters 1990). Indeed, by the late 1980s and into the mid-1990s, the extent to which local youth gangs were allied with precisely the traditional antimilitant community institutions that those gangs were imagined to be a reaction against was highly apparent. In particular, the manner in which physical discipline over young Asian women and their associates was exercised by members of gangs at the behest of mosques, *gurdwaras* and temples became an important manifestation of gang activity, as did a celebration of weapon culture, gang ritual and the orchestration of territorial combats (some of which had highly communal overtones) and sexual violence against women. Some of these formations became highly organized just in order to police women. The centrality of gender and the rehearsal

269

of both "tradition" and an elementary antiracism are important to these formations in constructing highly conservative masculinities and femininities. In a similar way, the religious and ethnic communal organization of gangs and youth formations also became more politicized in this period[11] and led to the murder of 20-year-old Christian student, Ayotunde Obonobi, at Newham Community College in east London after an increasingly polarized situation developed between Muslim students (mainly South Asian) and other students at the college (*The Guardian*, 1 March 1995).

The resistance to these developments represents a different cultural politics of affirmation and pleasure from young Asian women and men that has barely received attention from some of the more vanguardist politics of black socialism and feminism. These various transgressive and hybrid formations in Asian youth and young women's culture sharply pose the question of the relevance of older forms of black socialism and feminism to the remaking of their lives. These hybrid formations may be disagreeable to much of the left, but they have also shown the potential to criticize and disengage from the neofoundational and patriarchal groups that are claiming them, or disciplining them, as affiliates of an already-secured identity. However, the youths who chanted "Rushdie is the Devil! Kill the Devil!", the young people who attend RSS and VHP meetings or who have found their pleasure, fulfilment, integrity and perfection in new Islamic or Hindu identities are the other product of this hybrid process. Their impure and profane peers have this struggle to contend with for the future.

Importantly, the newness of authoritarian religious movements is also a demonstration of their contingent nature and thus the possibility is open for their political defeat. The political space that neofoundationalist ideologies have exploited is one that demonstrates a deep longing for justice, equality and liberation. Leila Ahmed notes that,

> Like the young women, the young men affiliating with Islam are hearing its ethical voice, a voice insistently enjoining Muslims to act justly and fairly, and constantly reiterating the equal humanity of all. The voice they hear is the voice virtually ignored by the framers of establishment Islam, which is the technical, legal, doctrinal Islam about which [young people] seem so little informed. (Ahmed 1992: 229)

This liberation impulse is genuine, a utopian passion that has also influenced socialism and feminism. Its tragedy is its articulation of emancipation through the themes of transcendentalism, purity, absolutism, an authoritarian masculinism, a fear of the sexual body and a will to power. Many of these themes are Enlightenment strands and their unfolding in neofoundationalist ideologies emphasizes, in a different way, that we cannot turn back from the Enlightenment, even if we wanted to. Whatever this utopian desire for emancipation, its combination with neofoundational strategies is quite concrete, effective and repressive. Neofoundational themes of liberation and purity can be opposed by stressing the value of human impurities, human dependencies and human solidarity. Their mythologies and transcendental fictions can be opposed by critical and realist engagements. But these seem incongruent and unsatisfactory outside of sustainable visions we can create for the future. Can we provide any content for that Kantian utopian space of freedom where the duty of all of humanity is towards itself, where humanity is its own end, and requires nothing above humanity for its realization? What is the relation between this space and the Marxist space of freedom from class exploitation and anti-imperialism?

Dogmatic forms of faith seem increasingly to have taken the place of progressive and emancipatory utopian vision. Their authoritarian methods suppress those real humanist, ethical and secular traditions that have existed in religion. Moreover, these new authoritarian religious formations demand a reverent attitude. Numerous writers have stressed how a reverent disposition by Rushdie towards Islam, rather than the profane position he took, would have been acceptable and would not have caused him any problems.[12] Revivalist Hindus make the same demand – a respectful and deferential approach towards their truth-claims. Those religious ideologies assert a legislative privilege that is denied to every other political ideology. We are not expected to criticize religion as we would any other discourse. Naïve relativism demands that we cannot attack its superstitions, its falsehoods, its brutalities and its profanities. Instead, we are expected to step around religion carefully and meekly. If the Enlightenment has taught us anything, it is surely that we have absolutely no reason to do so.

Notes

Chapter 1: Knowledge and its alternatives

1. Indeed, postmodernism theory can be seen as complicit in this move to naturalize an understanding of the West as equivalent to the Greeks plus the Enlightenment plus industrialization. This is perhaps where postcolonial discourse analysis can be useful, because it does interrupt modernist and postmodernist reconfirmations of the West's understanding of itself through its Aristotle–Marx philosophical lineage.
2. There seems to be considerable potential in elaborating how this trope of "superior" forms of "Western" reason, knowledge-science and technology can recreate racial superiority ("racisms") without needing to invoke either biology or ethnic culture.
3. See especially Gilroy's discussion of centrality of the master–slave relation to the foundation of Enlightenment philosophy (Gilroy 1993: 50–8).
4. Young Muslims UK, "Amnesty International Targets Islaam in Sudan", 20 February 1995, The Young Muslims UK.
5. The reference is to Amrit Wilson's book, *Finding a voice: Asian women in Britain* (London: Virago, 1978) and its review in *Race Today* (January 1979) by Mala Dhondy entitled "Voices already heard".
6. Amhad (1992: 13) suggests that Said's category of Orientalism makes for far greater ahistorical claims than Marxism has ever made for any mode of production. While the latter is debatable, the general point is valid.

Chapter 2: Authoritarian religious movements and modern civil societies

1. The demands of some orthodox Jewish organizations since 1991 to create an *eruv* (an enclosure marked by poles and wire encompassing

four square miles) in the London Borough of Barnet to legitimize certain activities outside the home during sabbath is a striking coincidence of social, physical and imagined space.

2. AIDS activism is the best contemporary example: the demand for medical, social, welfare and financial resources is coupled with a sophisticated disruption of the way sexuality and disease are signified in popular culture and institutional medical practice.

3. Primarily Rosa Luxembourg's discussion of spontaneity and agency, but see also Lenin (1978).

4. This view was especially relevant to the political practice of the Race Today Collective in the 1980s. It can also be fruitfully compared with the assumptions behind forms of feminist and gay organization in the 1970s and very early 1980s and the critique of the latter as the "tyranny of structurelessness". (See Rowbotham et al. 1979, part 1, and especially 71–82, Walter 1980: 15–19; see also James et al. [1958] 1974.)

5. Though it is important to keep in mind the highly pessimistic assessments of "mass society" that were developed during and after the fascist and Nazi periods, this being one of the reasons why Gramsci wrote about civil societies.

6. For examples, see respectively: Dworkin (1981) and Madhubuti (1990). *Capital Gay* in the week of 30 July 1993 had three separate stories and features on the genocide theme: page 8 had an article related to the drug AZT and criticizing the "genocidal mentality" among gay men; page 1 had the story of Lord Jacobovits urging Jewish people to undergo voluntary genetic "elimination" to remove the gay gene and ensure they have no gay or lesbian kids. The story and the subsequent protests were explicitly linked to the contemporary extermination of gays with direct comparisons to the Holocaust; page 2, carries responses to the organization "Gays Against Genocide" which had formed to protest against HIV/AIDS agencies and gay organizations that, they said, were complicit in the mass murder of gays.

7. The following phrases seem to crop up repeatedly in writings from *both* new social movements and authoritarian religious movements, and are frequently not actually concerned with a particular campaign or actual instance of violence but are general activist narratives about the condition of oppression: "pain", "suffering", "victimized", "hurt", "endurance", "survival", "alienation", "terror", "healing", "danger", "death", "silenced", "made invisible", "murder", "being erased", "fear", "survival of our people", "hostility" and so on. The point in highlighting this is not to deny or minimize the actual suffering and misery that oppression causes but to raise the question of what this says about the way these tendencies visualize their dystopian life-world.

Chapter 3: The modernity of Islamic movements

1. See, for example, Gellner (1992: 18–21). Though Gellner views "fundamentalism" as a reversion to what he calls "High Islam", and questions whether earlier Islam was the same as this, he essentially views all these as comprising essentially premodern, pre-industrial ideologies.
2. Ahmad (1992) seems to echo this view, though it is not clear what his understanding of postmodernity is, beyond some combination of multiculturalism and cultural iconoclasm. See also Jameson (1991: 388–91).
3. *Shari'a* is the form of legal system in Islam based on interpretations of the Qur'an, the Sunna (the practice of the Prophet) and the Hadith (the teachings of the Prophet) through various processes of consensus, independent judgement, reasoning, custom, public interest, analogy and so forth. Interpretations of the *shari'a* in particular cases leads to law (jurisprudence), opinion (*fatwa*) or judgement (as in a court). There are four main legal schools in Sunni Islam that interpret *shari'a* differently – the Hanafi (the most important for South Asian Sunni Muslims), the Hanbali (Saudi Arabia), Shafi'i and Maliki. Shi'a sects have different legal schools (the Ja'fari school of Twelver Shi'ites, and the Zaydi and Kharijite).
4. Pryce-Jones (1990) is a good recent example of the application of transcendental Western or "Orientalist" categories, such as the "shame–honour" or "power–challenge" dialectic that manages to explain all of Islamic history and sociology.
5. In *Shi'ite* belief, the rightful successor to Muhammad should have been his cousin and son-in-law, Ali, and not the three actual successor caliphs (Abu-Bakr, Umar and Uthman) who are seen as illegitimate usurpers. Ali, however, did become the fourth Caliph, but was assassinated. Sunnis accept the first four caliphs as "rightly guided". It is this difference in belief that is the basis of the two sects. In the dominant, "Twelver" Shi'ism, the next rightful successor after Ali should have been his son Hasan. Hasan claimed the caliphate but failed. His brother Husayn then tried to claim the caliphate against the Caliph's son Yazid. Husayn and his small group of followers were brutally massacred by Yazid's army when they refused to surrender. Husayn's "martyrdom", personal sacrifice and call to arms against all the known odds constitutes an immensely powerful trope for Shi'ism, just as Yazid symbolizes an evil figure. The next rightful successor for Twelver Shi'ites should have been Husayn's son, after which the rightful successors are traced to the Eleventh Imam who died in AD 874, also leaving a son. The son, the Twelfth Imam, mysteriously vanished and for 70 years only had contact with the Shi'ite community through an intermediary. This is the period of the "Lesser Occultation". After this period, he disappeared completely (the "Greater Occultation") but will return one day as a Messianic or "Mahdi"

figure. In traditional Twelver Shi'ite belief, only on his return can there be legitimate authority and government and all other worldly authority is, in principle, illegitimate.

6. This is a reference to the *usuli* school of jurisprudence. Briefly, the invasion of Iran in the early eighteenth century by Afghan Sunnis, the subsequent persecution of Shi'as and the fleeing of Shi'ite leaders to Ottoman Iraq created a confused and complicated situation in which the close alliance of clerics with the earlier Safavid rulers was broken and a power vacuum was created. Some clerics then made the claim that Shi'as should follow their authority.

7. A similar holistic construction of the East (the Soviet bloc) was also a manifest part of Khomeinism – "Neither West/Capitalism nor East/Communism but Revolutionary Islam!" – and illustrated its "third way" position.

8. The importance, in Khomeinism, of attaining *shahid* status (martyrs who have earned a place in Paradise) is such an example. This exact theme recurs in Hindu fundamentalism.

Chapter 4: The Rushdie affair and the deceptive critique of imperialism

1. Reproduced in Appignanesi & Maitland (1989: 58–60). The full text of this letter also includes several paragraphs of the earlier letter from the Leicester Islamic Foundation, illustrating again the influence of the Jamaati-i-Islami during these early stages of the campaign.

2. Such as the London-based Muslim Institute for Planning and Research, formerly headed by Kalim Siddique, which had supported the Khomeini regime in the 1980s and 1990s.

3. Set up with Saudi assistance through the World Muslim League and related to the Union of Muslim Organisations mentioned earlier.

4. Set up by Zaki Badawi, apparently with assistance from the Libyan al Dawaa (The Call) organization. It had influence among Barelwi community mosques who would object to the other Saudi-funded umbrella organizations (Nielsen 1992: 48).

5. A representative body for most of Bradford's 26 mosques as well as numerous other Muslim organizations, which was formed in 1980, in particular to enable formal representation of all Muslim interests to the City Council under whose auspices it was formed.

6. Nielsen (1992) points out that the number of registered mosques in Britain started to grow faster from 1974 after the OPEC oil price rise, which thus led to more generous funding from overseas. However, his data also suggest that the rate of increase was not particularly dramatic and suggests instead that the slow process of community formation may be more important than any external influences or sources of funding.

7. Black community campaigns in support of Rushdie were severely

limited and the reality was the considerable fear of direct intervention in the institutions of community (youth or religious organizations). Black Voices in Defence of Salman Rushdie and The *satanic verses*, a loose group formed to defend Rushdie, did some basic networking and published articles. Southall Black Sisters and Women Against Fundamentalism were the main groups that attempted to intervene at a community level.

8. The British Muslims Action Front was, however, campaigning on various levels to get the law changed to cover blasphemy against Islam. On 27 May 1989, it organized a massive demonstration of Muslims in London ("The Greatest March on Parliament") and took its case to the High Court but failed, in May 1990, to get a right of appeal to the House of Lords.

9. The Jamaat-i-Islami has been miserably defeated at every single poll, however rigged. In the 1985 Pakistani elections, during which all opposition and secular parties were banned and their leaders were in prison or out of the country, the Jamaati-i-Islami should have swept up the vote, but, even in these favourable conditions, it was resoundingly defeated. The Jamaati-i-Islami derives its power and influence from its close association with sections of the capitalist class, Saudi funding and the earlier Zia dictatorship. It also controls virtually every educational institution and university in Pakistan and uses paramilitary terror against opponents to achieve its objectives. (See Alavi 1988: 93–4.)

10. Yaqub Zaki (James Dickie), a convert to Islam, is an extreme example of this antisemitic tendency. See, for example, his contributions which the Islamic Foundation chose to reproduce (Ahsan and Kidwai 1991: 228–31). However, the themes of Jewish power, influence, money or conspiracy are reproduced in arcane forms in many other responses to Rushdie's book.

11. There are extremely important historical exceptions to this that stress essentially humanist and rationalist interpretations. Mernissi argues that these have been systematically suppressed in the interests of preserving not religious but political caliphate and court despotism. She argues that the current Islamic regimes are a continuation of two strands of Muslim political thought: the despotic and the oppositional terrorist (who opposed despots, but frequently installed their own despotic regimes). The rationalist humanist and *falasifa* ("philosopher") tradition in Islam has been suppressed (Mernissi 1993: 32–41).

Chapter 5: Neotraditional Hinduism and the fabrication of purity

1. Cf. Magas (1993: 49–72), who reports on the striking shift towards Serbian nationalism and anti-Albanian racism among the formerly acclaimed critical theorists of the Praxis International group in former Yugoslavia.

2. The new influence of Hindu symbolism in British cultures, and especially youth culture music, appears vast – Boy George as Krishna, LSD tabs called "Ganesh" or "Oms", the Mother Goddess or the Kali figure in Western feminist spirituality, healing, chakras, karma, self-realization, and innumerable New Age professional and self-help manuals.

3. For example, Knappert (1991: 38–9) on the Arya Samaj (AS) will give the reader a view of the AS as an extremely peaceful, loving organization rather than the fundamentalist mass movement it actually is. Sen ([1961] 1991), who would have known better, describes the AS as doing good social work, attempting to spread education and raising the standards of the "backward" classes. No mention is made of its major role in orchestrating a terrible period of mass communal violence in the Punjab in the early part of this century. The point is that it is not the AS that is important here but the selective fascination with Hindu metaphysics and beliefs to the exclusion of its history or politics.

4. See K. Elst, "Ramjanmabhoomi vs. Babri masjid: some political implications", in Mishra & Singh (eds) 1991, 36–72. Elst views Hindus as India's underdogs, defends a caste system which he will never live under, and has a "theory" that the Dravidians invaded India after the Aryans. (See also Gandhi 1992: 108–9.)

5. The dash-notation used in this and the following chapters emphasizes that the named deities are different but related figures, or alternative personalities of one God or Goddess, or regional name variations of the same deity.

6. Akali Dal Sikhs, including Sikh separatists, were among the most militant *kar sevaks* ("volunteers") during the destruction of the Babri masjid. See "The saffron unity: what accounts for the Sikh presence at Ayodhya", *Sunday* 3–9 January 1993. The paper reported that Sikh cries of "Jai Shri Ram" ("Victory to Ram") put "even the Hindu volunteers to shame".

7. See Goel (1991). This is a fairly typical RSS-Hindu nationalist text that barely conceals its hatred of secular or (what it calls) "Marxist" Hindus as well as Muslims (pp. 70–4, 438–41). It also emphasizes the selective and symbolic importance of historical texts for Hindu nationalism. Goel's text uses Islamic sources to "prove" that Mughals were only interested in religious domination of Hindus and nothing more. The historical method used is based almost entirely on highly selective non-contextual quotations from these sources. Goel is particularly irritated by criticisms of *brahmins* (p. 274). He even provides "evidence" that the Black Stone in the Ka'ba at Mecca (the most sacred site for Muslims) was originally a shrine to the Hindu God Shiva (pp. 429–34). Goel also demonstrates the importance of Brahminism for Hindu nationalism (p. 274).

Chapter 6: The land, the blood and the passion: the Hindu far-right

1. Which annoyed Christians, especially missionaries, who put consider-able labour into undermining these claims (see, for example, Lilling-ston 1901).
2. Deoras died in June 1996 and Professor Rajendra Singh was named *sarsangchalak* of the RSS.
3. China had a special and unique place in early "Hindu nationalism". Both Savarkar and Golwalkar compared Chinese civilization very favourably with Hindu-Aryan civilization. Indeed, it was considered to be the only real human civilization, apart from the Aryan one. However, following the Chinese invasion in 1962, Golwalkar changed his tune: "It is said that a man becomes what he eats. It is said of the Chinese that the only biped that they do not eat is man and the only quadruped they spare is a table! They eat rats, cats, pigs, dogs, serpents, cockroaches and everything. Such men cannot be expected to have human qualities. Therefore the technique used against *a civilized people like the British* is of no use in dealing with the Chinese" (Golwalkar 1966: 270, emphasis added).
4. See Atal Behari Vajpayee, "The Sangh is my soul", *The Organiser*, 7 May 1995: 61.
5. Uttar Pradesh contains not only Ayodhya but also Mathura, Krishna's alleged "birthplace" and numerous other sites that revivalist Hindus are contesting.
6. An RSS affiliate gymnasium instructor speaking to a group of young women being trained in Indian martial arts, quoted in *Assignment*, BBC 2 15 June 1993.
7. Madhu Kishwar, "Hindu nationalism and women", paper presented at the University of California at Berkeley, 5 May 1993.

Chapter 7: The new materials of ethnogenesis: communalism, the body and science

1. Leaflet distributed by Abu Bakr mosque, Southall, November/December 1993.
2. List of ethnic minority and community organizations, Community Relations Councils and specialist race and ethnic workers, Greater London Council Ethnic Minorities Unit (The Greater London Council 1983).
3. The Chinmaya Mission was founded by the now deceased Swami Chinmayananda who was also a key founder member of, and leading figure in the VHP (the VHP was formed by Golwalkar and several others at Chinmayananda's ashram in 1964). The Swaminarayan movement (the Akshar Purushottam Sanstha) is a Vaishnavite sect, based on the

worship and teachings of the nineteenth-century Sahajanand Swami (Swaminarayan), and especially his collection of codes, the Shikshapatri. The Mission, which built the extraordinary Hindu temple in Neasden, northwest London, is led by Swami Pramukh. In the UK the Mission has generally supported the VHP's broad Hindutva position, especially around Ayodhya, and would co-operate with VHP activities, but apparently does not and would not have formal institutional ties with the RSS and BJP. The Chinmaya and Swaminarayan Missions, together with the Ramakrishna Mission and the International Society for Krishna Consciousness, are perhaps the main modern Hindu missionary movements outside India. However, an interesting development in recent years has been the rise of "disorganized cult" movements that are based on no particular orthodox canon and have no formal memberships (and sometimes no formal organization). The personality at the centre of the cult is virtually an empty signifier and whatever spiritual realization, spiritual content, personality of the spiritual leader, or miracles are experienced by devotees are mostly created by the devotees themselves. The Sai Baba movement, the Osho cult, the Amritanandamayi movement and the Mother Meera cult are broad examples of this new phenomenon.

4. For recent appraisals of natural selection and evolution, and the consideration of different physical mechanisms in evolutionary processes, see Gould (1989). For a presentation of contemporary evidence of natural selection see Weiner (1995).

5. The principle that one cannot know the exact momentum and position of a particle, nor the exact energy of a particle within an exactly defined period of time.

6. The radical unpredictability of some non-linear dynamic systems for some ranges of their parameters based on the inability to measure initial or starting values of the system exactly (Gleick 1987). Hofstadter (1980), as well as Casti (1993) are good popular accounts of Gödel's theorem and its consequences.

7. This is concerned with the spontaneous and holistic self-organization of complex, chaotic systems, and with initial states or small events that can have dramatic consequences for the later shape of the self-organized system. Something similar to Althusser's conception of metonymic or holistic causality is rehearsed in complexity theory's (to be sure organicist) holistic epistemology.

8. For an enlightening discussion of the extremely complex conceptions of sin, evil and "the good" in Hinduism, see O'Flaherty (1976).

9. Though transgressive does not means progressive. The hybridization of ragga and bhangra may be important for its articulation of pleasure, cultural integration and antiracism but it can also be done within a misogynist idiom that elaborates and upholds, rather than criticizes, the most repressive articulations of masculinity and "tradition" in Asian communities.

10. Scotland Yard set up a surveillance and intelligence unit, which also involved the Special Branch, just to monitor Asian gangs in west

London following a series of highly publicized street battles in Southall and Hounslow in 1985. A dossier was produced by Scotland Yard on Asian gangs which was selectively released to the press in March 1986. Scotland Yard paper, "Asian gangs", not dated, *Evening Standard* 24 March 1986, *Southall Gazette* 6 December 1985.

11. See, for example, *The Guardian*, 9 August 1995. The communalization of some northern Muslim communities along national-ethnic and linguistic lines (Pakistani–Punjabi, and Indian–Gujarati/Urdu) has increasingly manifested itself through youth gang violence.

12. Though the contemporary situations of, for example, the Egyptian novelist, Naguib Mahfouz, the Bangladeshi novelist, Taslima Nasreen, and the Egyptian academics, Nasr Abu Zaid and Ibtihal Younis, illustrate the mendacity of such statements.

Bibliography

Abrahamian, E. 1991. Khomeini – fundamentalist or populist. *New Left Review* 186, 102–9.

Abrahamian, E. 1993. *Khomeinism*. London: I. B. Tauris.

Ahmad, A. 1992. *In theory: classes, nations, literatures*. London: Verso.

Ahmed, A. S. 1992. *Postmodernism and Islam*. London: Routledge.

Ahmed, L. 1992. *Women and gender in Islam: historical roots of a modern debate*. New Haven & London: Yale University Press.

Ahsan, M. M. & A. R. Kidwai (eds) 1991. *Sacrilege versus civility: Muslim perspectives on The Satanic Verses affair*. Leicester: The Islamic Foundation.

Ahuja, G. 1994. *The BJP & Indian politics*. New Delhi: Ram.

Akbar, M. J. 1991. *Riot after riot: a report on caste and communal violence in India*. New Delhi: Penguin.

Akhavi, S. 1983. Shariati's social thought. See Keddie (1983), 125–44.

Akhtar, S. 1989. *Be careful with Muhammad! the Salman Rushdie affair*. London: Bellew.

Akhtar, S. 1993. *The Muslim parents handbook – what every Muslim parent should know*. London: Ta-Ha Publishers.

Alavi, H. 1988. Pakistan and Islam: ethnicity and ideology. See Halliday & Alavi, (1988), 64–111.

al-Azmeh, A. 1993. *Islams and modernities*. London: Verso.

Althusser, L. 1979. *For Marx*. London: NLB/Verso.

Althusser, L. 1984. *Essays on ideology*. London: Verso.

Amos, V. & P. Parmar 1984. Challenging imperial feminism. *Feminist Review* 17, 3–19.

Andersen, W. K. & S. D. Damle 1987. *The brotherhood in saffron: the Rashtriya Swayamsevak Sangh and Hindu revivalism*. New Delhi: Vistaar.

Anderson, B. 1983. *Imagined communities: reflections on the origin and spread of nationalism*. London: Verso.

Appignanesi, L. & S. Maitland (eds) 1989. *The Rushdie file*. London: Fourth Estate/ICA.

Arrighi, G., T. K. Hopkins, I. Wallerstein 1989. *Antisystemic movements*. London: Verso.

Asad, T. 1990. Multiculturalism and British identity in the wake of the Rushdie affair. *Politics & Society* 18 (4), 455–80.

Asante, M. K. 1988. *Afrocentricity*. Trenton, NJ: Africa World Press.

Bachelard, G. 1969. *The poetics of space*. Boston: Beacon Press.

Bakhash, S. 1986. *The reign of the Ayatollahs: Iran and the Islamic revolution*. London: Unwin.

Bakhtin, M. 1981. *The dialogic imagination*. Austin, TX: The University of Texas.

Banton, M. 1987. *Racial theories*. Cambridge: Cambridge University Press.

Barker, M. 1981. *The new racism: conservatives and the ideology of the tribe*. London: Junction Books.

Basu, T., P. Datta, S. Sarkar, T. Sarkar, S. Sen 1993. *Khaki shorts and saffron flags*. New Delhi: Orient Longman.

Baudrillard, J. 1993. *The transparency of evil: essays on extreme phenomena*. London: Verso.

Bauman, Z. 1991. *Modernity and ambivalence*. Cambridge: Polity.

Bauman, Z. 1992. *Intimations of postmodernity*. London: Routledge.

Bauman, Z. 1993. *Postmodern ethics*. Oxford: Blackwell.

Beckford, J. A. (ed.) 1991. *New religious movements and rapid social change*. Paris/London: UNESCO/Sage.

Benedikt, M. 1991. *Cyberspace: first steps*. Cambridge, MA: MIT Press.

Benhabib, S. 1986. *Critique, norm and utopia: a study of the foundations of critical theory*. New York: Columbia University Press.

Benhabib, S. 1992. *Situating the self: gender, community and postmodernism in contemporary ethics*. Cambridge: Polity.

Bernstein, R. J. (ed.) 1985. *Habermas and modernity*. Cambridge: Polity.

Bhabha, H. K. 1988. The commitment to theory. *New Formations* 5, 5–23.

Bhabha, H. K. 1990a. The third space. See Rutherford (1990), 207–21.

Bhabha, H. K. (ed.) 1990b. *Nation and narration*. London: Routledge.

Bhabha, H. K. 1994. *The location of culture*. London: Routledge.

The Bhagavad Gita with the Sanatsugatiya and the Anugita 1882. [trans. K. T. Telang.] Oxford: Clarendon. [*The Sacred Books of the East*, translated by various Oriental scholars and edited by F. Max Muller, vol. VIII].

The Bhagavad Gita 1962. [trans. J. Mascaro.] Harmondsworth: Penguin.

Bharatiya Janata Party 1991. *Towards Ram Rajya – mid-term poll to Lok Sabha, May 1991: our commitments*. New Delhi: Bharatiya Janata Party.

Bharatiya Janata Party 1996. *Election manifesto 1996 – for a strong and prosperous India*. New Delhi: Bharatiya Janata Party.

Bhaskar, R. 1979. *The possibility of naturalism*. Brighton: Harvester Press.

Bhaskar, R. 1986. *Scientific realism and human emancipation*. London: Verso.

Bhaskar, R. 1991. *Philosophy and the idea of freedom*. Oxford: Blackwell.

Bhaskar, R. 1993. *Dialectic – the pulse of freedom*. London: Verso.

Brass, P. R. 1990. *The new Cambridge history of India, IV–1: the politics of India since Independence*. Cambridge: Cambridge University Press.

Brown, W. N. 1933. *The Swastika: a study of the Nazi claims of its Aryan origin*. New York: Emerson Books.

Brunn, S. D. & T. R. Leinbach (eds) 1991. *Collapsing space and time: geographic aspects of communications and information*. London: Harper Collins.

Burrell, R. M. (ed.) 1989. *Islamic fundamentalism – Royal Asiatic Society seminar papers no. 1*. London: Royal Asiatic Society.

Butler, J. 1993. *Bodies that matter: on the discursive limits of "sex"*. New York: Routledge.

Carr, E. H. 1990. *What is history?* Harmondsworth: Penguin.

Castells, M. 1983. *The city and the grassroots: a cross-cultural theory of urban social movements*. Berkeley: University of California Press.

Casti, J. L. 1993. *Searching for certainty*. London: Abacus.

Centre for Contemporary Cultural Studies (ed.) 1982. *The empire strikes back: race and racism in 70s Britain*. London: Hutchinson.

Chakrabarti, D. K. 1995. *The ancient archaeology of Indian cities*. Delhi: Oxford University Press.

Chatterjee, P. 1986. *Nationalist thought and the colonial world: a derivative discourse?* London: Zed Press.

Chhachhi, A. 1991. Forced identities: the state, communalism, fundamentalism and women in India. In *Women, Islam and the State*, D. Kandiyoti (ed.), 144–75. Basingstoke: Macmillan.

Chhatra-Yuva Sangharsha Vahini n.d. *The Shah Bano case and the right to maintenance*. Bombay: CYSV.

Chopra, D. 1990. *Quantum healing: exploring the frontiers of mind/body medicine*. London: Bantam.

Choueiri, Y. M. 1990. *Islamic fundamentalism*. London: Pinter Publishers.

Commission for Racial Equality (ed.) 1990a. *Law, blasphemy and the multi-faith society: report of a seminar*. London: CRE.

Commission for Racial Equality (ed.) 1990b. *Free speech: report of a seminar*. London: CRE.

Daniélou, A. [1964] 1991. *The myths and Gods of India*. Rochester, Vermont: Inner Traditions International.

Das, A. N. 1992. *The Republic of Bihar*. New Delhi: Penguin.

Das, V. (ed.) 1992a. *Mirrors of violence: communities, riots and survivors in South Asia*. Delhi: Oxford University Press.

Das, V. 1992b. Introduction: communities, riots, survivors – the South Asian experience. See Das (1992a), 1–36.

Dekmejian, R. H. 1995. *Islam and revolution: fundamentalism in the Arab world*. Syracuse, NY: Syracuse University Press.

Derrida, J. 1976. *Of grammatology*. Baltimore: Johns Hopkins University Press.

Dews, P. 1987. *Logics of disintegration: post-structuralist thought and the claims of critical theory*. London: Verso

Dews, P. (ed.) 1992. *Autonomy and solidarity: interviews with Jürgen Habermas*. London: Verso.

Diamond, S. 1989. *Spiritual warfare: the politics of the Christian right*. Boston: South End Press.

Dubashi, J. 1992. *The road to Ayodhya*. New Delhi: Voice of India.

Dworkin, A. 1981. *Pornography: men possessing women*. London: The Women's Press.

Dworkin, A. 1982. *Our blood: prophecies and discourses on sexual politics*. London: The Women's Press.

Eatwell, R. 1996. *Fascism: a history*. London: Vintage.

Engels, F. [1896] 1978. *The part played by labour in the transition from ape to man*. Moscow: Progress Publishers.

Enzenberger, H. M. 1988. *Dreamers of the absolute*. London: Hutchinson.

Eyerman, R. & A. Jamison 1991. *Social movements: a cognitive approach*. Pennsylvania: Pennsylvania State University Press.

Factsheet Collective n.d. *Communalism – the razor's edge*. Bombay: Factsheet Collective.

Fanon, F. [1967] 1982. *The wretched of the earth*. Harmondsworth: Penguin.

Femia, J. V. 1981. *Gramsci's political thought: hegemony, consciousness and the revolutionary process*. Oxford: Clarendon.

Feminist Review (ed.) 1984. Many voices, one chant: black feminist perspectives. *Feminist Review* 17.

Feyerabend, P. 1987. *Farewell to reason*. London: Verso.

Fischer, M. M. J. & M. Abedi 1990. *Debating Muslims: cultural dialogues in postmodernity and tradition*. Madison: University of Wisconsin Press.

Foucault, M. 1970. *The order of things: an archaeology of the human sciences*. London: Tavistock.

Foucault, M. 1980. *Power/knowledge: selected interviews and other writings 1972–1977 Michel Foucault*, ed. C. Gordon. Brighton: Harvester.

Foucault, M. 1981. *The history of sexuality*, vol. I. Harmondsworth: Pelican.

Freeman, J. (ed.) 1983. *Social movements of the sixties and seventies*. New York: Longman.

Gandhi, M. K. [1927/9] 1982. *An autobiography*. London: Penguin.

Gandhi, M. K. 1978. *Hindu dharma*. New Delhi: Orient Paperbacks.

Gandhi, R. 1992. *Sita's kitchen: a testimony of faith and inquiry*. New Delhi: Penguin.

Gellner, E. 1992. *Postmodernism, reason and religion*. London: Routledge.

Geuss, R. 1981. *The idea of a critical theory: Habermas and the Frankfurt School*. Cambridge: Cambridge University Press.

Giddens, A. 1979. *Central problems in social theory: action, structure and contradiction in social analysis*. London and Basingstoke: Macmillan.

Giddens, A. 1981. *A contemporary critique of historical materialism*. London and Basingstoke: Macmillan.

Giddens, A. 1985. *The nation state and violence*. Cambridge: Polity.

Gilroy, P. 1987a. *Problems in anti-racist strategy*. London: Runnymede Trust.

Gilroy, P. 1987b. *There ain't no black in the Union Jack: the cultural politics of race and nation*. London: Hutchinson.

Gilroy, P. 1990. One nation under a groove: the cultural politics of "race" and racism in Britain. See D. T. Goldberg (1990), 263–82.

Gilroy, P. 1991. It ain't where you're from, it's where you're at: the dialectics of diasporic identification. *Third Text* (13), 3–16.

Gilroy, P. 1993. *The black Atlantic: modernity and double consciousness*. London: Verso.

Giri, Y. [1894] 1977. *The holy science*. Los Angeles: Self-Realization Fellowship.

Gleick, J. 1987. *Chaos: making a new science*. London: Cardinal.

Glucksmann-Buci, C. 1980. *Gramsci and the state*. London: Lawrence & Wishart.

Goel, S. R. 1991. *Hindu temples: what happened to them. Part II – the Islamic evidence*. New Delhi: Voice of India.

Goldberg, D. T. (ed.) 1990. *Anatomy of racism*. Minneapolis: University of Minnesota Press.

Golwalkar, M. S. [1939] 1944. *We, or our nationhood defined*. 2nd edn. Nagpur: Bharat Publications.

Golwalkar, M. S. 1956. *Sri Guruji – the man and his mission*. Delhi: Bharat Prakashan.

Golwalkar, M. S. 1962. *Justice on trial: a collection of the historic letters between Sri Guruji and the government 1948–49*. 3rd edn. Bangalore: Rashtriya Swayamsevak Sangh.

Golwalkar, M. S. 1966. *Bunch of thoughts*. Bangalore: Vikrama Prakashan.

Gopal, S. (ed.) 1991. *Anatomy of a confrontation: the Babri masjid – Ramjanmabhoomi issue*. New Delhi: Penguin.

Gorz, A. 1989. *Critique of economic reason*. London: Verso.

Gould, S. J. 1989. *Wonderful life*. Harmondsworth: Penguin.

Gregory, D. & J. Urry (eds) 1985. *Social relations and spatial structures*. London: Macmillan.

Guha, R. & G. C. Spivak (eds) 1988. *Selected subaltern studies*. Oxford: Oxford University Press.

Habermas, J. 1990. *The philosophical discourse of modernity*. Cambridge: Polity.

Habermas, J. 1992. *Postmetaphysical thinking*. Cambridge: Polity.

Hall, S. 1979. The great moving right show. *Marxism Today* (April), 14–20.

Hall, S. & M. Jacques (eds) 1989. *New times: the changing face of politics in the 1990s*. London: Lawrence & Wishart.

Halliday, F. 1994. The politics of Islamic fundamentalism: Iran, Tunisia and the challenge to the secular state. In *Islam, globalisation and postmodernity*, A. Ahmed & H. Donnan (eds), 91–113. London: Routledge.

Halliday, F. 1996. *Islam and the myth of confrontation*. London: I. B. Tauris.

Halliday, F. & H. Alavi (eds) 1988. *State and ideology in the Middle East and Pakistan*. New York: Monthly Review Press.

Hampson, N. 1990. *The Enlightenment*. Harmondsworth: Penguin.

BIBLIOGRAPHY

Haraway, D. J. 1991. *Simians, cyborgs and women: the reinvention of nature.* New York: Routledge.

Harvey, D. 1989. *The condition of postmodernity: an enquiry into the origins of cultural change.* Oxford: Basil Blackwell.

Harvey, D. 1993. From space to place and back again: reflections on the condition of postmodernity. In *Mapping the futures: local cultures, global change,* J. Bird (ed.), 3–29. London: Routledge.

Hawthorn, G. 1987. *Enlightenment and despair: a history of social theory.* Cambridge: Cambridge University Press.

Heller, A. & F. Feher 1991. *The postmodern political condition.* Cambridge/Oxford: Polity/Blackwell.

Heuzé, G. 1995. Cultural populism: the appeal of the Shiv Sena. See Patel & Thorner (1995), 213–47.

Hiro, D. 1976. *Inside India today.* London: Routledge & Kegan Paul.

Hiro, D. 1987. *Iran under the Ayatollahs.* London: Routledge.

Hoare, Q. and G. Nowell Smith (eds) 1978. *Selections from the prison notebooks of Antonio Gramsci.* London: Lawrence & Wishart.

Hobsbawm, E. & T. Ranger (eds) 1984. *The invention of tradition.* Cambridge: Cambridge University Press.

Hofstadter, D. 1980. *Gödel, Escher, Bach: an eternal golden braid.* Harmondsworth: Penguin.

Hoodbhoy, P. 1991. *Islam and Science.* London: Zed Books.

Hughes, R. 1993. *Culture of complaint: the fraying of America.* Oxford: Oxford University Press.

Hume, D. [1888] 1978. *A treatise of human nature.* Oxford: Clarendon.

Institute for African Alternatives n.d. *Islamic fundamentalism: papers presented at a seminar held by the IFAA on 3 June 1989.* London: IFAA.

ISKCON. 1977. *The science of self-realisation.* Borehamwood: Bhaktivedanta Book Trust.

Ja'far, M. & A. Tabari 1984. Iran: Islam and the struggle for socialism. In *Forbidden agendas: intolerance and defiance in the Middle East,* Khamsin (ed.), 322–49. London: Al Saqi Books.

Jain, G. 1994. *The Hindu phenomenon.* New Delhi: UBS Publishers.

James, C. L. R. 1973. *Modern politics.* Detroit: Bewick/ed.

James, C. L. R. 1980. *Notes on dialectics.* London: Allison & Busby.

James, C. L. R., G. L. Lee, P. Chaulieu. [1958] 1974. *Facing reality.* Detroit: Bewick/ed.

James, W. [1902] 1982. *The varieties of religious experience.* London: Penguin.

Jameson, F. 1991. *Postmodernism, or the cultural logic of late capitalism.* London: Verso.

Jayawardena, K. 1986. *Feminism and nationalism in the Third World.* London: Zed.

Jeffreys, S. 1990. *Anticlimax: a feminist perspective on the sexual revolution.* New York: New York University Press.

Jordan, J. [1980] 1989. *Moving towards home.* London: Virago.

Kabbani, R. 1989. *Letter to Christendom.* London: Virago.

Kaviraj, S. 1993. The imaginary institution of India. *Subaltern Studies* VII, 1–40.

Keane, J. (ed.) 1988a. *Civil society and the state*. London: Verso.

Keane, J. 1988b. *Democracy and civil society*. London: Verso.

Keddie, N. R. 1980. *Iran: religion, politics and society*. London: Frank Cass.

Keddie, N. R. (ed.) 1983. *Religion and politics in Iran: Shi'ism from quietism to revolution*. New Haven & London: Yale University Press.

Keer, D. 1988. *Veer Savarkar*. Bombay: Popular Prakashan.

Khan, M. A. (ed.) 1985. *Islam, politics and the state: the Pakistan experience*. London: Zed.

Khomeini, R. M. 1981. *Islam and revolution: writings and declarations of Imam Khomeini* [trans H. Algar]. Berkeley: Mizan Press.

King, A. 1991. *Global cities: post-imperialism and the internationalisation of London*. London: Routledge.

Knappert, J. 1991. *Indian mythology: an encyclopaedia of myth and legend*. London: Aquarian Press/Harper Collins.

Kohli, A. 1990. *Democracy and discontent: India's growing crisis of governability*. Cambridge: Cambridge University Press.

Kohn, M. 1995. *The race gallery: the return of racial science*. London: Jonathan Cape.

Kosambi, D. D. [1964] 1992. *The culture and civilisation of ancient India in historical outline*. New Delhi: Vikas.

Kritzman, L. D. (ed.) 1990. *Michel Foucault – politics, philosophy, culture: interviews and other writings 1977–1984*. London: Routledge.

Kumar, P. (ed.) 1989. *Kautilya Arthasastra: an appraisal*. Delhi: Nag Publishers.

Laclau, E. 1990. *New reflections on the revolution of our time*. London: Verso.

Laclau, E. & C. Mouffe. 1982. Recasting Marxism: hegemony and new political movements. *Socialist Review* 12 (6), 91–113.

Laclau, E. & C. Mouffe. 1985. *Hegemony and socialist strategy: towards a radical democratic politics*. London: Verso.

The Laws of Manu. 1886. [trans. G. Buhler]. Oxford: Clarendon. [*The Sacred Books of the East*, translated by various Oriental scholars and edited by F. Max Muller, vol. XXV].

Lefebvre, H. 1991. *The production of space*. Oxford: Basil Blackwell.

The legends of Alexander the Great. 1994 [trans. R. Stoneman]. London: J. M. Dent.

Lenin, V. I. 1978. *What is to be done?* Moscow: Progress Publishers.

Levinas, E. 1969. *Totality and infinity: an essay on exteriority*. Pittsburgh: Duquesne University Press.

Levinas, E. 1987. *Time and the other*. Pittsburgh: Duquesne University Press.

Lewis, P. 1994. *Islamic Britain*. London: I. B. Tauris.

Lillingston, F. 1901. *The Brahmo Samaj and Arya Samaj in their bearing upon Christianity: a study in Indian theism*. London: Macmillan.

Lyotard, J-.F. 1987. *The postmodern condition: a report on knowledge*.

Manchester: Manchester University Press.

McDermott, M. Y. & M. M. Ahsan 1993. *The Muslim guide for teachers, employers, community workers and social administrators in Britain.* Leicester: The Islamic Foundation.

MacDonogh, S. & Article 19 (eds) 1993. *The Rushdie letters: freedom to speak, freedom to write.* Lincoln: University of Nebraska Press.

McGrew, A. 1992. A global society? In *Modernity and its futures*, S. Hall, D. Held, A. McGrew (eds), 61–102. Cambridge/Oxford: Polity/Open University Press.

Madan, T. N. (ed.) 1991. *Religion in India.* Delhi: Oxford University Press.

Madhubuti, H. R. 1990. *Black men – obsolete, single, dangerous? Afrikan American families in transition.* Chicago: Third World Press.

Magas, B. 1993. *The destruction of Yugoslavia.* London: Verso.

The Mahabharata of Vyasa. 1989 [trans. P. Lal]. New Delhi: Vikas.

Malkani, K.R. 1980. *The RSS story.* New Delhi: Impex India.

Mani, L. 1990. Contentious traditions: the debate on sati in colonial India. In *The nature and context of minority discourse*, A. R. JanMohamed & D. Lloyd (eds), 319–56. Oxford: Oxford University Press.

Mani L. & R. Frankenberg 1993. Crosscurrents, crosstalk: race, 'postcoloniality' and the politics of location. *Cultural Studies* 7(3), 292–310.

Manuel, P. 1993. *Cassette culture: popular music and technology in north India.* Chicago: University Press.

Massey, D. 1984. *Spatial divisions of labour: social structures and the geography of production.* Basingstoke: Macmillan.

Massey, D. 1985. New directions in space. See Gregory & Urry (1985), 9–19.

Massey, D. 1991. A global sense of place. *Marxism Today* (June), 24–9.

a῾la Mawdudi, S. A. 1991. *The Islamic movement: dynamics of values, power and change* [trans. K. Murad]. Leicester: The Islamic Foundation.

a῾la Mawdudi, S. A. 1982. *Let us be Muslims [Khutubat].* Leicester: The Islamic Foundation.

Mehta, G. 1990. *Karma Cola.* London: Minerva.

Melucci, A. 1989. *Nomads of the present: social movements and individual needs in contemporary society.* London: Hutchinson Radius.

Mernissi, F. 1993. *Islam and democracy: fear of the modern world.* London: Virago.

Milbank, J. 1993. Problematizing the secular: the post-postmodern agenda. In *Shadow of spirit: postmodernism and religion*, P. Berry. & A. Wernick (eds), 30–44. London: Routledge.

Mishra, V. C. & P. Singh 1991. *Ramjanmabhoomi/Babri Masjid – historical documents, legal opinions & judgements.* New Delhi: Bar Council of India Trust.

Mitra, A. 1993. *Television and popular culture in India: a study of the Mahabharat.* New Delhi: Sage.

Modood, T. 1988. "Black" racial equality and Asian identity. *New Community* 14 (3) 397–404.

Modood, T. 1992. British Asian Muslims and the Rushdie affair. In

"Race", culture and difference, J. Donald & A. Rattansi (eds), 260–77. London: Sage.

Mohanty, C. T. 1991. Under Western eyes: feminist scholarship and colonial discourses. In *Third World women and the politics of feminism*, C. T. Mohanty, A. Russo, L. Torres (eds), 51–80. Bloomington and Indianapolis: Indiana University Press.

Moin, B. 1994. Khomeini's search for perfection. In *Pioneers of Islamic revival*, A. Rahnema (ed.), 64–97. London: Zed.

Momen, M. 1989. Authority and opposition in Twelver Shi'ism. See Burrell (1989), 48–66.

Mottahedeh, R. 1987. *The mantle of the prophet: religion and politics in Iran*. Harmondsworth: Penguin.

Mouffe, C. 1979. Hegemony and ideology in Gramsci. In *Gramsci and Marxist theory*, C. Mouffe (ed.), 168–204. London: Routledge & Kegan Paul.

Mullatti, L. 1989. *The Bhakti movement and the status of women: a case study of Virasaivism*. New Delhi: Abhinav.

Mumtaz, K. & F. Shaheed 1987. *Women of Pakistan: two steps forward, one step back*. London: Zed.

Murphy, P. 1992. Socialism and democracy. In *Between totalitarianism and postmodernity: a thesis eleven reader*, P. Beilharz, G. Robinson, J. Rundell (eds), 12–31. Cambridge, MA: MIT Press.

Nadvi, K. S. 1993. *Darwinism on trial*, 2nd edn. London: Ta-Ha Publishers.

Nandy, A. 1983. *The intimate enemy: loss and recovery of self under colonialism*. Delhi: Oxford University Press.

Nasr, S. H. 1987. *Science and civilisation in Islam*. Cambridge: Islamic Texts Society.

Nasr, S. V. R. 1994. *The vanguard of the Islamic revolution: the Jamaʿat-i Islami of Pakistan*. London: I. B. Tauris.

Nielsen, J. 1992. *Muslims in Western Europe*. Edinburgh: Edinburgh University Press.

Norris, C. 1987. *Derrida*. Cambridge, MA: Harvard University Press.

Norris, C. 1991. *Deconstruction: theory and practice*. London: Routledge.

Norris, C. 1992. *Uncritical theory: postmodernism, intellectuals and the Gulf War*. London: Lawrence & Wishart.

Norris, C. 1993. *The truth about postmodernism*. Oxford: Blackwell.

O'Flaherty, W. D. 1976. *The origins of evil in Hindu mythology*. Berkeley: University of California Press.

Omi, M. & H. Winant 1986. *Racial formation in the United States from the 1960s to the 1980s*. London: Routledge & Kegan Paul.

Omvedt, G. 1990. *Violence against women: new movements and new theories in India*. New Delhi: Kali for Women.

Padgaonkar, D. (ed) 1993. *When Bombay burned*. New Delhi: UBS.

Pandey, G. 1992. *The construction of communalism in colonial North India*. Delhi: Oxford University Press.

Pandey, G. 1995. The appeal of Hindu history. In *Representing Hinduism: the construction of religious tradition and national identity*, V. Dalmia

& H. Stietencron (eds), 369–88. New Delhi: Sage.

Panikkar, K.N. 1991. A historical overview. See Gopal (1991), 22–37.

Parekh, B. 1990. The Rushdie affair and the British press: some salutary lessons. See Commission for Racial Equality (1990b), 59–78.

Parry, B. 1987. Problems in current theories of colonial discourse. *Oxford Literary Review* 9 (1–2), 27–58.

Patel, S. & A. Thorner (eds) 1995. *Bombay: metaphor for modern India.* Bombay: Oxford University Press.

Patel, V. 1989. Sex determination and sex preselection tests in India: recent techniques in femicide. *Journal of Reproductive & Genetic Engineering* 2 (2), 111–19.

Patel, V. 1992. Amniocentesis and female foeticide: misuse of medical technology. *Socialist Health Review* (Summer), 69–71, Bombay.

Penrose, R. 1989. *The emperor's new mind.* London: Vintage.

Pois, R. A. 1986. *National socialism and the religion of nature.* London: Croom Helm.

Poliakov, L. 1971. *The Aryan myth: a history of racist and nationalist ideas in Europe.* London: Heinemann.

Poulantzas, N. 1979. *Fascism and dictatorship: the Third International and the problem of fascism.* London: Verso.

Poulantzas, N. 1980. *State, power, socialism.* London: Verso.

Pryce-Jones, D. 1990. *The closed circle: an interpretation of the Arabs.* London: Grafton.

Qadir, C. A. 1988. *Philosophy and science in the Islamic world.* London: Routledge.

The Qur'an 1988 [trans. A. Ali]. Princeton/Karachi: Princeton University Press/Akrash Publishing.

Qureshi, S. & J. Khan 1989. *The politics of Satanic verses: unmasking Western attitudes.* Leicester: Muslim Community Studies Institute/Raza Academy.

The Rajanitisastra of Chanakya 1983. [trans. M.P. Joshi]. Almora: Sri Malika Publications.

Raleigh, V. S. 1996. Suicide patterns and trends in people of Indian Subcontinent and Caribbean origin in England and Wales. *Ethnicity & Health* 1 (1), 55–63.

Ramanujan, A. K. 1973. *Speaking of Siva.* Harmondsworth: Penguin.

Ramanujan, A. K. 1991. Three hundred Ramayanas: five examples and three thoughts on translation. See Richman (1991), 22–49.

The Ramayana of Valmiki 1990–91. 3 vols. [trans. R. P. Goldman & S. I. Pollock]. Princeton, NJ: Princeton University Press.

Rashtriya Swayamsevak Sangh 1983. rss *resolves: full text of resolutions from 1950 to 1983.* Karnataka: Rashtriya Swayamsevak Sangh.

Reagon, B. J. 1983. Coalition politics: turning the century. In *Home girls: a black feminist anthology,* B. Smith (ed.), 356–68. New York: Kitchen Table – Women of Color Press.

Reeves, G. 1993. *Communications and the 'Third World'.* London: Routledge.

Richman, P. (ed.) 1991. *Many Ramayanas: the diversity of a narrative tradition in South Asia.* Berkeley: University of California Press.

The Rig Veda 1992 [trans. R. T. H. Griffith 1896]. New York: Quality Paperback Book Club/Motilal Banarsidass.

Robinson, F. 1988. *Varieties of South Asian Islam in Britain.* Coventry: Centre for Research in Ethnic Relations.

Rorty, R. 1989. *Contingency, irony and solidarity.* Cambridge: Cambridge University Press.

Rose, G. 1983. Velayat-e-faqih and the recovery of Islamic identity in the thought of Ayatollah Khomeini. See Keddie (1983), 166–88.

Rousseau, J-. J. [1913] 1993. *The social contract & discourses.* London: J. M. Dent.

Rowbotham, S., L. Segal, H. Wainright. 1979. *Beyond the fragments: feminism and the making of socialism.* London: Merlin Press.

Roy, O. 1994. *The failure of political Islam.* London: I. B. Tauris.

Rushdie, S. 1988. *The Satanic verses.* London: Viking/Penguin.

Rushdie, S. 1991. *Imaginary homelands: essays and criticism 1981–1991.* London: Granta.

Rutherford, J. (ed.) 1990. *Identity: community, culture, difference.* London: Lawrence & Wishart.

Ruthven, M. 1990. *A satanic affair: Salman Rushdie and the rage of Islam.* London: Chatto & Windus.

Sahgal, G. & N. Yuval-Davis (eds) 1992. *Refusing holy orders: women and fundamentalism in Britain.* London: Virago.

Said, E. W. 1981. *Covering Islam.* London: Routledge & Kegan Paul.

Said, E. W. 1985. *Orientalism.* Harmondsworth: Penguin.

Said, E. W. 1993. *Culture and imperialism.* London: Chatto & Windus.

Sardar, Z. & M. W. Davies 1990. *Distorted imagination: lessons from the Rushdie affair.* London: Grey Seal.

Savarkar, V. D. [1923] 1989. *Hindutva – who is a Hindu?* 6th edn. Bombay: Veer Savarkar Prakashan.

Sen, K. M. [1961] 1991 *Hinduism.* Harmondsworth: Penguin.

Shaheed, F. 1992. The Pathan–Muhajir Conflicts, 1985–6: a national perspective. See Das (1992a), 194–214.

Sharma, A. 1991. New religious movements in India. See Beckford (1991), 220–39.

The Shikshapatri of Lord Swaminarayan 1994. Amdavad: Swaminarayan Aksharpith.

Shourie, A. 1993. *Indian controversies: essays on religion in politics.* New Delhi: ASA.

Siddiqui, K. 1984. Integration and disintegration in the politics of Islam and Kufr. In *Issues in the Islamic movement, 1982–83 (1402–03),* K. Siddiqui (ed.), 1–28. London: The Open Press.

Sirsikar, V. M. 1995. *The politics of modern Maharashtra.* Bombay: Sangam.

Sivanandan, A. 1982. *A different hunger: writings on black resistance.* London: Pluto.

Sivanandan, A. 1985. RAT and the degradation of black struggle. *Race & Class* 26 (4), 1–33.

Sivanandan, A. 1990. All that melts into air is solid: the hokum of New Times. *Race & Class* **31** (3), 1–30.

Smart, N. 1992. *The world's religions: old traditions and new transformations*. Cambridge: Cambridge University Press.

Soja, E. 1989. *Postmodern geographies: the reassertion of space in critical social theory*. London: Verso.

Solomos, J. 1989. *Race and racism in contemporary Britain*. Basingstoke: Macmillan.

Soper, K. 1995. *What is nature?* Oxford: Blackwell.

Southall Black Sisters 1990. *Against the grain: a celebration of survival and struggle*. London: Southall Black Sisters.

Spear, P. 1990. *A history of India*, vol. ii. London: Penguin.

Spivak, G. C. 1988a. *In other worlds: essays in cultural politics*. London: Routledge.

Spivak, G. C. 1988b. Can the subaltern speak? In *Marxism and the interpretation of culture*, C. Nelson & L. Grossberg (eds), 271–313. London: Macmillan.

Spivak, G. C. 1989. Who claims alterity? In *Remaking history*, B. Kruger & P. Mariani (eds), 269–92. Seattle: Bay Press.

Spivak, G. C. 1990. *The post-colonial critic: interviews, strategies, dialogues*. London: Routledge.

Spivak, G. C. 1993a. Foundations and cultural studies. In *Questioning foundations: truth/subjectivity/culture*, H. J. Silverman (ed.), 153–75. London: Routledge.

Spivak, G. C. 1993b. *Outside in the teaching machine*. London: Routledge.

Spivak, G. C. 1996. "Woman" as theatre: United Nations conference on women, Beijing 1995. *Radical Philosophy* 75, (Jan–Feb), 2.

Thapar, R. [1966] 1990. *A history of India*, vol. i. London: Penguin.

Thapar, R. 1991. A historical perspective on the story of Rama. See Gopal (1991), 141–63.

Theweleit, K. 1987. *Male fantasies volume 1: women, floods, bodies, history*. Cambridge: Polity.

Thompson, J. B. & D. Held (eds) 1982. *Habermas: critical debates*. London and Basingstoke: Macmillan.

Upadhyaya, D., M. Golwalkar, D. B. Thengdi 1979. *The integral approach*. New Delhi: Deendayal Research Institute.

The thirteen principal Upanishads 1995. [trans. R. E. Hume 1877]. 2nd edn. Delhi: Oxford University Press.

The Upanishads 1988. [trans. E. Easwaran]. Harmondsworth: Arkana/Penguin.

Vaniak, A. 1990. *The painful transition: bourgeois democracy in India*. London: Verso.

Wallerstein, I. 1983. *Historical capitalism*. London: Verso.

Walter, A. (ed.) 1980. *Come together: the years of gay liberation 1970–73*. London: Gay Men's Press.

Watt, W. M. 1988. *Islamic fundamentalism and modernity*. London: Routledge.

Weeks, J. 1981. *Sex, politics & society: the regulation of sexuality since 1800.* Harlow: Longman.

Weeks, J. 1995. *Invented moralities.* Oxford: Polity.

Weeks, J. (ed.) 1994. *The lesser evil and the greater good: the theory and politics of social diversity.* London: Rivers Oram.

Weiner, J. 1995. *The beak of the finch: a story of evolution in our time.* London: Vintage.

Weldon, F. 1989. *Sacred cows: a portrait of Britain, post-Rushdie, pre-utopia.* London: Chatto & Windus.

Welsing, F. 1991. *The Isis papers.* Chicago: Third World Press.

Werbner, P. & M. Anwar (eds) 1991. *Black and ethnic leaderships in Britain.* London: Routledge.

West, C. 1993a. *Prophetic reflections: notes on race and power in America.* Monroe, Maine: Common Courage Press.

West, C. 1993b. *Race matters.* Boston: Beacon Press.

West, C. 1993c. *Prophetic thought in postmodern times.* Monroe, Maine: Common Courage Press.

Wilson, T. [1895] 1973. *The Swastika: the earliest known symbol, and its migrations with observations on the migration of certain industries in pre-historic times.* Delhi: Oriental Publishers.

Wink, A. (ed.) 1991. *Islam, politics and society in South Asia.* New Delhi: Manohar Publications.

Yazdi, M. H. 1992. *The principles of epistemology in Islamic philosophy: knowledge by presence.* New York: State University of New York.

Young, R. 1990. *White mythologies: writing, history and the West.* London: Routledge.

Zaehner, R. C. [1961] 1992. *Hinduism.* Oxford: Oxford University Press.

Zakaria, R. 1989. *The struggle within Islam: the conflict between religion and politics.* Harmondsworth: Penguin.

Zizek, S. 1989. *The sublime object of ideology.* London: Verso.

Zohar, D. 1991. *The quantum self.* London: Harper Collins.

Zubaida, S. 1982. The ideological conditions for Khomeini's doctrine of government. *Economy & Society* **11** (2), 138–72.

Zubaida, S. 1993. *Islam, the people and the state: political ideas and movements in the Middle East.* London: I. B. Tauris.

Index

INDEX

sacred texts and epics 74, 158,
159–66
and science 75, 182–3, 259–63
Hindutva, Savarkar's concept of
186–94
Hindutva – Who is a Hindu? 186
historical methodology 16
history
in Hinduism 157, 168–70
impact of colonization on
indigenous 87
re–inscribing of 66–7
role in communal violence
224–5
see also temporality; tradition
HIV/AIDS, Hindu revivalist
discourse on 262–3
Hobsbawm, Eric 86
Hoodbhoy, Pervez 257, 258
Hume, David 1, 10
hybridity 28–34

identity
of difference 10–11
globalization and ethnic identity
formation 251–4
national and racial identity in
Rushdie affair 128–30,
132–3, 146–7
national and transnational
90–2, 105–6
and spatiality in social
movements 42–4
and temporality of social
movements 67–8
see also Hindu identity; *umma*
ijtihad 96
Imams 95, 96, 141
imperialism, Khomeini's opposition
to 98–9, 137, 138
Indian liberation, religious
influences on 180
Indian nationalism, and nineteenth
century Hindu revival 181–4
Institute of Race Relations (IRR)
266–7
integral humanism 216
internet, Hindu nationalism and

Islamicist use of 252–3
Islam
conceptualized as traditional,
modern or postmodern 78–9
identity of Islamic
fundamentalism 81
modernity of Islamic revival
79–85, 88, 100
relationship with Hinduism 173,
175
relationship with West 111–12
revivalism and science 257–9
revivalism and symbolism of
women's bodies 229
Rushdie as agent of West against
113–14, 128–9, 137–40, 143
and social policy 242–4
use of and views of
communication technology
252, 253
see also Jamaat–i–Islami;
Khomeinism; Muslim
communities
Islami Jami'at-i-Tulabah (IJT) 115
Islamic Foundation (Leicester) 115,
116
Islamic movements
concept of space 61, 62
impact on civil society 62
Islamic Republic of Iran (IRI),
modernity of 103–6

Jamaat-i-Islami (JI) 114–17, 118,
137
Jameson, Fredric 21, 38–9
Jan Sangh 215, 216
Jordan, June 37, 233

Kanwar, Roop 220, 221–2
Kaviraj, Sudipta 82
Khilafat movement 184
Khomeini, Ruhollah xii, 141
Khomeinism
assault on tradition 92–7, 100
invention of new tradition 98,
99, 100
modernity of 101–3, 104,
105–6

300

INDEX

rights of 221–2
role in Hindu nationalism
168, 199–200, 225–7
Women Against
Fundamentalism (WAF)
24–5
women's movement
identity and spatiality 44

see also black feminism

Young Muslims UK (YMUK)
19–20, 116
youth, Asian youth formations
127, 267–70

Zubaida, Sami 102